Alexander Marin Delavoye

Records of the 90th Regiment

With roll of officers from 1795 to 1880

Alexander Marin Delavoye

Records of the 90th Regiment
With roll of officers from 1795 to 1880

ISBN/EAN: 9783337268930

Printed in Europe, USA, Canada, Australia, Japan

Cover: Foto ©ninafisch / pixelio.de

More available books at **www.hansebooks.com**

RECORDS

OF THE

90th REGIMENT,

(PERTHSHIRE LIGHT INFANTRY),

WITH

ROLL OF OFFICERS FROM 1795 TO 1880.

BY

ALEX. M. DELAVOYE,

Captain 56th Foot (late 90th L.I.)

LONDON:
RICHARDSON & Co., PALL MALL;
MARCHANT SINGER & Co.,
INGRAM COURT, FENCHURCH STREET, E.C.

———

1880.

INTRODUCTION.

During the wars waged with France and Spain, prior to the establishment of the French Republic, it was the custom in England to raise regiments in cases of emergency, disbanding them when their services were no longer required.

On two occasions a 90th Regiment was so embodied, the first time being in 1760, the Corps appearing in the army-list of the following year as the 90th Regiment of Light Infantry.

This battalion served with credit in the West Indies, where, in 1762, it took part in the successful assault on the Castle of Moro, in the island of Cuba, on the 30th of July. The storming party was commanded by Lieut.-Colonel Stewart, of the 90th Regiment, and was composed as follows:—

	Officers.	Sergeants.	Rank and File.
Royal Regiment ..	6	5	102
Marksmen..	8	8	129
90th Regiment.. ..	8	2	50
	22	15	281

Lieutenant Holroyd, of the 90th, was killed on this occasion.

The Regiment was disbanded in March, 1763, on its return home.

In 1779, when Spain joined France in the war which was being carried on by the latter country against England, a 90th Regiment was again raised, and remained embodied, under the command of Colonel Loftus Anthony Tottenham, until peace was concluded at Versailles in 1783.

RECORDS

OF THE

90TH REGIMENT, LIGHT INFANTRY.

The end of the last century, remarkable for the overthrow of the French Monarchy, found England with a small army scattered over the face of the globe, and but ill prepared for the war which was declared by the French Convention in February, 1793. The unnecessary atrocities which had accompanied the rise of the Republic, and the persistent endeavours of the French to force their democratic principles upon the other nations of Europe, made the war, to a certain extent, popular in England; therefore, when it was found necessary to increase the army by the formation of new regiments, no difficulty was experienced in obtaining recruits; but, as is usual on the sudden augmentation of the peace establishment, the bounties demanded were enormously high.

Of the new corps, six were raised in Scotland; letters of service were granted to the Duke of Gordon, the Duke of Argyle, Lord Seaforth, Lieutenant-General Stewart Douglas, Sir James Grant, of Grant, and Mr. Thomas Graham, of Balgowan, who, on his return from Toulon, whither he had proceeded as a volunteer with the force under Admiral Lord Hood, had solicited permission to raise and command a regiment. This was reluctantly granted, owing to the king's dislike to give high commands to individuals who had had no previous military training, nor had held commissions in the army.

1794. The required authority, however, once obtained, Mr. Graham commenced his levy with an energy which proved both his loyalty and his taste for the profession he had adopted. Recruiting parties were sent into various districts in Scotland and England, the head-quarters of the regiment being established at Perth, whence, on being appointed Colonel-Commandant of his regiment, on the 10th of February, 1794, Mr. Graham, with a view to rousing the military spirit of his native county, issued the following address :—

" *To the Inhabitants of the County of Perth.*

" Being desirous that the regiment I have under-
" taken to raise, and which I am to have the honour to
" command, should bear the name of a county I am so
" much attached to, I have obtained His Majesty's leave
" that it should be called 'The Perthshire Volunteers.'
" While I flatter myself that the corps will prove worthy
" of so distinguished a name, allow me to hope that it will
" find in the spirit of the young men of the county, and
" in the zeal of the recruits, that preference and support
" which may make up for the want of the extensive
" influence which patronizes the other corps now recruiting.
" I need not assure all able-bodied volunteers that they
" will be received by the Commanding-Officer, at the head-
" quarters at Perth, with the greatest attention, and will
" meet with the most liberal treatment.
  " I am, with sincere regard,
   " Your devoted servant,
    " THOS. GRAHAM."

Colonel Graham's influence in Perthshire, and his liberality in other parts of Great Britain, enabled him to parade at Perth, on the 13th of May, 7 Officers and 746

Non-commissioned Officers and men, for the inspection of 1794. Lieutenant-General Lord Adam Gordon, the Commander-in-Chief in Scotland, who expressed himself highly pleased with the condition of the regiment, which was composed of:—

$$\left.\begin{array}{lr}\text{Highlanders} & 95 \\ \text{Lowlanders} & 430 \\ \text{English} & 165 \\ \text{Irish} & 56\end{array}\right\} 746$$

Being one of the first of the new levies reported as complete, the "Perthshire Volunteers" became the 90th Foot, and Lord Moira, who was greatly interested by Colonel Graham's exertions and zeal, obtained the King's leave that it should be enrolled as a Light Infantry Battalion, and as such it was equipped and drilled. While quartered in Perth the conduct of the regiment was most exemplary, its good behaviour being due to the strict, yet just, system of discipline which, introduced by Colonel Graham, has ever since been maintained.

In February, 1794, Brevet-Major George Moncrieffe, of the 11th Foot, was promoted Lieutenant-Colonel into the 90th, the Majority being offered by the Commandant to Captain Rowland Hill, afterwards Lord Hill, of the 53rd Foot, whom he had met at Toulon, where his conduct and gallantry had rendered him conspicuous. At the same time Captain John McNair was appointed Pay-master, and in that capacity, as in all others, proved himself to be an invaluable officer.

The vacancies in the 90th were given to officers who could raise a certain number of recruits, or were obtained by purchase, the sums paid becoming the property of Colonel Graham, who, however, from his desire to oblige his friends and to obtain officers of known character and ability, frequently gave away commissions, thereby entailing on himself a heavy loss.

By the 24th of June, the strength of the regiment had been increased to 29 Sergeants, 43 Corporals, and 1,042

1794. men, Major Hill becoming the second Lieutenant-Colonel, and Captains Mackenzie and Houston the Majors. The success attending the levy of the first battalion so elated Colonel Graham that he offered to raise a second of 1,000 men, this offer being eagerly accepted; notwithstanding the competition of innumerable recruiting parties, he was able in August to report its completion, and gave the command to Lieutenant-Colonel the Honourable Alexander Hope.

Being now anxious to test the capabilities of the corps he had organized, Colonel Graham requested to be sent to one of the camps formed in the South, and, accordingly, about the end of June he received orders to proceed to Southampton, to form part of the army encamped on Netley-common, commanded by Lord Moira.

On the 27th June, the 90th embarked at Kinghorn, in Fife, on board the following transports :—

The *Aid*.—Lieutenant-Colonel Moncrieffe, Lieutenant Napier, Ensign Francis Eddins, Surgeon Russel, 217 N.C.O. and men, and 32 women.

The *Disco Bay*.—Captain Lord Henry Murray, Ensign Thomas Webster, 192 N.C.O. and men, and 25 women.

The *Alliance*.—Lieutenant Fortescue, Ensign Cartwright, Ensign McDonald, Assistant-Surgeon Anderson, 83 N.C.O. and men.

The *Mary*.—Captain Mackenzie, Lieutenant Graham, 180 N.C.O. and men.

The *Sally*.—Ensign Drummond, Quarter-master David Hopkins, 130 N.C.O. and men, and 22 women.

On the 29th July, the regiment arrived at Netley camp, where it was joined with several parties of recruits and those officers who had been absent on duty. While in the camp it was announced in orders that the 90th would be among those regiments to be employed on service, when the Commandant took occasion to recommend to all classes the most unremitting attention to every point of duty and the most strict and prompt obedience, expressing his

determination to make the conduct and character of indi- 1794.
viduals of every rank the only title to indulgence or
promotion, as far as it depended upon him to give or
recommend it.

On the 6th November, the regiment marched to Winchester, where it was inspected by the Earl of Moira, who expressed his satisfaction at its appearance, and added that it afforded him great pleasure to be able to make so favourable a report of its state to His Majesty.

During its stay at Winchester, colours were presented to 1795. the 1st battalion—the anniversary of the King's birthday, the 4th of June, being chosen for the purpose. Colonel Graham, who presented them, addressed his Corps in the following terms:—

" Officers and fellow soldiers, I have chosen to deliver
" the Colours of the Regiment into your custody on this
" day, because I wish that it should be marked in every
" man's remembrance by its being the anniversary of the
" birth of our gracious Sovereign. The sentiments of
" loyalty to your King, and attachment to these Standards,
" blended together with happy enthusiasm on this day of
" national joy, will for ever remain engraven on your
" hearts. The defence of these colours is a sacred trust
" that I need not dwell on; the honour of the regiment is
" in your hands, and depends on the exertion of your
" attention, perseverance, and courage. Courage, how-
" ever, is the growth of the soil of Britain; cowardice and
" slavery are alike unknown in these isles, for the bravery
" of her sons is cherished and confirmed by the fostering
" hand of freedom. When I look then on this chosen
" band, can I doubt that the truest spirit of heroism per-
" vades its ranks? Who amongst you would not devote
" himself to death rather than abandon these banners, and
" who of you would not be ready to spill the last drop of
" his blood in defence of that constitution which equally
" secures the rights of the people and the throne of the
" King!

1795.
"I entertain no such doubts; on the contrary, I am sure
"that if I have the honour of leading you into the field
"against the enemy, I shall have more occasion to temper
"your ardour than to animate your courage. But I am
"most anxious that courage should be tempered and
"directed by the most perfect discipline, and I trust that
"none who think themselves worthy to belong to the
"90th Regiment will grudge the pains necessary to attain
"to that perfection. You must be distinguished not only
"in appearance, but in reality. It is highly gratifying to
"me to be at the head of a body of men on whose
"exertions as good soldiers I can rely, as I do with
"confidence. Accept my thanks for your past conduct;
"we shall soon be in company with other troops; let it be
"your constant object to excel. I wish not only to be
"proud of you, but to owe you my gratitude and affec-
"tion."

The 90th was inspected on the 5th of July by His Royal Highness the Duke of York, who conveyed to Colonel Graham his orders to thank the officers and men, in his name, for the handsome appearance they made. Shortly after the regiment moved to Nursling camp, whence it marched to Southampton, there to await the departure of the expedition to co-operate with the French Royalists, of which it was to form part.

After several delays the troops were embarked on board the ships commanded by Commodore Warren, the land forces being under the command of General Doyle, and the expedition, accompanied by the Comte d'Artois, started on the 18th of August for the coast of France, where it was proposed to land the regiments of French emigrants with a view to their joining the forces of General Charette, one of the royalist leaders, in La Vendée.

The first rendezvous was in Quiberon Bay, and the intention was to land the troops and stores on the peninsula of Noir Montier, but on arrival it was found that the stores, etc., would, if landed, be exposed to the attack of the overwhelming force which the Republican Generals could 1795. bring forward at that point. General Charette having also explained how dangerous it would be for him to expose his troops on an open beach were he to advance in the direction of Noir Montier, it was decided to seize upon l'Isle Dieu, and thence to throw supplies on to the main land as opportunity offered. On the 29th of September, the garrison of the island surrendered to the *Galatea*, *Anson*, *Concord*, and *La Trompeuse* frigates, and the troops, divided into two brigades, were immediately landed. Colonel Anson, of the 12th Foot, commanded the 1st Brigade, and Colonel Graham the 2nd, consisting of the 78th and 90th Regiments. During the two months that the island was occupied, good roads were made from La Bourg St. Sauveur to such bays and other places as offered favourable opportunities of landing to the enemy, the fortifications were repaired, and every preparation made to resist an attack. The Republicans, however, contented themselves with preventing General Charette from obtaining any of the supplies brought for him, and the British brigades being far too weak to assist him by any offensive movement they were recalled at the end of November.

Early in December the troops were successively embarked, and the transports sailed from l'Isle Dieu for Quiberon Bay. An accident which happened to the ship in which was a wing of the 90th, under Colonel Graham, is best described in his own words:—

"Captain Sir Edmund Nagle, commanding the *Artois*
"frigate, was appointed to see everything removed from
"the island, and as I had command of the rear-guard he
"offered me a passage in his ship. It blew very fresh,
"with a heavy sea along the coast towards Quiberon Bay,
"so that we had only a foresail set in order to keep
"astern of the convoy. On coming near Quiberon Bay
"two lights were discovered, which were supposed by
"Sir Edmund and the pilot to be for the purpose of
"directing the ships round the east end of the island of

1795. "Houat, and so as to keep clear of the Cardinal rocks that lie off the S.E. end of that island. These lights, however, were intended for the purpose of marking out the anchorage to the transports, but no communication had been made on this subject to Sir E. Nagle. The consequence had nearly proved fatal to us all. About 7 o'clock in the evening, while we were at dinner in the Captain's cabin (a number of the officers of the 90th Regiment in company), the first Lieutenant came down to announce that we were close in upon the shore at the back of the island of Houat. The mainsail was dropped as quickly as possible and the helm put down, but the ship had scarcely got way enough when breakers ahead made it indispensably necessary to put the ship about, when there was but little chance of her staying.

"Her head, however, did come round to the wind, and Captain Nagle came back into the cabin wishing us all joy of our narrow escape, which he said was entirely owing to the perfection of the *Artois*.

"Very soon after this, and while standing out from the land close-hauled, we struck on a reef, and after three severe blows the swell fortunately carried us over. Much damage had been received, however, and the water, which was heard gushing in, soon rose to a considerable height, and could hardly be kept under with all the pumps going. Four hundred men of the 90th Regiment, being on board, gave great assistance. At daybreak we stood back and got into Quiberon Bay. On examination by the carpenters of the fleet it was considered impracticable that anything effectual could be done to improve the condition of the ship, and Admiral Harvey determined to send her immediately home—the *Melampus* frigate, Captain Sir Richard Strachan, having orders to keep company with the *Artois*, and afford every assistance in his power.

"Three hundred men of the 90th, with a proportion of officers, were withdrawn and distributed on board of

"other ships. I had received such marked attention from 1795.
"Sir Edmund Nagle that I accepted his invitation to
"remain on board. Three days after we sailed from
"Quiberon Bay we fell in with some English frigates,
"which, from the signals not being seen, owing to thick
"weather, obliged us to clear for action. The night
"following it came on to blow very fresh, and we had a
"good deal of damage done to our sails and rigging, and
"lost our main-top-gallant mast. In addition to these
"untoward circumstances we lost sight of our friend the
"*Melampus*, and were thus left alone with a foul wind and
"a heavy swell. We never got an observation, but, from
"calculations, supposing that we had got sufficiently to
"westward to clear Ushant, we stood northward, with
"scarcely any sail set, as the wind increased as we opened
"the chops of the channel.

"Under these circumstances it was thought advisable,
"when the day closed, to lay to for fear of running foul of
"the Lizard Point; but at midnight we discovered we were
"quite on the other side of the channel, having distinctly
"made out the three Casquet lights off Guernsey. This
"was a great relief to Sir Edward Nagle's mind, and we
"accordingly shaped our course for Spithead; on rounding
"the east end of the Isle of Wight we discovered the
"*Melampus* frigate working up towards St. Helens. We
"were all most happy to get on shore after this dis-
"agreeable voyage . . . . The frigate was
"afterwards ordered into dock, when it was found that a
"considerable piece of rock had been broken off and was
"still sticking in the ship's bottom, providentially with
"such a hold as saved her from immediately going to the
"bottom."

On its return to England the 90th proceeded to Poole, 1796.
where it arrived on the 1st of January, 1796, and where
orders were received for it to hold itself in readiness to go
out to St. Domingo, to join Sir Ralph Abercromby. It

1796. was, however, shortly afterwards decided to abandon that expedition, and in March, the regiment returned to Southampton, whence, on the 12th of April it sailed for Gibraltar, which was reached on the 13th of May. The second battalion was at this time employed to act as marines on board the fleet, and thus seeing no chance of being engaged on active service with his regiment, Colonel Graham accepted the appointment of British Commissioner with the Austrian army in Italy, where he remained until the end of the year.

Lieutenant-Colonel Moncrieffe, in the absence of the Commandant, assumed command of the regiment, having as his second, Lieutenant-Colonel Rowland Hill. Early in the year, Major Kenneth Mackenzie had gone to Portugal with General Sir Charles Stuart, where, with the local rank of Lieutenant-Colonel, he was appointed to command a battalion formed of the flank companies of the regiments composing the British army in that country, which was disciplined by him as a battalion of light infantry on the model of his own regiment. So highly did Sir Charles Stuart approve of the system of that corps, that he made it the school of instruction for the whole army under his command.

Intelligence of the stirring events which were startling the civilized world was brought to Gibraltar by the ships which were continually arriving, and helped by the contrast to make the daily round of garrison duties more wearying to the different corps quartered there. Nothing of any importance happened to the 90th until the middle of 1798,

1798. when, a French force having seized upon Malta, in May, a counter-expedition was organized at Gibraltar—it was generally supposed for the recapture of the former stronghold. Colonel Graham, who had returned to England at the beginning of the preceding year, at once prepared to rejoin his regiment, his movements being hastened by a letter which he received from General O'Hara, the Governor of Gibraltar, dated,—

> "Gibraltar, the 30th of September, 1798,   1798.
>
> "My dear Colonel,
>
> "I very sincerely rejoice at the prospect of seeing you again upon this rock, and talking over the recent unfortunate events of this cursed war. You will find your regiment in good order in every respect, and sincerely consider with much satisfaction they are to be employed upon this secret expedition. They are themselves perfectly happy with having you once more at their head, and I am perfectly confident when tried they will answer your most sanguine expectations. May this expedition, to whatever part of the globe you are going, succeed fully and amply is the earnest wish of your most
>
> "Faithful and obedient servant,
>
> "CHA. O'HARA."
>
> "COLONEL GRAHAM."

General Sir Charles Stuart, who was appointed to the command of the expedition, directed Lieutenant-Colonel Mackenzie (90th Regt.) to proceed at once from Lisbon to Gibraltar, to superintend the embarkation of the stores and to carry out the duties of Deputy Adjutant-General. About the 19th of October, the troops embarked, the 90th going on board the *Calcutta*. The other regiments composing the force being the 28th, the 42nd, the 58th, two companies R.A., and one company Royal Military Artificers.

> "General Orders.
>
> "H.M. Ship *Leviathan*,
>
> "20th October, 1798.
>
> "No. 1.—The corps are to be brigaded as follows:—
> "The 28th and 90th Regts. will form the first brigade under the command of Brigadier-General Stewart, to which will be attached 69 rank and file of the Royal Artillery and 23 rank and file of the Royal Military Artificers.

1798.   " The 42nd and 58th Regts., under the command of
" Brigadier General Oakes, will form the second brigade,
" to which will be attached 70 rank and file of the Royal
" Artillery and 24 rank and file from the Royal Military
" Artificers.

" Detachments will be made in the following propor-
" tions from the above Regts. to form a reserve under
" the command of Colonel Graham, 90th Regiment, to
" which will be attached 46 rank and file from the Royal
" Artillery and 15 rank and file from the Royal Military
" Artificers, viz.—

" The flank companies of the 28th Regt. completed
" to 50 rank and file each.

" The 42nd flank companies and as many companies of the
" battalion as will form a detachment of 350 rank and file.

" The 90th flank companies and as many companies of
" the battalion as will form a detachment of 300 rank and
" file."

" Regimental Orders:—
                " On board the *Calcutta*,
                        " 25th October, 1798.
                        " Colonel Graham has had much satisfaction in
" receiving a very favourable report of the conduct of the
" 90th Regiment at Gibraltar from his Excellency the
" Governor, and from Colonel Moncrieffe.

" No regiment raised during this war has had equal
" opportunities, before meeting the enemy, of acquiring all
" the advantages which a thorough knowledge of a soldier's
" duty gives to old regiments. Much, therefore, will be
" expected of the 90th Regiment, and Colonel Graham
" entertains no doubt of their justifying and confirming by
" their behaviour in this expedition the high character they
" have already obtained.

" He flatters himself that it is unnecessary for him to
" assure the Regiment that no other command could have
" been more agreeable to him, and in considering the last

1798 "General Orders, by which he is appointed to the com-
"mand of the reserve, he feels very sincere pleasure in the
"reflection that that corps is to be composed in part of a
"considerable detachment of the 90th Regiment. He
"cannot conclude without most earnestly pressing upon
"the mind of every officer and every soldier of the regi-
"ment the strictest attention to the important precepts
"contained in the Rules and Regulations of the 18th
"instant, issued by the Commander-in-Chief, and the
"explanatory observations contained in the General Orders
"of the 20th instant.*

"To gain distinction, to stamp in indelible characters
"the reputation of the 90th Regiment, the conduct of
"every man belonging to it must be equally distinguished
"by implicit obedience to superiors, by the most deter-
"mined enterprise, and by the most punctual execution of
"every military duty.

"Agreeable to the General Orders a detachment to join
"the reserve will be prepared, consisting of the following
"officers and companies, with the sergeants and drummers
"belonging to them:—

"Lieutenants Edden, Preedy, Colberg, Carter, Wright,
"and Holland.

        "Lord Ruthven's Company.
        "Captain McNair's Company.
        "Captain Cholmondeley's Company.
        "Major Mackenzie's Company.

"These Companies are to be completed to 75 rank and
"file each, and the above-mentioned officers will be posted
"to them as follows:—

        "Lieutenants Edden and Carter to Lord Ruthven's
        "Company.
        "Lieutenant Preedy to Captain Cholmondeley's
        "Company.

---

* Rules and Regulations for the guidance of the army when in the field, issued by Sir C. Stuart, on board H.M.S. *Argo*, Octr. 18th, 1798.

1798.   " Lieutenant Wright to Captain McNair's Company.
" Lieutenants Colberg and Holland to Major Mac-
" kenzie's Company."

" H.M.S. *Leviathan,* at sea.
" Octr. 26th, 1798.

" G.O. No. 1.

" From some unforeseen circumstances relative to
" the order of disembarking the troops, the reserve, as
" mentioned in the order No. 1 of the 20th inst., will not
" be established previous to landing ; the officers, therefore,
" and companies named to compose that corps will land
" with their respective regiments, and the distribution of
" the artillery and artificers will be, for the present, as
" hereafter stated."

* * * * * * * * * * *

" G.O. No. 3.
" Order of disembarkation :—
" 1st Division of the 28th Regiment and one captain, one
" Lieutenant, one Sergeant, one drummer, and 30 rank and
" file of the Royal Artillery, with two light six-pounders.

" 2nd Division.—800 men of 90th Regiment, including
" officers, non-commissioned officers and drummers, and
" one Lieutenant, one Sergeant, one drummer, and 30 rank
" and file from the Royal Artillery, with two light six-
" pounders.

" 3rd Division.—The remainder of the 90th Regiment,
" part of the 42nd Regiment, and one Lieutenant, one
" Sergeant, one drummer, and 30 rank and file of the
" Royal Artillery, with two light six-pounders.

" 4th Division.—The remainder of the 42nd Regiment
" and 400 men of the 58th Regiment, including officers,
" non-commissioned officers, and drummers ; and one
" Lieutenant, one Sergeant, one drummer, and 30 rank
" and file of the Royal Artillery, with two light six-
" pounders.

" 5th Division.—The remainder of the 58th Regiment, 1798.
" the remainder of the Royal Artillery and the Royal
" Military Artificers, with two 5½-inch howitzers and such
" stores as will be particularly specified to the heads of the
" following departments, viz., Engineers, Artillery, Deputy
" Commissary General of Provisions, and Inspector Gene-
" ral of Hospitals."

" Regimental Orders :—
                    " On board the *Calcutta*,
                          " 28th October, 1798.
" The Commander-in-Chief having signified that,
" on account of some unforeseen circumstances relative to
" the disembarkation of the troops, the Reserve cannot be
" established previous to landing, and having directed
" that two companies of the 90th Regt. shall meanwhile
" be completed to 100 rank and file each, the 3rd, Lord
" Ruthven's, Company, under the command of Lieutenant
" Edden, and the 7th, Captain McNair's Company, under
" the command of Captain Napier, are to be immediately
" completed to that number, and it being necessary that
" every man of those two companies should be capable of
" undergoing the fatigue of the most active service, Lieu-
" tenant Edden and Captain Napier are directed to choose
" each respectively for the company under his command
" four men from each of the other companies of the
" regiment, which will enable them to draft from their
" companies respectively some of the least active men
" belonging to them, so as, on the whole, to complete these
" companies to 100 rank and file each, and the men so
" drafted from these two companies will be equally
" distributed among the remaining companies of the
" regiment."

The fleet anchored off the north-east side of the island
of Minorca on the 6th of November, and on the following
day the landing was effected in the Bay of Addaya, with

1798. the greatest regularity and despatch, and was promptly followed up by movements, described in the following despatch, which in a very short time brought about the surrender of the island.

" Ciudadella, Novr. 18th, 1798.

" Sir,

" I have the honour to acquaint you that His
" Majesty's forces are in possession of the Island of
" Minorca, without having sustained the loss of a single
" man.

" As neither Commodore Duckworth or myself could
" procure any useful information relative to the object
" of the expedition at Gibraltar, it was judged advisable
" to despatch the *Petrel* sloop of war to cruize off the
" harbour of Mahon for intelligence, where, after remaining
" a few days, she joined the fleet near the Colombrites,
" without having made any essential discovery. So cir-
" cumstanced, it was agreed to attempt a descent in the
" Bay of Addaya, and the wind proving favourable on the
" 7th instant, a feint was made by the line-of-battle ships
" at Fornelles, and boats were assembled for that purpose
" under the direction of Captain Bowen, Captain Polden,
" and Captain Pressland. Previous to the landing of the
" troops, a small battery at the entrance of the bay was
" evacuated by the enemy, the magazine blown up, the
" guns spiked, and shortly after, the first Division, consist-
" ing of eight hundred men, was on shore. A considerable
" explosion to the westward indicated that the Spaniards
" had also abandoned the works at Fornelles. Nearly at
" the same moment two thousand of the enemy's troops
" approached in several different directions, but were
" repulsed with some loss on the left, while the guns of the
" *Argo* checked a similar attempt on the right flank, and
" the post was maintained until the debarkation of the
" different divisions afforded the means of establishing a
" position, from whence the enemy's troops would have

" been attacked with considerable advantage, had they not 1798.
" retired in the beginning of the night.

" The strength of the ground, the passes, and the bad-
" ness of the roads in Minorca are scarcely to be equalled
" in the most mountainous parts of Europe ; and what
" increased the difficulty of advancing upon this occasion
" was the dearth of intelligence, for although near one
" hundred deserters had come in from the Swiss regiments,
" and affirmed that the remaining force upon the island
" exceeded four thousand men, no particular account of
" the enemy's movements was obtained. Under this
" uncertainty it was for a few minutes doubtful what
" measure to pursue, but as quickly determined to proceed
" by a forced march to Mercadel, and thereby separate the
" enemy's force by possessing that essential pass, in the
" first instance, and from thence advancing upon his
" principal communications to either extremity of the
" island, justly depending upon Commodore Duckworth's
" zeal and exertions to forward from Addaya and Fornelles
" such supplies of provisions and ordnance stores as
" might favour subsequent operations.

" To effect this object, Colonel Graham was sent with
" six hundred men, and by great exertion arrived at
" Mercadel a very few hours after the main force of the
" enemy had marched towards Ciudadella, making several
" officers and soldiers prisoners, seizing various small
" magazines, and establishing his corps in front of the
" village.

" The persevering labour of 250 seamen, under the
" direction of Lieutenant Buchanan, during the night
" having greatly assisted the artillery in forwarding the
" battalion guns, the army arrived at Mercadel on the
" 9th, where, learning that Mahon was nearly evacuated, a
" disposition was instantly made to operate with the whole
" force in that direction, and Colonel Paget was detached
" under this movement with three hundred men to take

C

1798. " possession of the town. Upon his arrival he summoned
" Fort Charles to surrender, and made the Lieutenant-
" Governor of the island, a Colonel of Artillery, and one
" hundred and sixty men prisoners of war; he removed
" the boom obstructing the entrance of the harbour, and
" gave free passage to the *Cormorant* and *Aurora* frigates
" which were previously sent by Commodore Duckworth
" to make a diversion off that port.

" But these were not the only advantages immediately
" resulting from this movement—it favoured desertion,
" intercepted all stragglers, and enabled the different
" departments of the army to procure beasts of burthen
" for the further progress of His Majesty's arms.

" Having ascertained that the enemy's troops were
" throwing up works and entrenching themselves in front
" of Ciudadella, it was resolved to force their position on
" the night of the 13th instant, and preparatory to this
" attempt, Colonel Paget, with two hundred men, was
" withdrawn from Mahon; Colonel Moncrieffe (90th) was
" sent forward with a detachment to Ferarias; three light
" twelve-pounders, three five-and-a-half-inch howitzers,
" and ninety marines were landed from the fleet ; when, in
" consequence of its having been communicated to Com-
" modore Duckworth, that four ships, supposed of the line,
" were seen between Majorca and Minorca, steering
" towards the last-mentioned island, he decided to pursue
" them, and requested that the seamen and marines might
" re-embark, and signified his determination of proceeding
" with all the armed transports to sea. But weighing the
" consequences which would result to the army from the
" smallest delay on the one hand, and the advantages to be
" reasonably expected from a spirited attack on the other,
" it was thought advisable to retain them with the army,
" and on the 12th inst. the whole force marched to Alpinz,
" and from thence proceeded on the 13th to Jupet—Colonel
" Moncrieffe's detachment moving in a parallel line on the

"Ferarias road to Mala Garaba. These precautions, and the
"appearance of two columns approaching the town, induced
"the enemy to retire from their half-constructed defences
"within the walls of Ciudadella, and in the evening of the
"same day a small detachment, under Captain Muter,
"was sent to take possession of the Torré den Quart,
"whereby the army was enabled to advance on the 14th,
"apparently in three columns, upon Kane's, the Ferarias,
"and Fornelles roads to the investment of the town at
"daybreak, occupying ground covered by the position the
"enemy had relinquished. Thus situated, in want of heavy
"artillery, and every article necessary for a siege, it was
"deemed expedient to summon the Governor of Minorca
"to surrender, and the preliminary articles were im-
"mediately considered, but doubts arising on the part
"of the enemy, whether the investing force was superior
"in number to the garrison, two batteries of three twelve-
"pounders, and three five-and-a-half-inch howitzers were
"erected in the course of the following night within eight
"hundred yards of the place, and, at daybreak, the main
"body of the troops formed in order of battle considerably
"to the right of Kane's road, leaving the picquets to
"communicate between them and Colonel Moncrieffe's
"post. This line, partly real and partly imaginary,
"extended four miles in front of the enemy's batteries,
"from whence two eighteen-pound shot were immedi-
"ately fired at the troops; but a timely parley, and the
"distant appearance of the squadron, occasioned the
"cessation of hostilities, and renewed a negociation which,
"through the address of Major-General Sir James St.
"Clair Erskine, terminated in the capitulation.

* * * * * * * * * * *

"The zeal, spirit, and perseverance of both the
"officers and men of the different regiments under my
"command have eminently contributed to the success of
"the expedition, and authorize me to represent their

1798.

1798. " services as highly deserving His Majesty's most gracious approbation.

* * * * * * * * * * *

" I have the honour to be, etc., etc.,
"CHS. STUART."
" The Right Honourable Henry Dundas."

The reduction of Minorca once completed, Colonel Graham obtained leave of absence, and proceeded to Sicily, there to employ himself in the service of its legitimate monarch. The command of the regiment was again assumed by Colonel Moncrieffe, the troops being actively employed in placing the island in a state of defence.

1799. In May, 1799, the state of Sir Charles Stuart's health rendered it necessary for him to return to England, the chief command devolving on Major-General Sir James St. Clair Erskine.

" General Orders.

" Mahon, May 2nd, 1799.

" As the state of the General's health does not permit him at present to command the army with that activity which the service may require, he resigns that important trust to Major-General Sir James St. Clair Erskine, with full confidence that under his care, both the officers and men will be directed in a manner to maintain the high opinion which the King has formed of their services.

" If their good conduct was so conspicuous as to be judged worthy of his Majesty's distinct approbation upon the reduction of the island, the orderly behaviour and discipline of the troops at the outposts, the unparalleled efforts of the forces at Fort George, with the indefatigable labour of the several departments employed at the different fortresses is an equal and no less eminent proof of their zeal and spirit, and the General trusts that when he lays before

"the King an account of the extraordinary efforts whereby 1799.
"this important possession is enabled in four months to
"meet and resist the most daring attempts of the enemy,
"His Majesty will feel a superior degree of satisfaction in
"having troops so determined to defend the territory they
"have obtained, as they were firm and resolute in effecting
"the conquest.

"Impressed with these truths, though the General
"cannot refrain from expressing his sincere regret at
"leaving the army, he feels a degree of pleasure in having
"an opportunity of laying their just representation at the
"feet of His Majesty, and he cannot help entertaining
"hopes that his health will once more enable him to
"direct their proceedings upon some future and no less
"important occasion."

On the 2nd of May, Captain McNair was appointed Deputy Judge-Advocate of the army in Minorca, and about the same time Lieutenant-Colonel Hill obtained leave of absence and returned to England.

Colonel Graham having satisfactorily concluded his duties in Naples, was appointed to the command of the troops who were sent to wrest Malta from the French, with the rank of Brigadier-General. Soon after his arrival on that island he applied for the 90th Regiment to be sent to him, receiving the following reply from General Fox, who was commanding at Minorca.

"Mahon, 2nd February, 1800.   1800.

"Dear Sir,
    "I am honoured with your private letter of the
"12th Decr., the contents of which I conceived it necessary
"that Mr. Dundas should be acquainted with, and being
"aware that you were in the habit of correspondence with
"him, I enclosed it to him in a private letter from myself.
"As Mr. Dundas has received my letter from Gibraltar,

1800. "and from hence upon my arrival, before the *Constance* left
"England, in which I fully stated to him that I did not
"think myself authorized to detach troops from hence, I
"am to presume my intentions were approved of, or the
"*Constance* would have brought an order to detach them.
"You may be assured, should I receive such an order, not
"a moment's time shall be lost in sending them, and if it
"is left to me, and the numbers can be brought to agree,
"the 90th Regiment shall be sent. In the event, I shall
"send Brigadier-General Moncrieffe with it, who is per-
"fectly aware that, as senior Colonel, and your being
"appointed a Brigadier-General, he will be entirely under
"your command.

* * * * * * * * *

"I have the honour to be, dear Sir,
"Your faithful and obedient servant,
"G. FOX."
"BRIGADIER-GENERAL GRAHAM,
"etc., etc., etc."

The 90th was not sent to the assistance of its gallant chief, Colonel Moncrieffe proceeding alone to Malta, there to assume command of a corps of Maltese, which had been raised by Colonel Graham.

The state of the 90th Regiment on the 23rd of March, 1800, was as follows:—

"*Officers and men doing duty with the regiment in Minorca.*

"1 Lieutenant-Colonel, Lyde Browne.
"2 Captains, Alex. Murray and the Honble. Mark
"Napier, 16 subalterns, 1 adjutant, 1 quarter-master,
"1 surgeon, and 1 assistant-surgeon, 51 serjeants, 22
"drummers, and 748 privates.
"Colonel Thomas Graham, Brigadier-General to the
"forces serving in Minorca.

"Lieutenant-Colonel George Moncrieffe, Brigadier-General to the forces in Minorca. 1800.

"Lieutenant-Colonel Rowland Hill, absent on leave.

"Lieutenant-Colonel Kenneth Mackenzie, Deputy Adjutant-General to the forces in Minorca.

"Captain John McNair, Deputy Judge-Advocate to the forces in Minorca.

"Captain Thomas Bligh St. George, Brigade-Major to the forces in Minorca.

"Captain John Graham, Aide-de-Camp to the Earl of Chatham.

"Captain James Lord Ruthven, recruiting.

"*General state of casualties, 90th Regiment, from April, 1796, to April, 1800 :—*

"Dead	{ In Gibraltar	44	
	{ In Minorca	50	94
"Discharged	{ In Gibraltar	2	
	{ In Minorca	1	3
"Deserted	{ In Gibraltar	8	
	{ In Minorca	4	12
"Invalided from Gibraltar		40	
"Left in Gibraltar		12	
"Invalided from Minorca		9	61
"Drafted in Gibraltar		67	67
"On Furlough	{ From Gibraltar	9	
	{ From Minorca	4	13
"Total casualties in Gibraltar and Minorca			250

"*General state of men joined the 90th Regiment from April, 1796, to April, 1800 :—*

"1796	{ From 2nd battalion, Gibraltar	35
	{ From Hospital, England	12
	{ Recruit	1
		48

1800.

"1797	Recruits . . . . 23 From 2nd battalion 31	54	
"1798	Recruits . . . . 20 From 37th Regiment . . . . 3 From 70th Regiment 9	32	
"1798	Recruits in Minorca	3	
"1799	Recruits in Minorca . . . . 8 From Furlough in ditto . . . 3	11	
"1800	Recruits in ditto. 3	3	
	" Total joined in Gibraltar and Minorca	151 "	

In April, the officers of the regiment were gratified by a most unexpected piece of good fortune. Captain McNair had, when in London some time before, taken a ticket in one of the State lotteries in the name of the regiment, and on looking through the papers of March he came upon the following announcement in the *Times* newspaper of the 27th (Thursday) :—

" The ticket, No. 34,925, drawn a prize of £20,000, was
" purchased by Geo. Leckie, Esq., of Artillery-place,
" Finsbury-square, for Captain John McNair, of the 90th
" Regiment, now at Gibraltar, and was chequed with its
" counterpart at Guildhall by Mr. Leckie, in order to
" ascertain its validity and render it negociable."

Captain McNair, in a letter to Colonel Graham, thus alludes to this most gratifying event.

" Minorca, 5th May, 1800.

" Dear Sir,

* * * * * * * * * *

" You will have observed in the papers of the 27th
" March that a £20,000 prize in the lottery belongs to the
" 90th ; we anxiously look for an official notification of it ;

"7/85 shares is your proportion of it—perhaps sixteen- 1800.
"hundred pounds. A grand expedition to the Mediter-
"ranean is much talked of, but nothing certain is known
"respecting it; there is not any appearance of movement
"in this island. Since Colonel Stuart's return Colonel
"Mackenzie has applied to return to the Regiment and
"been refused—it is to be regretted.

   "I have the honour to be, dear Sir,
      "Yours most faithfully,
        "JOHN McNAIR."
"BRIG.-GENL. GRAHAM,
 "etc.,   etc."

 The expedition mentioned in the foregoing letter was that of Sir Ralph Abercromby, which left England in May, and was accompanied by Lieutenant-Colonel Rowland Hill, who, hearing that the 90th was to be actively employed, immediately proceeded to rejoin. Captain McNair in a letter, dated May 26th, says, "Our good fortune in the "lottery is confirmed."

 In June, Sir Ralph Abercromby arrived at Minorca with troops to form an expedition, and Lieutenant-Colonel Kenneth Mackenzie was requested to continue in his situation on the staff, but, as the 90th Regiment was to form part of the expedition, he resigned his staff appointment and rejoined. On the following day he was appointed by Sir Ralph Abercromby to command a secret expedition with the flank companies of the army, to be embarked on part of Lord Keith's squadron, but the arrival of orders from England, in the course of the night, put a stop to it. About the 25th of June, the 90th went on board H.M.S. *Alkmaar*, and proceeded with Sir Ralph Abercromby to Genoa, with a view to make a diversion in favour of Austria, then at war with France, and hard pressed by her armies.

 Suchet commanded and held Genoa obstinately against the Austrian General Ott and Lord Keith with the British fleet, till compelled to capitulate on the 5th of June; the

1800. issue of the battle of Marengo, however, caused its restoration to the French, and the troops, under General Abercromby, arrived too late to be of service.

On the 4th of July 200 men of the 90th were sent on board the *Pallas* and 100 on board the *Zephyr* transports. While at Leghorn, Colonel Rowland Hill rejoined and assumed command of the regiment.

" Leghorn, 11th July,
" 4 o'clock in the morning.
" My dear Sir,
" We are this moment ordered to sail for Minorca,
" so there is only time to go on board the Admiral's ship
" with your letters, which Lord Keith has promised to
" forward the very first opportunity. You will of course
" hear all that has passed here. I am rejoiced to hear the
" 90th is in so fine order.

* * * * * * * * * * *

" I have the honour to be,
" Your sincere and much obliged,
" R. HILL."
" COLONEL GRAHAM."

Sir Ralph Abercromby inspected the regiment on the 6th of August, at Minorca, where the whole of the troops were actively preparing for service.

" Minorca, 7th August, 1800.
" Dear Sir,
" I only received your letter of the 15th July two
" days ago; I wrote to Mr. Buller yesterday, agreeable to
" your request, about the prize in the lottery. I have sent
" by the *Pegasus* three boxes for you, I suppose from
" England. Our clothing is making up with every possible
" expedition, and I hope will be finished before we can
" leave this island. The army of the expedition is bri-
" gaded anew; the 42nd, 90th, and De Rolle's form one

"brigade, under General Oakes, in General Moore's Division; Colonel Paget commands a brigade in General Hutchinson's Division. We are still in the lazzarette and uncommonly healthy; three other regiments are with us. I am just setting off for Ciudadella to attend a General Court Martial, but I shall write you by very first ship.

  "I have the honour to be,
    "Dear Sir, yours most faithfully,
      "JOHN McNAIR."

"BRIGADR.-GENL. GRAHAM.
 "etc., etc., etc."

1800.

Despatches from England were received on the 25th of August by Sir R. Abercromby, and on the 27th the troops, amounting to 9,000, embarked for Gibraltar, which was reached on the 11th of September; while there, the army was augmented by the arrival of Sir James Pulteney with 12,000 men. The whole force thence proceeded to Cadiz, off which place the fleet arrived on the 4th of October, and anchored about four leagues from the shore.

The army was divided into wings, the right was commanded by Major-General Hutchinson, and the left by Major-General Morshead. On the 5th, the reserve of the right wing made a feint by hovering about the shore, but did not leave their ships. On the 6th, they were ordered to land, and part embarked in the flat boats, but were obliged to return to their ships, a sufficient number of boats not having been sent to convey them on shore. On the 8th, they were again ordered to land, and to be on shore before eight o'clock in the morning, but the wind being high, and dead on shore, together with a very heavy sea, the signal was made from the Admiral to hoist in and secure the flat boats, which was immediately done, and by eleven o'clock the fleet put to sea,—appearing off Gibraltar about midnight on the 11th of October, and finally anchored in Tetuan Bay early on the 12th. On the 14th, a severe gale of wind began to blow from the

1800. eastward, which so increased in violence that it became necessary for the fleet to stand out to sea. On the 20th, most of the scattered ships were anchored off Cape Spartel, the rendezvous, Sir Ralph Abercromby joining the fleet on the 21st. After waiting for a favourable wind for some time, on the 27th a start was again made for Tetuan Bay, which was reached the following day.

On the 24th, the following general order was published, which was carried into effect on arrival at Tetuan.

" G. O.

" October 24th, 1800.

" The service requiring a separation of the army under " the command of Sir Ralph Abercromby, the general " officers are attached in the following manner :—

" Major-Generals Hutchinson, Coote, Craddock, Ludlow, " Moore, and Lord Cavan, Brigadier-Generals Stewart, " Hope, Doyle, and Oakes, are to be attached to the " troops that will serve under the immediate command of " Sir R. Abercromby.

" Major-Generals Morshead and Manners, Brigadier-" Generals Fisher and Maitland, will serve under the " immediate command of Sir James Pulteney."

" G. O.

" On board H.M.S. *Diadem*,

" 25th October, 1800.

" The army under the command of Sir Ralph Aber-" cromby is brigaded as follows :—

" 1st Battn. Coldstream Guards . }	Major-General
" 1st do. 3rd Guards . . . . }	Ludlow.

" 1st Brigade of the line.

" 54th (two battalions) . . . . }	
" 92nd Highlanders . . . . . }	Major-General
" 2nd Royals . . . . }	Coote.

"2nd Brigade.

"8th Regiment. ⎫
"13th do.   ⎬ Major-General
"18th do.   ⎪ Craddock.
"90th do.   ⎭

"3rd Brigade.

"27th (two battalions) ⎫
"50th Regiment   ⎬ Lord Cavan.
"79th do.   ⎭

"4th Brigade.

"2nd Queen's   ⎫
"40th (two battalions) ⎬ Brigr.-General
"41th Regiment   ⎭ Doyle.

"5th Brigade.

"Stuart's Regiment ⎫
"De Rolle's do.   ⎬ Brigr.-General
"Dillon's do.   ⎭ Stewart.

"Reserve.

"23rd, 28th, 42nd, 58th Rifle Corps, Corsican Rangers, "Detachment 11th Dragoons, Detachment Hompech's "Mounted Riflemen, under Major-General Moore and "Brigadier-General Oakes."

On the 8th of November, the whole sailed from Tetuan Bay, Sir James Pulteney going to Lisbon with the corps under his command, while Sir Ralph Abercromby and his troops steered for Malta and Minorca; the former place was reached by one division on the 10th, the remainder following in about a fortnight.

The 90th remained at Minorca until the 16th and arrived at Malta on the 20th, when it disembarked and went into barracks.

It being now determined to interrupt the French in their occupation of Egypt, and orders being received by Sir Ralph Abercromby to that effect on the 25th of October, every preparation was made by the troops, during their stay in Malta, for the anticipated struggle.

1800. " G.O.

" Malta, December 11th, 1800.

" The army under the command of Sir Ralph
" Abercromby is to be considered as forming two lines
" and a reserve.

" The 1st line will consist of the brigade of Guards, the
" 1st, 2nd, and 3rd brigades of the line.

" The 2nd line will consist of the 4th and 5th brigades
" of the line.

" The corps under Major-General Moore will form the
" reserve from which a battalion or adequate corps will
" occasionally be taken to cover each flank of the army."

1801. The expedition left Malta, in two divisions, for Marmorice Bay, a magnificent land-locked harbour on the coast of Karamania, in Turkey; the first sailed on the 20th and arrived on the 29th, the second reached the Bay on the 5th of January, 1801.

On arrival, the sick were landed, and the regiments were also successively disembarked while the ships were cleaning, and the whole army was frequently exercised to those manœuvres they were shortly to practice before the enemy in landing.

On the 8th of February, commenced the most violent thunder and hail storm ever remembered, and which continued two days and nights intermittingly. The hail, or rather the ice, stones were as big as walnuts. The camps were deluged with a torrent of them, two feet deep, which, pouring from the mountains, swept every thing before it. The scene of confusion on shore, by the horses breaking loose, and the men being unable to face the storm or remain still in the freezing deluge, surpasses description. The ships in the harbour were in no less disorder from drifting, loss of masts, etc., and the *Swiftsure* was struck by lightning. At night the firmament was, from the increasing flashes, in a state of constant and vivid illumination. To add to the terrific grandeur of this concussion of elements, signal-guns of distress were frequently heard, and the howlings of wolves, jackalls, etc., re-echoed through the mountains at the back of the camp in the intervals, whenever the thunder ceased. It is not in the power of language to convey an adequate idea of such a tempest.

1801.

Every effort was made to procure horses for the cavalry and artillery, and mules and camels for the stores, but the Turks, who had promised much, gave but little, consequently the cavalry was only in part mounted, and then badly. The Captain Pacha, who was to have joined with a flotilla of gunboats, did not keep time, and only a few gunboats came round; it then became evident that the Turkish contingent would not be ready.

" G. O.

" February the 16th, 1801.

" As nearly as circumstances will permit, the dis-
" embarkation of the army will take place in the following
" order :—

" 1st. The infantry of the reserve with ten pieces of
" Light Artillery.

" 2nd. The brigade of Guards.

" 3rd. The remainder of the first line with six additional
" pieces of Light Artillery.

" 4th. The infantry of the second line.

" 5th. The mounted detachment of cavalry of the re-
" serve and Brigadier Finch's brigade.

" 6th. The dismounted part of the same brigade.

" 7th. The pioneers of the army, the horse detachment
" of the artillery, and such additional pieces of ordnance
" and ammunition as may be wanted.

* * * * * * * * * * *

" The Commander-in-Chief has much satisfaction in
" observing the behaviour of the troops in their transac-
" tions with the inhabitants during the stay of the army at
" Marmorice."

1801. The army embarked on the 20th of February, but it was not until the 23rd that the fleet could weigh anchor, when it sailed with a very fresh breeze. The number of vessels was such, about 175 sail, as to require a complete day for the whole to assemble in the roads.

A great misfortune was the total want of information respecting Egypt. Not a map to be depended upon could be procured, and the best draft from which information could be formed, and which was distributed to the generals, proved ridiculously incorrect.

Sir Sydney Smith was the only officer who knew anything of the locality of the coast, and he certainly, as far as he had seen, gave perfect information. Colonel Rowland Hill was by him furnished with a map, which was found invaluable in the subsequent operations.

On the 1st of March, the leading frigate made the signal for land, which proved to be the coast near Arab's Tower, and on the next morning the whole fleet anchored in Aboukir Bay.

The state of the weather was such as to prevent the possibility of landing, but on the 7th, the weather having moderated, Sir Ralph Abercromby went in a boat to reconnoitre the shore. The wind continuing to moderate, and the swell of the sea subsiding, on the morning of the 8th, at two o'clock, the first division of the army, consisting of the reserve under the orders of Major-General Moore, the brigade of Guards, under Major-General Ludlow, and part of the 1st brigade, the whole amounting to about five thousand five hundred men, under the command of Major-General Coote, assembled in the boats, the remainder of the 1st and 2nd brigade being put into ships close to the shore, that a support might be given after the first landing was effected. At three o'clock, the signal was made for their proceeding to rendezvous near the *Mondovi*, anchored about gun-shot from the shore; but the extent of the anchorage was so great that the assembling and arrangement of the boats could not be completed till near nine o'clock.

At nine, the signal was made for the boats to advance, 1801. which they did swiftly and with regularity, notwithstanding the heavy fire which was brought to bear upon them by the enemy's artillery advantageously posted on the sand-hills which skirted the beach, and also from the Castle of Aboukir. Undismayed by the hail of shot with which they were greeted, the men leaped on shore the moment the boats grounded, and forming up as they advanced, stormed the heights, which were in some parts very steep, and drove the French battalions before them, who, finding that the British were in full possession of the ridge, retreated behind the rear sand-hills, whence, for about an hour and a-half, they kept up a desultory fire. In the meantime the boats returned for the remainder of the army, which was all landed before night.

The French loss amounted to three hundred men and eight guns; that of the British to five hundred men.

As soon as the whole force had landed, a position was taken up about three miles distant from Aboukir, with the right resting on the sea, and the left on Lake Maadie. On the 12th, Sir Ralph Abercromby moved the army to Mandora Tower, about four miles, where it encamped in three lines. A body of French cavalry skirmished the whole way with the advanced guard, but no serious opposition was made.

On the 13th, the army marched to attack the French who were posted on a ridge of hills, the approach to which was perfectly open, and afforded a clear field of fire to their numerous artillery. As Sir Ralph Abercromby determined to turn their right, their left being refused, the English army marched in two lines and columns of regiments from the left, the reserve covering the movement on the right, and keeping parallel with the first line.

It had not advanced far out of the wood of date trees in front of Mandora Tower, before the enemy left the heights on which they had been formed, and moved down by their

D

1801. right, commencing a heavy fire of musketry and artillery upon the advanced guards of the British columns. The 92nd Regiment led the left, and the 90th the right column, under Colonel Rowland Hill. The advance of the advanced guard, consisting of the flank and two battalion companies, commanded by Lieutenant-Colonel Kenneth Mackenzie, had only moved forward a short distance when the enemy opened fire, and a strong cavalry corps was observed preparing to charge; the advance was joined by the rest of the regiment, which forming up, as if on parade, awaited the onset of the French cavalry.

The 90th, wearing helmets at that time, was mistaken by the enemy for a body of dismounted cavalry; anticipating an easy victory over those whom they imagined would be fighting under difficulties, they charged boldly on, led by General Bron, and were allowed by the 90th to approach to within a few yards, when a withering volley broke their ranks, and a second forced them to retire—those who were carried forward by the impetuosity of the charge were bayoneted as they came up. The determined front shewn by the 90th on this occasion, was the means of saving Sir Ralph Abercromby from being made prisoner. He had had his horse shot under him, and was nearly surrounded by the enemy's troopers when he was rescued by a party of the regiment which moved forward to his assistance. Colonel Hill was struck from his horse early in the action by a musket bullet which hit the rim of his helmet, and wounded him in the head. Colonel Mackenzie took command of the regiment, which, on the retreat of the French cavalry, was formed up with the remainder of the brigade by Major-General Craddock.

The army now formed in two lines, the reserve continuing in column on the right, the Guards in rear of the right of the second line as a support to the centre, and General Doyle's brigade moving in rear of the left in column. In this order the army pushed on with the greatest vigour, preserving always the strictest regularity 1801. of formation. The French kept up a constant fire of musketry and artillery, but did not afterwards oppose in line. As the army continued to advance, the French were compelled to quit their position, and retreat over the plain into their own lines on the heights before Alexandria. Sir Ralph Abercromby, wishing to follow up his success, and by a *coup de main* to carry the important position the French had now retired on, advanced across the plain, ordering General Hutchinson, with the second line, to move forwards to the left, and secure a projecting rising ground; General Moore was directed to the right, that both flanks might be assaulted at the same time. The first line remained in the plain rather to the right. General Hutchinson advanced upon the green hill, and occupied the whole of it. The enemy now opened fire from all their field artillery and heavy ordnance. General Hutchinson's column found some shelter from the inequalities of the ground, and the reserve was protected by the broken surface of the soil on the right. The centre remained totally exposed.

Whilst Sir Ralph Abercromby reconnoitred, the army continued under the most terrible and destructive fire from the enemy's guns to which troops were ever exposed. The work of death was never more quick, nor was greater opportunity offered for destruction. The French, no longer in danger, had only to load and fire; aim was unnecessary; the bullets could not but do their office and plunge into the lines. For several hours did the English remain patiently suffering this exterminating fire. At length Sir Ralph Abercromby deemed it prudent not to attempt the forcing of the heights, and the army was, therefore, withdrawn at sunset, still marching as if on parade, and occupied the position it had won.

The loss of the English was about 1,100 men killed and wounded. The French did not suffer so much, but above

1801. 500 of them were put *hors de combat*. The casualties in the 90th were as follows:—22 rank and file killed; 8 Officers, 11 Sergeants, 203 rank and file wounded. The names of the officers wounded were Colonel Hill, Lieutenant-Colonel Vigoureux, Captains Austin and Edden, Lieutenants Jisdell, Cartwright, and Wright, Asst.-Surg. Lamerte.

The next day the Commander-in-Chief published the following order:—

" Camp, four miles from Alexandria,
" 14th March, 1801.
" The Commander-in-Chief has the greatest
" satisfaction in thanking the troops for their soldier-like
" and intrepid conduct in the action of yesterday; he feels
" it incumbent on him particularly to express his most
" perfect satisfaction with the steady and gallant conduct
" of Major-General Craddock's brigade, and he desires
" that Major-General Craddock will assure the officers and
" men of the 90th Regiment that their meritorious conduct
" commands his admiration. To the 92nd and Regiment
" of Dillon an equal share of praise is due, and, when it
" has been so well earned, the Commander-in-Chief has
" the greatest pleasure in bestowing it."

The army, independently of its severe military duties, was now incessantly and most laboriously at work in constructing the batteries, bringing up the guns, and forming a dépôt of heavy artillery and ammunition. The Captain Pacha, with the remainder of the cavalry, arrived on the 17th, and on the same day Aboukir Castle surrendered, it having been blockaded since the 13th.

Sir Ralph Abercromby's despatch, referring to the landing in Aboukir Bay and to the battle of Mandora, was not received until the 9th May.

1801.

"Camp, before Alexandria,
"March 16th, 1801.

"Sir,
"Although it was not originally my intention to
"have commenced the operations of the British army in
"Egypt on the side of Alexandria, yet circumstances arose
"which induced me to change my opinion. We were
"much longer delayed on the coast of Asia Minor than
"we had at first any reason to apprehend, and we were
"ultimately obliged to sail for Marmorice in a very im-
"perfect state of preparation. I am fully sensible of the
"exertions of his Majesty's Ambassador at the Ottoman
"Porte, as well as of the Quarter-Master-General and the
"other officers who were sent forward to provide for the
"necessities of the army. Our delays originated from
"other causes. For a considerable time previous to our
"sailing the weather was extremely boisterous and the
"winds contrary. The moment that it became practicable
"to sail with so large a fleet, Lord Keith put to sea; we
"left Marmorice on the 22nd of February, and came in
"sight of Alexandria on the 1st of March.

"On the 2nd, the fleet anchored in Aboukir Bay. Until
"the 7th the sea ran high, and no disembarkation could
"be effected; on that day every arrangement was com-
"pleted, and on the 8th, the troops forming the first
"division, * * * * * * * * *
"got into the boats early in the morning; they had, in
"general, from five to six miles to row, and did not arrive
"at the point of landing till ten o'clock. The front of
"disembarkation was narrow, and a hill, which commanded
"the whole, seemed almost inaccessible. The enemy were
"fully aware of our intention, were in force, and had every
"advantage on their side. The troops, however, notwith-
"standing their being exposed to a very severe cannonade,
"and under the fire of grape shot, made good their landing,
"ascended the hill with an intrepidity scarcely to be

1801. "paralleled, and forced the enemy to retire, leaving behind him seven pieces of artillery and a number of horses.

＊　＊　＊　＊　＊　＊　＊　＊　＊　＊　＊

"The disembarkation of the army continued on that and the following day.

"The troops which landed on the 8th, advanced three miles the same day; and on the 12th, the whole army moved forward, and came within sight of the enemy, who was formed on an advantageous ridge, with his right to the canal of Alexandria, and his left towards the sea.

"It was determined to attack them on the morning of the 13th, and, in consequence, the army marched in two lines by the left, with an intention to turn their right flank.

"The troops had not long been in motion before the enemy descended from the heights on which they were formed, and attacked the leading brigades of both lines, which were commanded by Major-General Craddock and Major-General the Earl of Cavan.

"The 90th Regiment formed the advanced guard of the front line, and the 92nd of the second; both battalions suffered considerably, and behaved in such a manner as to merit the praise both of courage and discipline. Major-General Craddock immediately formed his brigade to meet the attack made by the enemy; and the troops changed their position with a quickness and precision which did them the greatest honour. The remainder of the army followed so good an example, and were immediately in a situation not only to face, but to repel the enemy.

＊　＊　＊　＊　＊　＊　＊　＊　＊　＊　＊

"I have the honour to be, etc.,
"R.A. ABERCROMBY."

Captain McNair in a letter to Colonel Graham, dated the 17th of March, thus describes the battle of Mandora.

"Near Alexandria, 17th March, 1801.

"Dear Colonel,

"With the most heartfelt satisfaction I congratulate you on the unparalleled gallantry of your regiment in the action of the 13th inst. The Commander-in-Chief was pleased to say we had gained immortal honour; we proved to our own army and also the enemy how futile the attempts of the most determined cavalry is on infantry that meet them with resolution. Col. Mackenzie, who commanded three companies for the support of the light company which was in front, behaved with singular coolness and most determined heroism. I had Mr. Wright wounded badly, and twenty-nine men killed and wounded of the light company; tho' unavoidably a good deal scattered, they individually stood firm to the cavalry and bayoneted some of them; I had five men cut with sabres, but none killed. Col. Vigoureux was wounded early in the day, and Colonel Hill soon after; our wounded in general are doing well. The fire the cavalry received from the regiment when formed, and their charge, astonished the whole army . . . . Captain Napier was not touched; his company suffered severely.

"In haste, I have the honour to be,
"Dear Sir,
"Yours most faithfully,
"JOHN McNAIR."

Colonel Hill, after the action of Mandora, was taken on board the *Foudroyant*, the flagship of his friend Lord Keith, from which, when partially recovered from his wound, he wrote to Colonel Graham the following letter :—

"*Foudroyant*, Aboukir Bay,
"April 4th, 1801.

"My dear Sir,

"Although the surgeons have desired me not to

1801. "write in consequence of the wound I have received in
"my head, yet I cannot resist this opportunity of sending
"you a few lines to give you some little account of your
"regiment. The public despatches will give every public
"information, therefore what I am able to say shall be
"confined principally to the 90th. We anchored here on
"the 2nd of March, the landing was gallantly made near
"Aboukir on the 8th; our brigade, Major-General Crad-
"dock's, was not engaged; in the evening we marched about
"two miles in the country and remained quiet till the 12th,
"when the whole army moved forward about three miles,
"and we perceived the enemy strongly posted on high
"ground near three miles in our front. It was then agreed
"to attack him next morning; accordingly the whole of
"our army was under arms at daybreak; the 90th was
"ordered to lead the first line, and the 92nd the second.
"About seven the whole marched in column of companies,
"the left in front; the light company was advanced and
"was furiously attacked by the cavalry, but McNair, his
"officers and men, were steady and firm, and gave them
"such a reception with musketry that many were killed
"and others thrown into the greatest confusion. I in-
"stantly formed line on the left, and the whole regiment
"was engaged. The enemy was on commanding ground,
"and kept up a very heavy fire of grape and musketry.
"We advanced and drove the French from the first
"position. I then, with the bugle-horn, halted the
"regiment and ceased firing, and, correcting our line,
"advanced with the greatest regularity to the second hill,
"where we were opposed with a very heavy fire; we had
"nearly gained the height, when I was wounded and fell
"from my horse, and carried out of the field. The enemy
"continued to retreat till he arrived at his present position.
"I am convinced it will give you great pleasure to hear
"that your regiment behaved well, I shall, therefore, not
"only give you my opinion of the 90th, but likewise
"inclose you the orders given out in consequence of the

"action of the 13th instant. Every officer of the regiment
"behaved so extremely well, that I cannot particularise
"anyone; when I mention officers, I am sure I may include
"non-commissioned officers and men, for I am certain
"every individual showed the greatest bravery. Col.
"Mackenzie's merits you are well acquainted with I know;
"but at the same time, I think it is my duty, as well as
"my inclination, to represent him to you as a most
"deserving and valuable officer, his conduct on every
"occasion has been for the good of the regiment and the
"service.

"Our loss has been very great; I have not yet got an
"exact return, but hope to have one before the *Flora* sails,
"and will inclose it you. My wound, thank God! is not
"much; my helmet saved my life; a ball struck me in the
"front, just on the peak, which is covered with brass and
"resisted the ball so much that it did not enter my head,
"but flattened the helmet, which made a small wound, but
"violent contusion. I suffered a great deal of pain for
"some days, but am now much better; my right eye is
"very weak, and I must, by the advice of the surgeon,
"remain some days longer on board this ship with your
"friend, and mine, Lord Keith.

"Colonel Vigoureux's wound is in the knee, and I am
"afraid is bad; the surgeons say there is little chance of
"his recovering without the loss of his leg. Capts. Edden
"and Austin are slightly wounded. Messrs. Cartwright,
"Wright, and Lamerte, I hope, are not in danger. Your
"friend, Genl. Hope, is in the cabin with me, he has
"lost the fore finger and part of the next on the right
"hand, he seems to suffer pain, but I understand he is
"doing well. Genls. Moore and Oakes are both wounded
"in the leg, neither of them dangerously.

* * * * * * * * * *

"Your much obliged
"and very sincere,
"R. H."

1801.

1801. On the 20th, a column of infantry and cavalry was perceived passing over the ground adjacent to Lake Mareotis into Alexandria, and an Arab chief sent in a letter to Sir Sidney Smith, acquainting him of the arrival of General Menou, with a large army, and that it was his intention to surprise and attack the British camp the next morning. The intelligence so forwarded, though not fully credited, was true, for at 4 a.m. on the morning of the 21st, the French columns moved forward to the attack, General Menou's plan being to make a feint against the British left wing, and occupy its attention while the main part of his army forced their centre, and wheeling round to the right drove the British troops into Lake Maadie. This plan, though able, was not carried out, for General Craddock's brigade prevented any forward movement against the left; while Generals Moore and Oakes defeated all attempts made upon an old Roman camp, which formed a main feature on the right. Towards the end of the battle the English regiments lacked ammunition, and General Menou, finding that every one of his movements had failed, and that the British lines had suffered no serious impression to justify the hopes of an eventual success, determined on a retreat, and retired in good order under the heights of their position.

In this action the 90th had one man wounded, the total British loss being 6 officers and 233 men killed, 60 officers and 1,190 men wounded, 3 officers and 29 men missing. On the ground were found 1,700 French killed and wounded, 1,040 of whom were buried two days after on the field of battle.

The conduct of the troops cannot but excite wonder in military men, of whatever nation they may be. Surrounded, partly broken, without ammunition, still to continue the contest, and remain conquerors, is an extraordinary evidence of intrepidity, discipline, and inherent good conduct. This splendid victory was clouded by the news which passed from corps to corps at the end of the struggle, that the noble old chief, who had posted them so judiciously and led them so gallantly, was dangerously 1801. wounded. Ever foremost in the fight, he was struck in the thigh by a bullet early in the morning, but continued walking about and directing the battle until the retreat of the enemy's columns assured him that the victory was his, then he acknowledged the severity of his sufferings and allowed his wounds to be dressed. He was taken on board the *Foudroyant*, and placed in the same cabin as Colonel Hill, who, with the deepest sorrow, saw him sink gradually until the 28th, when he breathed his last, mourned for by every soldier in the army he had so gallantly commanded.

While on board ship, Colonel Hill had an interview with the Captain Pacha, who presented him with a sabre, a gold box, and a handsome shawl, as a testimony of admiration of the gallant manner in which he had led the 90th Regiment on the 13th.

On the death of Sir Ralph Abercromby, the command devolved upon Lieutenant-General Hely Hutchinson, who began by fortifying and strengthening his position. Colonel Spencer, with a small force, was sent on the 2nd of April to endeavour to obtain possession of Rosetta, which place he captured on the 8th, the French retiring on El Hamed.

In order to secure the left and part of the front of his army, General Hutchinson gave orders to cut through the canal of Alexandria, and so let the waters of the sea into the dry bed of Lake Mareotis. The men set to work with pleasure, an eye-witness observing,—" Never did a working " party labour with more zeal ; every man would have " volunteered with cheerfulness to assist. Four cuts were " made of six yards in breadth, and about ten from each " other, a little in advance of the farthest redoubt, but only " two could be opened the first night. At seven o'clock in " the evening the last fascine was removed, and joy was " universal. The water rushed in with a fall of six feet, " and the pride and peculiar care of Egypt, the con- " solidation of ages, was in a few hours destroyed."

1801. On the 13th, in consequence of this inundation, the 18th, 79th, 90th, and a detachment of the 11th Light Dragoons marched to support Colonel Spencer. Colonel Rowland Hill joined the 90th the next day at El Hamed, where it remained until the 5th of May, when a force, composed of the brigades of Generals Craddock and Doyle, and four thousand Turks under Caia Bey, and twelve field pieces, moved forward under the command of General Hutchinson. After advancing twelve miles, the army encamped, remaining stationary until the 8th, when it took possession of El Aft, a strong position on the canal which had been evacuated by the French the night before. The next morning the army moved towards Rhamanieh, and when within about four miles of the place, was attacked by the French cavalry and light troops, the remainder of their forces being advantageously posted near the town. General Hutchinson imagining that the enemy might endeavour to retreat on Alexandria, advanced with General Craddock's and General Doyle's brigade in line, that the canal might be completely gained, inclining to the right as he approached the canal, refusing his left, to rest that flank upon the Turks.

The French cavalry, when they saw the army advancing, deployed into line, taking post between Lacana and Mehallet Daout, so as to menace in flank and rear any movement made across the canal. During this deployment two British guns cannonaded them. General Hutchinson seeing the movement of the enemy's cavalry, determined now to wait until Colonel Stuart, who had proceeded towards Dessong, might be enabled to erect batteries which must force the enemy to leave their camp. In the meantime a smart fire was kept up by the French sharpshooters upon our line, to check which, flankers from each regiment were sent out to cover the front. At night-fall all firing ceased, and the men, tired with the excessive fatigue of the day, lay down to rest on the ground. A considerable time before daylight the whole were under arms. As soon as day dawned, the troops moved to occupy their appointed positions, previous to the attack. While these movements were going on, an officer with a flag of truce came out from the fort and offered, on the part of his commander, to surrender it at discretion. According to General Hutchinson's despatch, one hundred and ten men marched out of the fort; the remainder of the French force, amounting to about four thousand infantry and eight hundred cavalry, retreated in the direction of Cairo, whither General Hutchinson determined to follow them. Accordingly, on the 11th of May, the army advanced, halting in the evening on the banks of the Nile, at Shibraghite, about twelve miles distant from Rhamanieh. The next morning the troops marched to Kaf Haudrig, at which place they remained on the 13th to enable the gunboats to come up.

1801.

On the 14th, the columns pushed forward to Shabour, on the 15th to Zowaff, and on the 16th to Algam, where, on the 17th, news was brought that a considerable body of the French was advancing to a point on the Nile about a league in rear of the English head-quarters. It proved to be a convoy of 600 French, with 400 camels, coming from Alexandria. They surrendered to General Doyle, who, with some cavalry, had moved off to intercept them. The army remained at Algam until the 1st of June, when it moved to Mishlee, Colonel Stuart with his force keeping pace on the opposite bank, where it remained until the 4th, when it marched to Lochmas, advancing the next day to Verdam.

The sickness of the troops now increased to an alarming degree, there being at this time one thousand who had returned to Rosetta or were in two days afterwards in such a state as to render expedient the establishment of an hospital camp on the point of the Delta. Notwithstanding the sufferings to which they were exposed, the British troops pushed on with determination, their spirits rising more and more as they neared Cairo. On the 7th, they

1801. were at Erhoue; on the 9th, at Burtos; on the 15th, at Tinash; and on the 16th, encamped at Shubrah, a suburb of Cairo, where they remained until the 21st, when the English army advanced to within a mile and a-half of Giza, encamping in two lines with their left on Dochi, and the right on Zaneen. Night and day the troops were occupied in dragging up the heavy guns and requisite ammunition, and every preparation was made for an attack, when early on the 22nd, a French officer from Giza, with a flag of truce, was brought in to the General. He came from General Belliard to require that an English officer might be sent to a conference he proposed. Accordingly General Hope met a French Colonel of Engineers, Touissard, near Giza, the result of their meeting being that the French General Morand visited General Hope the next morning to arrange for the evacuation of Cairo, and the return of its garrison to France. The articles were definitely agreed to on the 26th, and the capitulation was signed the following day.

" The capitulation of Cairo crowned the daring march " which General Hutchinson's judgment planned, and his " resolution persevered in. Its conquest secured Egypt, " and, without the most improbable misfortunes, the " speedy fall of Alexandria."

" Camp near Cairo, July 13th, 1801.
" Lieutenant-General Sir John Hely Hutchinson,
" K.B., has received His Majesty's orders to return the
" general officers and soldiers of the army his thanks for
" the brilliant services they have rendered their country,
" and for the manner in which they sustained and in-
" creased the honour of the British name and the glory of
" the British arms. You landed in Egypt to attack an
" enemy, superior in numbers, provided with a formidable
" body of cavalry and artillery, accustomed to the climate,
" flushed with former victory, and animated by a con-
" sciousness of hard and well-earned renown. Notwith-

"standing these advantages, you have constantly seen a
" warlike and victorious enemy fly before you, and you
" are now in possession of the capital. Such are the
" effects of order, discipline, and obedience; without which,
" even courage itself must be unavailing, and success can
" be but momentary. Such, also, are the incitements,
" which ought to induce you to persevere in a conduct
" which has led you to victory, has acquired you the
" applause of your sovereign, the thanks of parliament,
" and the gratitude of your country.

" To such high authorities it would be superfluous in
" me to add my testimony, but be assured your services
" and conduct have made the deepest impression on my
" heart, and never can be eradicated from my memory.
" During the course of this arduous undertaking, you
" have suffered some privations, which you have borne
" with the firmness of men and the spirit of soldiers. On
" such painful occasions, no man has ever felt more
" sensibly than I have done. But you yourselves must
" know that they are the natural consequences and effects
" of war, which no human prudence can obviate; every
" exertion has been made to diminish their extent and
" duration—they have ceased, and I hope are never likely
" to return.

" Nothing now remains to terminate your glorious
" career but the final expulsion of the French from Egypt,
" an event which your country anticipates, and a service
" which, to such troops as you are, can neither be doubt-
" ful nor difficult. The prevalence of contrary winds has
" prevented the arrival of ships from England with money.

" Your pay has been in arrear, but this inconvenience is
" now at an end, and everything that is due shall be put in
" a course of payment, and discharged as soon as possible.
                    " J. H. HUTCHINSON."

At the same time as the publication of the above, the following message was communicated to the troops:—

1801.

"May 18th, 1801.
"By the Lords Spiritual and Temporal in Parliament
"assembled,
RESOLVED,
"That this House doth highly approve of, and
"acknowledge the distinguished regularity, discipline,
"coolness, and valour displayed by the non-commissioned
"officers and private soldiers of the army serving under
"the command of the late Sir Ralph Abercromby, K. B.,
"in the memorable and brilliant operations in Egypt, and
"that the same be signified to them by the commanders
"of the several corps, who are directed to thank them for
"their distinguished and exemplary conduct."

While in camp near Cairo, the officers and men of the 90th were gladdened by a letter from their Colonel, who wrote to Colonel Rowland Hill from London.

"May 23rd, 1801.
"Dear Hill,
"I rejoice to hear you are doing so well, and
"sincerely congratulate you on the conduct of the regi-
"ment, which I never doubted would distinguish itself,
"though certainly the occasion was the most trying
"possible, and its behaviour has established its reputation
"for ever. I am extremely hurried, and have only time
"to request you will assure them all of the pride and
"satisfaction I have felt on this glorious occasion.
"With the best and sincerest wishes,
"I remain,
"Ever most truly yours,
"THOS. GRAHAM."

This letter was soon after followed by Colonel Graham in person. On his arrival in England from Malta, hearing of the gallant deeds of his regiment, he quickly made arrangements for rejoining it, and on the 22nd of July issued the following order:—

"22nd July, 1801.

"Though Colonel Graham took the first oppor-
"tunity to express to the officers and men of the regiment,
"when under arms this morning, the sense he entertained
"of their conduct, yet, desiring that his acknowledgment
"may be known to every individual belonging to it, and
"that it may stand recorded, he cannot refrain from
"repeating it to them in orders.

"The applause of the late Commander-in-Chief given
"in general orders, after the action of the 13th of March,
"has stamped the character of the regiment. The im-
"partial judgment of that great officer, himself an eye-
"witness of their steadiness and intrepidity on that
"trying occasion, can never be questioned, and it must
"ever afford the most heartfelt gratification to those who
"merited such a distinction. Colonel Graham is aware
"that after such a testimony, nothing he can say can add
"to their satisfaction; but having been prevented, by
"circumstances, from sharing in their glory, he assures
"them that he most sincerely participates in all their
"feelings, and those of exultation must be mingled with
"regret for the loss of so many brave men as fell on that
"day. It is impossible in remarking on the circumstances
"of an action where the most determined valour would
"not have been sufficient to prevent confusion without the
"aid of the most perfect discipline, not to request the
"field officers, who have during Colonel Graham's absence
"maintained and improved that system, to accept his
"sincere and cordial thanks for their unremitting exer-
"tions. The regiment will feel the loss of one of them
"Lieutenant-Colonel Mackenzie, promoted in another
"corps, but His Majesty's gracious attention to the merit
"of the regiment in filling up the vacancies in succession
"will be an additional incitement to all to exert them-
"selves, and the 90th Regiment will ever support the
"high character they have so justly acquired."

1801. During the night of the 10th, the French evacuated Cairo, but it was not until the 15th, at daybreak, that they gave up possession of Giza, and with the allied army began their march for Rosetta. The Turks preceded, the British army followed; then the French, numbering 14,200 men, with flanking parties of their own cavalry on the left, and the English cavalry, with two beydoms of mamelukes, closed the rear. Owing to the sickness of Generals Hutchinson and Craddock, General Moore commanded the army.

At Déronte, the French passed the English in order to be ready for embarkation. The real effective state of their army was then ascertained, as the principal English officers posted themselves at a narrow pass to see them file by. They could scarcely, however, credit their own sight when they beheld so large an army, with fifty pieces of artillery and its complement of ammunition, defile before them. It was now that, connecting this unexpectedly formidable power with the rising of the Nile, which at this time began to reach the top of its banks, the true importance of the capitulation was acknowledged.

On the 28th, the armies encamped at El Hamed, and on the 31st, the first division of the French, marched to the point of embarkation. Their departure occupied ten days, the divisions of shipping sailing as soon as each was ready.

The army was redistributed on the 9th of August, the 90th forming part of the 3rd Brigade, commanded by Brigadier-General Hope, which joined the camp at Alexandria on the 11th; General Hutchinson resumed command on the 15th, and expressed his intention of immediately besieging Alexandria; General Hope's brigade moving into the front line on the following day. The siege was vigorously carried out, and on the 30th, General Hope went into the town to sign the capitulation. On the 3rd of September, the 90th took possession of one of the gates of the city, and the Egyptian campaign was terminated. The garrison of Alexandria, from a return furnished by General Menou, amounted to 10,528 men of all ranks. 1801.

Colonel Graham left Egypt for Constantinople on the 6th of September, and before his departure, was presented with a sabre taken at Mandora.

"Camp before Alexandria,
"16th August, 1801.

"Sir,

"It is highly gratifying to my feelings to have
" the honour, at the request of the officers of the Ninetieth
" Regiment in Egypt, to present to you in their names a
" Damascus sabre—taken in the action of the thirteenth
" of March last, when the French cavalry 'so much
" celebrated in Europe, charged your regiment, and was
" so gallantly repulsed by it alone, although in a situa-
" tion the most advantageous for the enemy—in testimony
" of the high sense they entertain of the great obligations
" they are under to the zealous patriotism and military
" abilities displayed by you in establishing that systematic
" order and discipline in the regiment, that has enabled it,
" under circumstances the most trying that, perhaps, ever
" presented themselves to a corps, to acquire honourable
" laurels to itself, and to contribute to the glory of the
" Empire.

"I have the honour to be,
"With highest respect and regard, Sir,
"Your most obedient servant,
"R. HILL, Lt.-Col. 90th Regt.
"and Colonel."

"COLONEL GRAHAM,
"90th Regiment."

The 90th Regiment was inspected by General Hope on the 8th, who, at the conclusion of the inspection, said to Colonel Hill:—

1801. "Sir,—Considering the service your regiment has gone through, it is impossible a regiment can be more complete than the 90th is at present; I have minutely inspected into every part of it, and it is with pleasure I tell you that the whole corps does you and the officers the greatest credit."

The first division of the French troops left Egypt on the 14th, and were followed by the remainder as fast as ships could be procured for their transport. The English regiments embarked as soon as possible, some proceeding to Gibraltar for further service, others to Malta.

For their services in the campaign, each regiment was allowed to carry in their colours the emblem of a Sphinx, and to have the word " Egypt " inscribed.

The whole of the officers present in Egypt received gold medals from the Sultan, to perpetuate the services rendered to the Ottoman empire, those of the 90th being :—

Colonel	Rowland Hill.
Major	John McNair.
,,	George Vigoureux.
Captain	Mark Napier.
,,	Francis Eddins.
,,	William Cartwright.
,,	William Austin.
Lieutenant	Andrew Wood.
,,	Richard Butler.
,,	Hormer Tisdall.
,,	Samuel Colberg.
,,	John Patterson.
,,	Thomas Webster.
,,	Anthony Power.
,,	Thomas Wright.
,,	John Hales.
,,	Richard Butler.
,,	Benjamin Preedy.
,,	William Scholey.

1801.

Adjutant Dolittle.
Surgeon James Anderson.
Asst. Surgeon M. Lamerte.

On the 21st of September, the 90th marched from Alexandria and embarked on board the *Europa* for Malta, at which place the regiment arrived on the 9th of October, remaining in quarantine until the 15th, when it landed and took up its quarters in Fort Manuel.

" G.O.
" Hd.-Qrs., 17th October, 1801.
" No. 1.—The infantry of the line to be divided
" into three divisions, under Major-Generals Coote,
" Craddock, and Villette, until further orders, who will
" take immediate superintendence and inspection of them.
" 2nd Division—Major-Gen. Craddock.
  " 27th Regiment.
  " 30th   do.
  " 35th two battalions .
  " 90th   do."

The following regimental order describes the uniform worn by the officers and men of the regiment at that date.

" Regimental Order.
" Octr. 27th, 1801.
" As General Fox intends to inspect the regiment
" on Thursday morning, Colonel Hill desires every officer
" will exert himself for the good appearance of the regi-
" ment, and take care that the men's arms, accoutrements,
" and clothing are clean and in good order, that the blankets
" are well washed and neatly folded up, that the men's hair
" is well tied and dressed at the sides, and that the officers
" themselves are properly regimentally dressed. Uniform-
" jacket, red waistcoat, and buff breeches, long gaiters,
" helmet, and regimental sword and feather. This regu-
" lation of dress to be strictly observed at all times till
" further orders. The officers are likewise desired to wear
" powder."

1801.   During the stay of the 90th in Malta, Colonel Hill exerted himself to ensure the comfort and happiness of all under his command. The accompanying order shews fully how deep an interest he took in the welfare of the non-commissioned officers and privates.

" Regimental Order.
" 17th November, 1801.
" The plan adopted in Minorca for the Serjeants
" to mess together was so respectable and advantageous,
" that Colonel Hill is desirous of establishing it again,
" and, in order to put it on the most comfortable footing,
" every encouragement and assistance will be given. The
" internal regulation of the mess will be formed by its own
" members, but subject to the inspection and approbation
" of the commanding officer of his regiment. Colonel
" Hill is likewise anxious to re-establish a school, and he
" promises every encouragement to those who are desirous
" of improving themselves by so useful an institution.
" The school and mess will commence immediately;
" Corporal Anderson, who is appointed Lance Serjeant,
" will instruct the scholars in reading, writing, and
" accounts. Assistant-Serjeant-Major McFarland will
" superintend the school, and likewise give his assistance
" in the management of the Serjeant's mess. Serjeant
" McFarland's conduct on all occasions has been so meri-
" torious, that the commanding officer regrets he cannot
" be more actively employed; but although Serjeant
" McFarland from the wound he has received will for
" some time be prevented from doing his duty in the field,
" yet Colonel Hill is convinced that his example and
" services will be of advantage to the regiment, particu-
" larly in the situation he is now placed."

On the 26th of November, the 90th moved from Fort Manuel to Fort St. Elmo, where it remained during the rest of the stay in the island. In December, the regiment was startled and annoyed by a rumour that the men were to be called on to volunteer for some of the older regiments, with a view to the reduction of the corps. In consequence of these reports, Colonel Hill applied to General Fox, the officer in command of the forces in the Mediterranean, from whom he received a letter distinctly contradicting them.

"Head-Quarters, Malta, 12th Dec., 1801.
" Sir,
" General Fox being informed that a report has
" been circulated that the men of the 90th Regiment
" would be allowed to enlist in the older regiments, I am
" directed by His Excellency to say that such report is
" without any foundation, and that the reason of the 90th
" not being included in the number of regiments allowed
" to enlist men from the ancient Irish Fencibles, is that
" the 90th being looked upon as a national regiment, the
" recruiting of it is to be confined as much as possible to
" North Britons.
" I have the honour to be,
" etc., etc., etc.,
" (Signed) J. HOPE, D.A.G."

At this time a compliment was paid to the regiment by the selection of one of the non-commissioned officers for promotion to the rank of Sergeant-Major in another corps.

" R.M.O.
" Malta, 13th Decr., 1801.
" Colonel Hill has made the following pro-
" motions :—
" Serjeant Goddard to the Light Infantry, vice Serjeant
" Millar promoted to be Serjeant-Major in the 8th Regi-
" ment."

* * * * * * * * * *

On the 25th of February, 1802, the 90th embarked on board the *Alexandria* frigate, and the *Orpheus* and *Ranger*

1802. transports for conveyance to England. After a long and rough voyage, the regiment landed at Chatham on the 15th of April, and proceeded at once by march to take up quarters at Chelmsford, where it remained for a few months. About the middle of the year, the 90th marched from Chelmsford to Fort George, in Scotland, under the impression that on arrival it would be disbanded. The unsettled state of Europe at that time, however, rendered it necessary to increase rather than reduce the army, and orders were received for recruiting parties to be sent out both in England and Scotland. The regiment was now **1803.** raised to its full strength, and on the 23rd of March, 1803, proceeded from Fort George to Belfast, where it arrived on the 29th.

On the 21st of August, the 90th marched from Belfast to Athlone. While quartered there, Colonel Hill was appointed a Brigadier-General, and was ordered to proceed to Loughrea.

Before retiring from the regiment which he had so long ably commanded, the officers presented him with the following address :—

"Athlone, 1st September, 1803.

" The officers of the 90th Regiment in expressing
" to Colonel Hill their unfeigned and heartfelt pleasure on
" learning of his appointment of Brigadier-General to the
" forces, must, at the same time, assure him that his
" resigning the command of the regiment fills them with
" sentiments of the most lively and deep regret.

" On their taking their farewell of an officer who has
" ever stood so high in their estimation, they feel them-
" selves called upon to declare that the discipline he
" maintained in the regiment has ever gained it the
" distinguished praise and approbation of all the General
" Officers they have ever served with—a discipline so
" tempered with mildness that must have endeared him
" to every individual in the regiment, as well as his
" attention to their individual interests.

"But their gratitude and private feelings must now give
"way and be subordinate to the public service, and it is
"only left for them to indulge the hope that it may be
"their good fortune to serve under his command, and
"eventually in his brigade.

"They are proud to think and reflect on the distinguished
"honours they gained in Egypt, when he gloriously fell
"wounded at their head, and hope under his command
"they may acquire additional glory in future and no less
"important services.

"They finally beg leave to assure him that their best
"wishes for his welfare and happiness ever attend him;
"and that in every honour he may acquire, they will,
"though absent, always participate.

"Signed in the name, and at the request, of all the
"officers of the 90th Regiment.
    "RUTHVEN,
    "Major, commanding the 90th Regiment."

From Athlone the 90th proceeded to Ballinasloe on the 9th of September, whence, after a sojourn of a few weeks, it moved in three divisions to Tuam, where, on arrival, it was inspected by the Commander of the Forces in Ireland, and the next day the following order was published by Brigadier-General Hill.

"Divisional Order.
        "Tuam, 1st November, 1803.
"After the very high manner in which the Com-
"mander of the Forces was pleased to express his approba-
"tion of the appearance and discipline of the 90th Regiment
"yesterday, any encomium of Brigadier-General Hill is
"unnecessary, yet he cannot miss the opportunity of
"requesting Major McNair's, the officer's, and regiment's
"acceptance of his warmest thanks for their steady
"perseverance in discipline, and to assure them that it

1803. " will ever afford him sincere satisfaction to bear testimony
" of their good conduct.
> " By order of Brigadier-General Hill,
>> " (Signed)   EDWARD CURRIE,
>>> " Brigade-Major."

1804. The regiment remained at Tuam until the 11th of April, 1804, when it was ordered to Dublin, where, shortly after its arrival, it received a most gratifying proof of the estimation in which it was held by the inhabitants of the district in which it had been lately stationed.

" Regimental Orders.
> " Dublin, 1st May, 1804.
" The commanding officer has much satisfaction
" in directing the following address from the principal
" inhabitants of Tuam to be inserted in the orderly books
" of the regiment, and he has no doubt that the 90th will
" always support the character they have justly acquired."

At a meeting of the principal inhabitants of Tuam, Sir Thomas French, Bart., in the chair; it was unanimously agreed that the following address be signed by the chairman and presented to Major McNair, commanding the 90th Regiment.

" Sir,
" We feel it highly incumbent on us to express
" our great regret at your removal from this garrison,
" though it affords us an opportunity of publicly declaring
" that the conduct of both officers, non-commissioned
" officers, and privates of the 90th Regiment during the
" time they were quartered here, was such as has engaged
" the warm wishes and attachment not only from us, but
" from all ranks in this town and neighbourhood.

"Resolved,—
"That the above address, with Major McNair's answer,
"be published in the Dublin Evening Post.
            "(Signed)   THOMAS FRENCH."

Answer.

"Sir,
        "I have the honour of acknowledging, with high
"consideration, the receipt of an address from the principal
"inhabitants of Tuam, and have to request that you, as
"chairman of the meeting, will be pleased to signify to
"the members thereof, that the officers of the 90th Regi-
"ment are highly sensible of the honour conferred on them
"by the good opinion of gentlemen whose urbanity and
"polite hospitality they will have sincere pleasure in
"holding in grateful remembrance.
"I receive with great satisfaction such honourable
"testimony of the propriety of conduct of the non-
"commissioned officers and privates of the regiment
"during their residence at Tuam, at the same time I
"gratify my own feelings in saying that they experienced
"every friendly attention from the inhabitants of all ranks
"of the town and neighbourhood.
        "I have, etc., etc.,
            "(Signed)   JOHN McNAIR,
                "Comdg., 90th Regiment."

When on the staff in Ireland, Colonel Graham had many opportunities of superintending the management of his regiment, and particularly interested himself in its training as a Light Infantry battalion.

"Regimental Orders.
                    "Tuam, 29th Jan., 1804.
    "Colonel Graham is always highly gratified by
"seeing the 90th Regiment. He is proud of his attach-
"ment to it, and he feels confident that the same spirit

1804. " which has raised its character so high will ever main-
" tain it unsullied.

" In an open country, the readiness and precision with
" which every movement, under the immediate guidance
" of the officers, is performed, would give the bravery of
" the regiment every advantage that could be wished for,
" but in meeting an enemy in a broken and enclosed
" country, such as Ireland is from one end to the other,
" every means should be taken to prevent victory costing
" the lives of more gallant men than is necessary. To
" obtain this important object, the regiment ought not
" only to be perfect in Light Infantry movements which
" are so peculiarly adapted to the circumstances of service
" in this country, but as great extension may be often
" necessary, and as on these occasions the attention of the
" officers cannot be given to every man's conduct, the
" soldiers must learn how most to annoy the enemy with
" the least risk to themselves. In time of action they
" must individually possess themselves, maintaining that
" coolness which distinguishes true courage, so as to be
" able to take advantage of any favourable circumstance
" that will enable them to advance under cover, at the
" same time paying a strict obedience to any signals that
" may be made them by their superiors. By much
" practice across the country a knowledge of ground will
" be acquired both by the officers and men; they will
" individually become acquainted with the nature of this
" kind of service, and on all occasions, knowing what is
" best to be done, will acquire confidence so as not to be
" too anxious if separated for a short time from their
" comrades; officers are expected to be unremitting in
" their exertions to become perfectly masters of every
" part of their duty, and on their intelligence and activity
" the instructions of the men must depend relative to the
" objects which are recommended as so necessary and
" important. This instruction must be given on the spot;
" it is scarcely possible to explain by any general rule what

"must vary according to the circumstances of the moment; but the leading principle that should govern the conduct of all officers in the command of detachments, great or small, is to prevent their men being exposed in close order to the fire of an enemy that is not seen. It is evident that a few men scattered along and covered by a fence will successfully maintain their ground against an infinitely greater number drawn up in close order and remaining stationary in the middle of the field, for their fire is ineffectual, while every shot from the fence must strike a collected body. An extended line must, therefore, always cover the front of the main body till a favourable opportunity offers of advancing rapidly and charging the enemy. The skirmishers must avoid, too, as much as possible, remaining stationary in an open situation, but will gain ground from a flank under cover where it can be found, or, if necessary, advance to the front in extended line with as much rapidity as possible from one fence to another.

"Colonel Graham need not recommend it to the commanding officer to lose no opportunity when the weather will permit of carrying on the usual instruction of the young officers and recruits, and the important exercise of Light Infantry movements across the inclosures. He will be extremely anxious to receive information of the progress of the regiment, and he requests that on the back of the weekly states sent him, a memo. should be made of the days of such practice, noticing if any of the officers are absent, and why.

"(Signed)   THOS. GRAHAM."

On the 8th of August, orders were received from London directing that a second battalion should be formed from the men to be raised under the Defence Act, in place of that drafted into the Navy as marines in 1796.

On the 20th of October, the 90th 1st batt. marched

1805. from Dublin to Youghal, whence it embarked on the 26th of January, 1805, under the command of Lieutenant-Colonel John McNair, for service in the West Indies. On arriving at Barbadoes in March, the regiment was detained on board the transports for upwards of three weeks to be in readiness for immediate service, and then proceeded to St. Vincent, where it was quartered.

In the first year of its service in the West Indies, *i.e.*, from the 11th of April, 1805, to the 11th of April, 1806, the regiment suffered very severely from the climate, no fewer than eight officers and 136 men falling victims to it.

1806. In September, 1806, Lieutenant-General Bowyer inspected the corps.

" General Order,
" 18th September, 1806.
" Head-Quarters, St. Vincent.

" The Commander of the Forces having com-
" pleted his inspection of the troops, barracks, hospitals,
" and fortifications at Fort Charlotte and Dorsetshire hill,
" takes the earliest opportunity of expressing his appro-
" bation of the high order and condition in which he has
" found the whole to be, and it affords him great satis-
" faction to have it in his power in the execution of the
" most pleasing part of his duty to report to His Royal
" Highness, the Commander-in-Chief, the system esta-
" blished for carrying on the duties and discipline of
" this garrison by his Excellency Lieutenant-General
" Beckwith, as well as the soldier-like appearance of the
" troops in general, particularly the 90th or Perthshire
" Regiment, which he has no doubt, whenever opportunity
" offers, will add fresh laurels to those it has so gloriously
" gained in Egypt.

" Signed   ADOLPHUS HUMBER,
          Depy. Adjt.-General."

1807. During the years 1807 and 1808, the 90th remained at
1808. St. Vincent, performing the duties of the garrison to the

satisfaction of all. The strength of the regiment was kept up to its full complement, as, although the West Indian islands had been comparatively quiet for the past few years, still, the war with France continuing, the troops forming their garrisons might at any moment be called upon to act either in attack or defence.

In the latter part of 1808, it was decided that the Island of Martinique should, if possible, be wrested from the French, and as Sir George Beckwith, the Commander-in-Chief of the forces in the Windward and Leeward islands, had a large body of troops at his disposal, no doubts were entertained of his ultimate success.

Before leaving the island, the following letters were received by the 90th Regiment, and prove that the conduct of the corps had been most exemplary during its stay at St. Vincent.

Letter from Sir Charles Brisbane, Governor of St. Vincent.

"Government House,
"12th January, 1809.

" Sir,
"I beg leave, before your departure from this 1809.
" island, to express the very great regard and respect I
" entertain for you, the officers and men, and every person
" attached to the 90th Regiment, and to signify my sincere
" and best wishes for your success and prosperity in every
" arduous undertaking. The very correct and proper line
" of conduct by which you and the corps have regulated
" themselves since their arrival in this island, merits the
" warmest acknowledgments from every inhabitant in this
" colony, and I sincerely hope that your military career
" may be crowned with glory and receive the well-merited
" approbation of your king and country.

"CH. BRISBANE.
" LIEUT.-COLONEL McNAIR,
"Comdg. 90th Regiment."

1809.
"12th January, 1809.

"The Speaker and Members of the House of Assembly
"to Lieutenant-Colonel McNair and officers of the
"90th Regiment.

"Gentlemen,

"Permit us, previously to your departure from
"this colony, to pay our tribute of acknowledgment for the
"exemplary discipline evinced during your residence in
"this island, and of our high esteem of your conduct as a
"corps and as individuals.

"With a high military character already obtained under
"the lamented Abercromby, you have united and blended
"the qualities of good and peaceful citizens; nor can we
"forbear now declaring that since you have been in the
"colony, no instance has occurred of a deviation from the
"laws of the country.

"Our regret at parting with so distinguished a regiment
"is lessened by the assurance of the success and honour
"that awaits it, and we shall look forward with solicitude
"for your glory and speedy return.

"'Signed E. SHARPE.
"Speaker."

"St. Vincent.
"At a meeting of His Majesty's Council, held at Kingston,
"on Wednesday, the 18th of January, 1809.
"Present :—
"The Honourable Henry Haffey, President.
"Charles Grant.
"Joseph Warner.
"John Roach Dasent.
"William John Struth.

"Resolved,—
"That the thanks of this House be conveyed
"through the President to Lieutenant-Colonel McNair and
"the officers of the 90th Regiment for the high discipline
"they have preserved in that regiment during the time in

"which they have remained in this colony, and also to the 1809.
" non-commissioned officers and privates of the regiment
" for the peaceable and orderly manner in which they have
" demeaned themselves during the same period, by means
" whereof the internal security of the colony has been
" preserved; and the inhabitants confiding in the dis-
" tinguished valour and courage heretofore displayed by
" the regiment in the plains of Egypt, have relied upon
" the successful exercise of the same in repelling any
" hostile attack on the sovereignty of this island.
  " By command,
    " (Signed) M. REILLY,
     " Dy. Clerk of the Council."

     " Council Chamber,
      " January 18th, 1809.
" Sir,
  " I am directed to transmit to you a copy of the
" Resolution of the Council passed this day.
  " I feel particular satisfaction in making this communi-
" cation to you, in a small degree of pride, having had the
" honour of being on the most intimate terms of friendship
" with your very correct and much distinguished regiment
" from the period of your arrival at Barbadoes in April,
" 1805. The sentiments of the Council coincide with those
" of the whole community, and if the service of the 90th
" Regiment should be required to act against the enemy,
" with solicitude we shall look forward for your return
" with addition to the very high military character you
" have acquired.
   " I remain, etc., etc.,
    " (Signed) HENRY HAFFEY,
     " President of the Council."
" To LIEUT.-COLONEL MCNAIR,
  " Comdg. 90th Regiment."

  On the 28th of January, the army, formed in two

1809. divisions, commanded respectively by Lieutenant-General Sir George Prevost and Major-General Maitland, sailed from Carlisle Bay and landed on the Island of Martinique on the 30th.

The first division, consisting of between six and seven thousand men, landed at Bay Robert on the windward coast, without opposition, and, notwithstanding the difficulties of the country, occupied a position on the banks of the Grande Lézard River before daybreak on the 31st.

The second division, in which was the 90th Regiment, disembarked near St. Luce and Point Solomon, on the morning of the 30th, meeting with no resistance, and marched at once to Anse Ceron, and on the following day to Rivière Sallée. On the 2nd of February, the division moved to Lamantin, where the main body of the enemy's militia was overtaken, and where it surrendered, the men agreeing to disperse and return to their plantations. From Lamantin, General Maitland advanced, on the 3rd, to within gun-shot of Fort Dessaix. Batteries were at once constructed, and opened fire that night on Pigeon Island, which surrendered on the 4th. On the 5th, the troops marched to La Coste, and, uniting with the first division, completed the investment of Fort Royal on the west side.

" Camp la Coste, Febry. 8th, 1809.

" Sir,

* * * * * * * * * * *

" I have every reason to be highly satisfied with
" the troops I have the honour to command; neither
" officers nor soldiers have failed in exertion, and in
" bearing the great fatigues of the march with exemplary
" fortitude.

" I have the honour to be, etc.,

" FRED. MAITLAND, Maj.-Gen."

" LIEUTENANT-GENERAL BECKWITH,

" Commanding the Forces, etc., etc., etc."

On the 9th, the town of St. Pierre was taken possession 1809. of by the troops of the second division, and the next day the French hospitals in the town of Fort Royal were seized by 300 men of the 90th Regiment.

" Camp la Coste, Feb. 10th, 1809.
" Sir,
" Lieutenant-Colonel McNair, commanding the " 5th Brigade, was detached last night at twelve o'clock, " with three hundred men of the 90th Regiment, for " the service you had desired relative to the enemy's " hospitals.
" What was ordered has been well performed.
" F. MAITLAND, M. G."
" LIEUTENANT-GENERAL BECKWITH."

" General Order.
" Febry. 12th, 1809.
" The Commander of the Forces having com-" mitted to Major-General Maitland to adopt such " measures as should appear to him most effectual to " take possession of the hospitals in the town of Fort " Royal, and to place all the sick and wounded officers " and men, as also the medical department serving there, " on their parole, the General desires to express his ap-" probation of the able arrangements made by the Major-" General for the execution of this important object upon " the 9th inst., and to assure Lieutenant-Colonel McNair, " the officers, and men of the 90th Regiment, that their " exertions on this service afforded the General great " satisfaction."

" Divisional orders by Major-General F. Maitland:—
" Martinique, 22nd Febry., 1809.
" The Major-General is perfectly sensible of the " good order and discipline observed by the several corps " of the second division; he has particularly noticed the

1809. " merit of the 90th Regiment. The quickness with which
" they got under arms last night and advanced is a proof
" of the discipline of the regiment, for which the Major-
" General returns his best thanks."

The operations were now confined to the bombardment of Fort Dessaix and the reduction of Fort Royal, to which places the whole of the enemy's regular forces had withdrawn.

General Beckwith's despatch, announcing the surrender of both the above-named strongholds, gives an account of the means by which this brief yet brilliant campaign was brought to a close.

" Head-Quarters, Martinique,
" Febry. 28th, 1809.

" My Lord,
" In my letter of the 15th instant I had the
" honour to transmit to your Lordship the details of our
" operations to the 11th preceding; from that period until
" the 19th, we were incessantly employed in the construc-
" tion of gun and mortar batteries, and in the landing
" cannon, mortars, and howitzers, with their ammunition
" and stores, in dragging them to the several points selected
" by the engineers, and in the completion of the works,
" and in mounting the ordnance . . . . .
" The enemy during the interval fired upon our encamp-
" ments with shot and shells, but fortunately with little
" effect, and his picquets, when pressed, constantly fell
" back under the protection of his works.
" On the 19th, at half-past four in the afternoon, we
" opened from six points upon the enemy's fortress with
" fourteen pieces of heavy cannon, and twenty-eight
" mortars and howitzers, and the cannonade and bom-
" bardment continued with little remission until noon of
" the 23rd, when the French General sent a trumpet
" with a letter to our advanced posts, near the Bouillé

" Redoubt, in front of attack. In this communication, **1809**.
" General Villaret proposed, as the basis of negociation,
" that the French troops should be sent to France free
" from all restriction as to future service; but this being
" inadmissible, the bombardment recommenced at ten at
" night, and continued without intermission until nine
" o'clock of the 24th, when three white flags were dis-
" covered flying in the fortress, in consequence of which
" our fire from the batteries immediately ceased.

" It is with the most heartfelt satisfaction I have now
" the honour to report to your Lordship, for His Majesty's
" information, that, supported by the talents of the General
" Officers,

* * * * * * * * * *

" the experience and zeal of all the other officers, and the
" valour and unremitting labour of this army,

* * * * * * * * * *

" the campaign, notwithstanding incessant rains, has
" been brought to a glorious conclusion in the short
" space of twenty-seven days from our departure from
" Barbadoes.

" The command of such an army will constitute the
" pride of my future life. To these brave troops conducted
" by Generals of experience, and not to me, their King and
" country owe the sovereignty of this important colony, and
" I trust that by a comparison of the force which defended
" it and the time in which it has fallen, the present
" reduction of Martinique will not be deemed eclipsed by
" any former expedition.

* * * * * * * * * *

" After the embarkation of the French troops, I shall
" have the honour to command the eagles taken from
" the enemy to be laid at the King's feet.

" Captain Preedy of the 90th Regiment, one of my
" aides-de-camp, has the honour to be the bearer of this
" despatch. He is an officer of service, and I beg leave to

1809. " recommend him to His Majesty's favour, and to your
" Lordship's protection.

* * * * * * * * * * *

" I have the honour to be, etc.,
" GEO. BECKWITH, Com. Forces."

After the embarkation of the French garrison, the British troops were stationed in different parts of the island awaiting the arrival of transports. The greater part of the force returned to the several islands from which it had been collected; the 90th Regiment, amongst others, being retained by Sir George Beckwith as a temporary garrison for the captured island.

" Camp, Point Negro,
" Martinique, 7th April, 1809.
" Sir,
" As General Beckwith retains the 90th Regi-
" ment and you, the time of our separation is very nearly
" arrived; it is a satisfaction to me to express to you my
" good opinion of yourself and your regiment; the steadi-
" ness and discipline of the 90th is conspicuous, and is in
" the highest degree creditable to you and to them. I
" request you will accept my best thanks, and with best
" wishes to you and the regiment,
" I have the honour to be, etc.,
" F. MAITLAND."
" LIEUT.-COL. McNAIR,
" 90th Regiment."

The following complimentary and highly gratifying messages from Parliament were published in the order-books of the regiments which had taken part in the capture of Martinique.

"Veneris, 14 die Aprilis, 1809.   **1809.**

"Resolved, *Nemine Contradicente*,—

"That this House doth highly approve and acknowledge the distinguished services of the non-commissioned officers and soldiers in the army serving under Lieutenant-General George Beckwith, in the attack upon the Island of Martinique, and that the same be signified to them by the commanders of the several corps, who are desired to thank them for their gallant behaviour.

"Ordered,—

"That Mr. Speaker communicate the said resolutions to Lieutenant-General Beckwith.

"I. LEY,
"C. S. D. Dom. Com."

"Die Luna, 17 Aprilis, 1809.

"Resolved, *Nemine Dissentiente*, by the Lords Spiritual and Temporal in Parliament assembled, that this House doth highly approve and acknowledge the distinguished services of the non-commissioned officers and soldiers in the army serving under Lieutenant-General George Beckwith, in the attack upon the Island of Martinique, and that the same be signified to them by the commanders of the several corps, who are desired to thank them for their gallant behaviour.

"GEORGE ROSE, Cler. Parliamentor."

The inhabitants of Martinique being quite willing to submit to the mild and easy rule of their conquerors, but little time was necessary for arranging the government of the island; and after garrisoning the different forts, the regiments which had been retained for the preservation of order were withdrawn, the 90th returning to St. Vincent, where it was inspected on the 21st of October.

1809. " General Order.

"St. Vincent, 21st October, 1809.

" Brigadier-General Orde feels peculiar pleasure
" and satisfaction in expressing in general orders his high
" approbation of the discipline of the 90th Regiment,
" evinced this day under his immediate inspection.

" Their manœuvres were performed with great exact-
" ness in quick and slow time. Their firings were close
" and excellent, their wheelings regular, and their dis-
" tances well preserved.

" Major Napier, commanding the regiment 'pro. tem.',
" merits the Brigadier-General's warmest thanks. To
" Major Burrell his thanks are equally due, and likewise
" to every officer in the regiment.

" Brigadier-General Orde will not fail to report the
" regiment to the Commander of the Forces in strong
" and flattering terms."

The capture of Martinique was but the forerunner of a larger and still more important conquest. The Island of Guadaloupe still remained in possession of the French, who had lately strengthened the numerous works by which it was guarded, and had received considerable reinforcements.

At the end of the year, Sir George Beckwith, by a despatch from the Earl of Liverpool, dated the 2nd of November, received the King's orders to attack the island, and immediately concentrated his forces at Dominica.

The army was formed into five brigades, which were arranged in two divisions and a reserve. The first division, commanded by Major-General Hislop, was composed of the third and fourth brigades; the second, commanded by Brigadier-General Harcourt, comprised the first and second brigades, and the fifth brigade formed the reserve.

The third brigade, commanded by Brigadier-General Maclean, consisted of five hundred Light Infantry, five

hundred men of the 90th Regiment, including their flank **1809.**
companies, and four hundred men of the 8th West India
Regiment, including their flank companies.

The second division sailed from Dominica on the morn- **1810.**
ing of the 26th of January, 1810, and anchored at the
Saintes. The first division, with the reserve, sailed in the
course of the afternoon, and anchored on the 27th at Isle
Gosier Grande Terre, and early in the morning of the 28th,
proceeded across the bay to St. Mary's, in Capesterre, in
the smaller vessels of war, other craft, and flat boats,
where a landing was effected without opposition in the
course of the day, and in the afternoon the first division
moved forward, the third brigade proceeding to Capesterre.

On the 29th, the first division marched to the Bannaniers River, where it took post. On the 30th, it advanced by the strong pass of Trou-au-Chien, which was not defended, and the head of the column reached Three Rivers about eleven o'clock, pushing back small detachments of the enemy.

The French seemed inclined to defend the heights D'olet, and other places which they had strengthened with field artillery, but in the afternoon they abandoned all their posts with precipitation, leaving their ordnance behind.

In order to obtain provisions for five days from the fleet, the first division remained at Three Rivers until the 2nd of February, when it moved forward and seized the heights of Palmiste. On the morning of the 3rd, the first division crossed the River Gallion in one column at the only practicable pass; the fourth brigade taking post in the centre, about a mile from the bridge of Vozière, on the river Noire; and the third brigade, occupying M. Pelletier's house and estate, where the enemy abandoned a magazine of provisions. By this distribution of the forces the communication between the town of Basseterre and the enemy's camp was intercepted. The right of the first division now rested on the buildings of the above-mentioned estate, and the left extended towards the

1810. ravine which separated it from the enemy's position at the park.

A strong picquet having been placed in a redoubt evacuated by the enemy at this point, about 5 o'clock in the evening attention was drawn towards the right by a heavy fire of musketry in the woods between Morne Hoel and the post occupied by the enemy on the same heights, as well as from the quick fire he kept up from his batteries commanding the road towards the bridge of Vozière. The York Light Infantry, supported by the flank companies of the 90th Regiment, were ordered forward to divert the enemy's attention from what proved in the end to be a movement against his left by the reserve, and having advanced close to the enemy's posts, maintained their position through the night.

The second division landed near the River du Plessis on the 30th, and marching immediately towards the enemy's right, inclining to his rear, excited his alarm to such a degree, as to induce him to abandon his defences at Three Rivers and Palmiste, where he was already threatened by the first division.

The enemy was now in position behind the River Noire, with his left extended into the mountains, and secured by abattis and and stockaded redoubts.

On the 4th, the river was crossed by the reserve, and the left flank of the enemy was successfully assailed, to the utter confusion of the French Chief, General Ernouf, who instantly had white flags hoisted at his own quarters, and other places in token of surrender.

On the 5th, a capitulation was agreed upon, which was ratified on the morning of the following day, when General Beckwith issued his general order.

" Head-Quarters, Beau Vallon,
" Guadaloupe, Febry. 6th, 1810.
" The capitulation of the Island of Guadaloupe
" and its dependencies was signed by the commissioners

1810.

" on both sides last night, and ratified this morning at
" 8 o'clock by the Admiral and Commander of the Forces.

" The enemy are prisoners of war, to be sent to England,
" not to serve until duly exchanged.

" Thus, by the general exertion and co-operation of the
" fleet and army, has been effected the important conquest
" of this colony in nine days from the landing of the first
" division, and with a loss which, however to be lamented
" from the character and merits of the parties, is compara-
" tively small from the nature of such a service.

* * * * * * * * * * *

" The Commander of the Forces also returns his public
" thanks to the officers of all ranks for their meritorious
" exertions, and to the non-commissioned officers and
" soldiers for the cheerfulness with which they have
" undergone the fatigues of a march, difficult in its nature,
" through the strongest country in the world, and the
" spirit they have manifested upon all occasion to close
" with the enemy."

Extract from the despatch of Lieutenant-General Sir George Beckwith, K.B., to the Earl of Liverpool, dated Guadaloupe, February 9th, 1810 :—

" When the uncommon strength of this country,
" generally, is considered, and the nature of the enemy's
" position, which had been selected with great attention,
" covered with redoubts and furnished with artillery, I
" trust the advance of one column of the army without a
" single field-piece, and of the other equally unprovided,
" until within range of the enemy's principal works, will
" be held by military men a bold and arduous enterprise,
" where the defence possessed a force, in the first instance,
" of 3,500 men, notwithstanding which the campaign ter-
" minated in eight days.

* * * * * * * * * *

" I hope the services of this army will be honoured with
" His Majesty's approbation, and the confidence of their
" country.

1810.   " Captain Wilby (90th Regiment), one of my aides-de-
"camp, who was entrusted with the eagles taken from the
"enemy at Martinique last campaign, has the honour to
"be the bearer of this despatch, and of the eagle of the
"sixty-sixth Regiment, which has fallen into our possession
"on the present occasion, to be laid at the king's feet.

"I beg leave to recommend this officer to His Majesty's
"favour and your Lordship's protection for the rank of
"Major in the army.

* * * * * * * * * * *

"I have the honour to be, etc.,
"G. BECKWITH, Commander of the Forces."

After the capture of Guadaloupe, the Islands of St. Martin, St. Eustatius, and Saba surrendered to the fleet, and the French and Dutch had no longer dominion over any part of the West Indies. Their duty over, the troops returned to their respective stations overjoyed at having been able, in these distant colonies, to emulate the gallant deeds of their comrades in Europe.

1811.   The 90th returned to St. Vincent, whence, in 1811, Lieutenant-Colonel Mark Napier returned home to assume command of the second battalion, which was then quartered in Ireland.

1812.   In April, 1812, the Island of St. Vincent was visited by an earthquake, descriptions of which were given in letters received from the island, dated May 17th. "On the 28th,
"29th, and 30th of April, the island was visited by an
"earthquake, and at the same time one of the mountains
"vomited forth large quantities of lava. Strong detach-
"ments of the 90th Regiment stationed at Olivia, and
"close to the mountain whence the fluid first issued, had
"a most miraculous escape. The barracks in which they
"were quartered were completely demolished by stones
"falling on them, the arms and clothing totally destroyed,
"but most fortunately not an European perished. Upwards
"of twenty negroes who did not desert their huts fell
"victims to the awful visitation. The 90th Regiment

" (upwards of 1,000) are in good spirits, and the island is 1812.
" considered healthy."

The 90th had ample occupation for some time after the catastrophe in assisting the inhabitants to repair the damages which it had occasioned.

The strength of the two battalions of the regiment numbered at this time 2,144 men, composed of English 1,097, Scots 538, Irish 485, and foreigners 24.

At the end of 1813, orders were received directing the 1813. 90th to proceed to Canada in the following year. This news, naturally gratifying to the regiment, was the source of unfeigned sorrow to the inhabitants of St. Vincent, who, from its lengthened stay, had begun to look upon the corps as part of the community. Determined that their friends should not leave without some memento of their sojourn and of the friendly feelings with which they were regarded, on the 26th of September, the Committee of both Houses of Legislature waited on Colonel McNair at Fort Charlotte, when the following address was delivered by the Honourable Edward Jackson :—

" Colonel McNair,

" We are deputed, as a Committee of the Council
" and Assembly of this Island, to wait upon you to com-
" municate the thanks of both Houses, unanimously voted
" to you, the officers, and privates of the 90th Regiment,
" for the very meritorious and exemplary conduct of the
" corps during a period of upwards of eight years' residence
" amongst us. As a mark of the high sense they entertain
" of your individual merits, we are desired by the Legis-
" lature to request your acceptance of a sword ; to the other
" officers of the regiment we are directed to offer the
" concurrent thanks of the Legislature, and to present a
" piece of plate for the use of their mess, and we beg they
" will inform the committee in what shape they would
" prefer it, that the necessary orders may be given to
" forward the same with the least possible delay to the
" regiment.

1813. "In common with the other inhabitants of this Island,
"permit us, Sir, to regret the loss we shall sustain by
"your removal, but, convinced as we are that your going
"into more active service will but add the laurels of
"America to the palms of Egypt, we sacrifice our private
"feelings to the general cause, and sincerely hope that
"health, happiness, and honour may follow your colours
"wherever they are displayed.
                "Signed   E. JACKSON.
                          "JOHN ROSS.
                          "WM. HEPBURN."

Address of the Merchants of St. Vincent to Colonel McNair, and the officers of the 1st battalion, 90th Regiment :—

"We are deputed by the mercantile body of
"St. Vincent, to express to you their sincere regret at
"your departure from this colony, and to assure you of
"their lasting esteem and attachment, in token of which,
"they request your acceptance of a piece of plate, value
"one hundred guineas.

"It is a pleasing reflection that during a period of nearly
"nine years, such has been the harmony and friendship
"that have prevailed between every individual of the
"90th Regiment and all ranks of the community, that no
"one solitary act of disagreement has occurred between
"them from their first arrival to the present day. Much
"as it may be attributed to the well-known good order
"and military discipline of the regiment, they cannot
"fail to observe that it strongly marks its moral character,
"which, while it beams peace and harmony to its friends,
"makes it more to be feared by its enemy.

"We shall hear of the welfare and success of the
"90th Regiment with the highest satisfaction, well assured
"that in their destined place of active warfare, the Sphinx's
"Head will be entwined with additional laurels to those
"already so nobly won.

" We sincerely hope that you will have a pleasant and 1814.
" prosperous passage to the shores of America.

"(Signed) {
W. BASSNETT CROPPER.
JAMES GRANT.
C. PANNETT.
JAS. STECL.
J. DALZELL."
}

Prior to the embarkation of the 90th, on the 5th of May, 1814, Sir George Beckwith issued the following farewell order :—

" General Order.

" Barbadoes, 5th May, 1814.

" The Commander of the Forces desires to express " his approbation of the long and respectable West Indian " service of Brevet Colonel McNair, commanding 1st bat- " talion, 90th Regiment, and of this corps now proceeding " to North America, and wishes the officers and soldiers a " favourable occasion of maintaining that just reputation " which they possess in the army.

"(Signed) H. BERKELEY,

"D. A. G."

The regiment arrived at Quebec on the 20th of June, at Montreal on the 29th of the same month, and at Kingston on the 8th of July, whence, after a stay of three months, it commenced its march for Upper Canada on the 13th of October. On its arrival at Fort George, the 90th at once crossed over to Fort Niagara, in the United States territory, which it occupied until the 22nd of May, when, hostilities 1815. having ceased, the fort was given up, and the regiment returned to Fort George, from which it marched on the 1st of June, on its way to England.

After an uneventful voyage, Spithead was reached on the 3rd of August, where despatches awaited the regiment, ordering it to Ostend to form part of the army of occupation in France, and conveying the gratifying intelligence that

1815. the Prince Regent had conferred on the 90th the distinction of Light Infantry.

> "Horse Guards,
> "1st May, 1815.
>
> "My Lord,
>
> "I have had the honour to lay before the Comr.-in-Chief your Lordship's letter of the 18th ultimo, and am directed to state in reply, that H.R.H. the Prince Regent has been pleased, in the name and on the behalf of His Majesty, to approve of the 90th Regiment, or Perthshire Volunteers, being formed into a Light Infantry corps, and of the clothing, arming, and drill of the regiment being the same, in all respects, as the 43rd, 51st, 52nd, 68th, 71st, and 85th Regiments.
>
> "I have, etc.,
> "(Signed) "H. CALVERT.
> "A. G."
>
> "GENERAL LORD LYNEDOCH, G.C.B.,
> "Colonel, 90th Regiment,
> "Grafton Street."

On the 9th of August, 1815, the 90th Light Infantry disembarked at Ostend, and pushing forward immediately on arrival, reached the camp of St. Denis, near Paris, on the fourth of September, and next day was attached to the 7th division.

Extract from general orders, dated Paris, the 17th of September:—

> "The 9th, 57th, 81st, and 90th are to be the 16th British brigade."
>
> "The 15th and 16th British brigades will be formed in the Plaine de Sablons, facing the road leading from Porte Maillot to St. Denis, to-morrow morning at half-past seven for the inspection of the Field Marshal."

1816. The regiment moved into quarters at Garches on the 30th of October, where it remained until the spring 1816, when it marched to Calais, embarking on the 1st, and landing at Dover on the 2nd of June, whence it marched the following day for Plymouth, where it arrived on the 30th.

1816.

In 1817, the second battalion was disbanded, the first battalion being made up to its full strength.

1817.

"Horse Guards, 19th March, 1817.

"Sir,

"I have the honour to acquaint you, by direction
" of the Commander-in-Chief, that the Prince Regent has
" been pleased, in the name and in the behalf of His
" Majesty, to grant permission to the 90th Regiment of
" Light Infantry, or Perthshire Volunteers, to bear on its
" colours and appointments, in addition to any other
" badges or devices which may have been heretofore
" granted to the regiment, the words 'Mandora,' 'Mar-
" tinique,' and 'Guadaloupe,' in commemoration of the
" services of the regiment when leading the right column
" of the army in its advance on Mandora on the 13th
" March, 1801, in the capture of Martinique on the 8th of
" February, 1809, and of Guadaloupe on the 3rd of
" February, 1810.

"I have, etc.,
"(Signed) HARRY CALVERT.
"Adjt.-General."

" Officer Commanding
" 90th Regt. of Light Infantry,
" or Perthshire Volunteers,
" Plymouth Dock."

New colours were received by the regiment in May, the old ones being presented to Lord Lynedoch.*

---

* They are now in the possession of James Maxtone Graham, Esqre., of Cultoquhey.

G

1818.   Extract from the General Orders, dated,

"Plymouth Dock, 25th April, 1818.

"Major-General Browne cannot take leave of the 90th
"Regiment without expressing his marked approbation
"of the uniform good conduct of the officers, non-com-
"missioned officers, and privates whilst under his command
"for a period of two years and three months.

"The Major-General is sensible that unremitting atten-
"tion has been paid by Colonel McNair and Lieutenant-
"Colonel Burrell, who have commanded, to the comforts
"and discipline of the soldier; he is equally so that the
"officers and non-commissioned officers have ably per-
"formed their several duties.

"Major-General Browne has not heard a single com-
"plaint against the regiment; he is grateful for this
"laudable adherence to order, and most sincerely wishes
"success and honour to the officers, non-commissioned
"officers, and privates of the 90th Light Infantry."

The regiment marched from Plymouth dock on the 29th of April in three divisions, and arrived at Chatham on the 18th, 19th, and 20th of May, where it was inspected in July by H.R.H. the Commander-in-Chief. The Colonel of the regiment, Thomas Graham (Lord Lynedoch), was present at the inspection, and heard with delight the flattering terms in which His Royal Highness addressed the 90th at the termination of the review.

"Crown Inn, Rochester,
"30th July, 1818.

"Dear Colonel,

"Though anything which I can say in praise of
"the regiment can be but little felt after the high appro-
"bation which all the officers have had the gratification
"of hearing expressed by H.R.H. the Commander-in-
"Chief, yet I should not feel satisfied with myself if I left

" this without requesting you to accept yourself, and
" convey to the officers and men of the 90th Light Infantry,
" my best thanks for their attention to good discipline,
" which the appearance of the regiment has evinced.

" I may be permitted to observe, that it was ever the
" object (which the valuable officers who assisted me in
" the first formation of the regiment had also in view to
" impress upon every individual that the character and
" conduct of the regiment depended on his feeling satis-
" faction and pride in belonging to a corps where honour
" was the leading principle.

" In every situation this principle has carried with it the
" character of distinction which I am confident the regi-
" ment will ever retain.

" I am proud to think that I owe everything in my
" military career to the 90th Regiment. Accept for the
" regiment my sincerest good wishes.

"" I remain,
"" Truly and obediently yours,
"" Signed, LYNEDOCH.
"" Colonel 90th Light Infantry."

" LIEUT.-COL. BURRELL,
"" Comdg. 90th Light Infy."

Brighton was the next station visited by the 90th Light Infantry, at which town it arrived in two divisions on the 22nd and 26th of December, and where it remained until April, 1819, when the right wing marched to Hilsea barracks, being followed by the remainder of the corps in May.

From Hilsea it proceeded to Shrewsbury, where it arrived on the 31st of October, and whence it marched to Macclesfield on the 18th of the following month.

From Macclesfield the regiment moved to Stockport, and thence to Plymouth, which was reached on the 18th of September, 1820, and where orders were received for it to proceed at once on foreign service, after a stay in England of four years.

1820. The destination of the regiment was Malta, for which place it sailed in three transports, viz., the *Aurora* on the 6th of October, the *Nautilus* on the 13th of October, and the *Chapman* on the 7th of November, which arrived at Malta—the *Aurora* on the 28th of October, the *Chapman* on the 3rd of December, and the *Nautilus* on the 5th.

" Horse Guards,
" 11th November, 1820.
" Sir,
" I have received and laid before the Commander-
" in-Chief your letter of the 7th, and His Royal Highness
" has read with great satisfaction the favourable report
" which you made of the manner in which the last division
" of the 90th Regiment embarked, and from the good
" disposition which has been manifested by the corps after
" its arrival at Plymouth, and the acknowledged zeal and
" attention of the officers of all ranks, H.R.H. is con-
" vinced that it will under all circumstances maintain its
" former high and distinguished character.
" I have, etc.,
" (Signed) H. TAYLOR."
" LIEUT.-COL. BURRELL,
" 90th Regiment."

1821. While at Malta, the regiment was inspected by Major-General Sir Manley Power, K.C.B., on the 18th of January, 1821.

" Division Orders.
" Malta, 18th January, 1821.
" The Major-General having completed the half-
" yearly inspection of the 90th Regiment, considers it his
" duty to express in Division Orders his approbation of
" that corps. Their very soldierlike appearance, and cor-
" rectness of manœuvres in the field, as well as the
" interior arrangements of the corps, and their regular

" conduct in quarters since they landed in the island of **1821**.
" Malta, have been reported in the most favourable manner
" to His Royal Highness the Commander-in-Chief.

" For the Brigade-Major,
" (Signed)   G. RAITT.
" D. A. G."

Towards the end of the year, disturbances arose in the Ionian islands requiring the presence of troops for their suppression. For this purpose two companies of the 90th Light Infantry embarked on board *H.M.S. Seringapatam*, and landed at Cephalonia on the 1st of October. They were followed by five companies in the *Chapman* transport, which arrived at Zante on the 10th of November. The remainder of the regiment leaving Malta on the 30th of October, and reaching Zante before the others.

Immediately on arrival, the 90th was employed in disarming the inhabitants and quelling the insurrection, which was fortunately accomplished without bloodshed.

Prior to the departure of the corps from Malta, the following divisional order was issued by Sir Manley Power, K.C.B., commanding the forces in the islands.

" Malta, 24th October, 1821.

" The 90th Light Infantry being upon the eve of
" leaving this command, the Major-General commanding
" has to express his very sincere regret at losing a corps
" whose conduct has been so uniformly correct and credit-
" able to themselves as to merit his most perfect and
" unqualified approbation.

" (Signed   N. BROWNE.
" M. B."

Extract from General Orders, dated,
" Head-Quarters, Zante, 15th November, 1821.
" The Commander of the Forces (Lieut.-General
" Sir Frederick Maitland, G.C.B.) having already, in a

1821. " proclamation bearing date the 15th ultimo, expressed the
" very deep sense he entertains of the firm and judicious
" conduct of Major-General Sir F. Adam, K.C.B., and of
" the good behaviour of the officers and men of His
" Majesty's 8th and 90th Regiments, employed in dis-
" arming the population of the island, a measure now
" happily completed without the smallest accident, etc.". .

For some time one wing of the regiment was stationed in Cephalonia, where Colonel Charles Napier was commandant (afterwards Sir Charles Napier, the conqueror of Scinde), the other wing being quartered in Zante.

1825. While the regiment was thus separated an event took place which tended greatly to enliven the dullness of garrison routine. A Greek pirate had for some time been hovering about Zante and had captured several small coasting vessels, when it was determined to put an end to its mischievous career.

A small detachment of the 90th, under the command of Lieutenant Wilson, formerly a midshipman in the Royal Navy, was placed on board one of the country vessels. The men wore their white fatigue dresses and were hidden under sails, canvass, etc. After cruising about for some time the pirate was at last sighted, and soon after bore down upon his, seemingly helpless, prey. At the word of command the men rose up and poured in a volley at close quarters with such deadly effect that a second was not required.

The regiment remained in the Ionian islands until 1830, for the greater part of the time under the command of Lt.-Colonel Sir Frederick Stovin, K.C.B. Nothing occurred during its stay in the Mediterranean to disturb its quiet enjoyment of these charming stations, which it quitted, after a sojourn of nine years, regretted by all.

On its voyage home, one wing of the regiment, under the command of Captain Boulby, was shipwrecked on the coast of Sicily, owing to the misconduct of the crew of the hired transport in which it was embarked. Thanks to the indefatigable exertions of the officers and men of the 90th, all the baggage and public stores were saved. **1830.**

On its arrival in Great Britain, the 90th proceeded to Edinburgh where it remained for a year, under the command of Lieut.-Colonel Lord G. W. Russell, and then moved on to Glasgow, which station it left at the end of 1832 for Ireland.

The regiment was now commanded by Lieut.-Colonel Arbuthnot, who had exchanged with Lord G. W. Russell.

On the 21st of January, 1833, new colours were presented to the 90th Light Infantry, in the square of the Royal Hospital, Kilmainham, by Lieutenant-General Sir Hussey Vivian, the Commander of the Forces in Ireland, who addressed the regiment in the following terms :— **1833.**

"Colonel Arbuthnot, officers, non-commissioned "officers, and soldiers of the 90th Light Infantry, the "purpose for which we are here assembled this day, is to "perform one of the most solemn, one of the most inte- "resting, and one that ought to be rendered one of the "most imposing of our military ceremonies.

* * * * * * * * * * *

"On such an occasion it is customary, it is right, to "refer to those opportunities the corps, to which the "colours are to be presented, has had of distinguishing "itself before its enemies. It is right, I say, that this "should be the case; it brings to the recollections of the "old soldiers days of honour and of glory of which they "have reason to be proud. It stimulates the young "soldiers to emulate the conduct of the old in those days "that are to come, and in referring to such opportunities, "although in the case of this regiment they have not "occurred so frequently as in the case of some of its more "fortunate fellow-soldiers, still it is gratifying to recollect "that when such opportunities have occurred they have "been nobly taken advantage of, and the steadiness and

1833. "courage of the corps has been proudly asserted. At an
"early period of my military life it was my good fortune
"to become intimately known to that distinguished indi-
"vidual who raised this regiment, who at an advanced
"period of his own life I mean advanced for first com-
"mencing that of a soldier, quitted his home at his
"country's call, and whose whole career was one of con-
"tinued and eminent services—who, to use the words of
"the Duke of Wellington, closed that career in the
"Peninsula, after having established within the French
"territory the troops of the allied British and Portuguese
"army, which had been so permanently distinguished
"under his command, and who afterwards, having been
"again called into service, planned and carried into effect
"that most extraordinary military enterprise, the surprise
"of Bergen-op-Zoom—an enterprise which may be said
"to have been completely successful, as far as regarded
"the General under whose orders it was undertaken, and
"which failed solely from some unfortunate and accidental
"misunderstanding of orders by the troops engaged—an
"enterprise designated by Buonaparte as one of the
"boldest and first military exploits ever imagined or
"attempted.

"It was my fortune also, in early life, to be quartered
"for two years with this regiment in the garrison of
"Gibraltar; there I had the happiness to form an ac-
"quaintance, and, I may add, a friendship—a friendship
"that I am proud to say has existed and exists up to the
"present time—with that amiable and excellent man, that
"admirable officer at the head of His Majesty's army,
"General Lord Rowland Hill. I there also became
"acquainted with the other officers of the corps—I there
"became acquainted with the merits of the corps itself.
"The friendship, thus established, led me naturally, when
"parted from it, still to regard its progress with anxiety,
"and to look with interest to all such events as were con-
"ducive to its success and its honour. It was, there-

" fore, with great pleasure that I learnt it was one of those
" regiments brought together to form the army, when
" England put forth that wonderful instance of her power
" and assembled her legions from the four quarters of the
" globe in order to expel the invading enemy from the
" territories of an ancient and faithful ally.

" The regiment, I say, then formed part of that force so
" assembled on the burning plains of Egypt—on those
" burning plains where in days of yore the lion-hearted
" king of England led his chivalry to feats of arms, by
" which they have been immortalized—on that holy land,
" where, for the first time, a check was given to the career
" of that extraordinary man whose victories in Italy had
" already rendered him so celebrated by a British naval
" chief—a Christian knight who raised the union flag of
" England on the walls of Acre. It was, I say, on the
" burning sands of that country that this regiment, under
" the command of Colonel, now Lord, Hill, formed the
" advanced guard of the army, and for the first time
" meeting the enemy, whilst severely engaged and under
" a fire of artillery and musketry, suddenly finding them-
" selves assailed by a large body of the enemy's cavalry,
" received the attack with all the coolness of veterans, gave
" their fire, defeated and dispersed them.

" After that, in the great victory, in which fell one of
" the oldest and bravest of our generals—nobly fell at the
" head of the army he commanded, and from which re-
" sulted the evacuation of Egypt by the enemy—this
" regiment again was eminently distinguished by its
" valour, its steadiness, and its good conduct ; the grand
" memorials of these two occasions are borne on your
" colours. Subsequently I find its services were called for
" in the West Indies, that inhospitable climate to which,
" in support of her commercial interests and political
" power, England is under the necessity of calling for the
" services of her soldiers—that climate in which, although
" honour was not so readily to be gained as it was by

1833.

1833. " those who had the good fortune to serve elsewhere,
" danger was infinitely greater. There I find this regi-
" ment composing part of the few which wrested from the
" power of France those important colonies of Guadaloupe
" and Martinique, and there also was the regiment dis-
" tinguished for its discipline and good conduct, the
" honourable testimony to which is most handsomely
" expressed in the orders of the civil and military au-
" thorities of the country, and borne on your record books.
" In Ireland also, where, during the war, the regiment,
" 2nd battalion, was for many years stationed, the same
" flattering and highly honourable testimony is borne to
" its admirable conduct on all occasions and under all
" circumstances.

" Having thus referred to the discipline of the corps, let
" me impress on your officers that discipline is best
" preserved by a constant and viligant attention to those
" under your orders. Let me beg of you at all times to
" recollect that the British soldier, who at an early period
" quits his home, his parents, and his friends to serve his
" country, is entitled to expect that you will, as far as
" possible, replace those parents and those friends. It is
" your duty to administer to his wants, to look to his
" comforts, to consult over his wishes as far as you pos-
" sibly can consistent with the good of the service, to
" watch over his conduct, to control those who miscon-
" duct themselves, and to indulge those who merit to be
" indulged.

" Soldiers! it is your business to look to the officers as
" your parents and friends; let your only fear be the fear
" of offending them. But why do I refer to discipline?
" Is it that the regiment, now before me, requires such a
" reference? No, Colonel Arbuthnot, it stands a proud
" instance—a proud and honourable testimony to you,
" and to your officers and men—of the perfection to
" which discipline may be carried, with the smallest
" degree of punishment; it stands, as does the army,

" giving a proud contradiction to those who, speaking of 1833.
" matters of which they can know nothing, charge us with
" cruelty in our punishments—those who, thus pretending
" to be the soldier's friend, never, that I am aware of,
" stepped forward in any way to prove that they really
" were such; on the contrary, they are those who are
" always the first to exclaim against the weight of that
" provision a liberal country has made for the maintenance
" of those old soldiers whose services have well and truly
" deserved it; they are those who, if unhappily any
" instance does occur in which there is a lapse of discipline,
" are the first to come forward and loudly to complain of
" it. But so far is it from being true that the punishments
" of the British army are severe, there is not in Europe an
" army in which they are so light—there is not in Europe
" an army in which the soldier is in every respect, and at
" all times, so well and so kindly treated—there is not in
" Europe an army in which such perfect discipline is so
" constantly preserved. I refer to discipline also, in order
" that I may have an opportunity of pointing out its
" advantages. Who is there amongst us, let me ask, that
" does not look back with pride to the many glorious
" occasions in which, during the late war, the discipline
" of our army shone triumphantly victorious.

* * * * * * * * *

" They raised the British Standard in the territories of
" France, and by their conduct and discipline caused such
" a feeling in their favour, that the French people them-
" selves received them as protectors, and the French
" writers, in describing the invasion, admit that the
" admirable behaviour of the British soldiery valued the
" army, in its effects, at least ten thousand men. And
" may I be permitted to add, who is there amongst us that,
" now belonging to the army in Ireland, is not proud of
" the results which have arisen from the excellent conduct
" it has everywhere observed. Called upon to perform the
" most vexatious and harassing duties, subjected at all

1833. " times to insult, and even to outrage, such has been the
" temper and forbearance—such the firmness of the troops,
" that they are everywhere looked upon as friends, and
" from one end of Ireland to another are respected and
" admired. Such then are the advantages of preserving
" discipline; it is by this alone that you can do honour to
" your colours.

" I will now detain you but a very short time longer,
" but before I conclude, I must impress upon you that at
" all times the watchward of a soldier ought to be
" ' Honour and Fidelity.' To attain this, the governing
" principle of his conduct must be—obedience to the
" orders of his superiors. I will remind you of the last,
" that most impressive order of that great naval comman-
" der, who fell in the most glorious victory ever gained by
" the navy of England, and who in falling scaled the
" maritime ascendency of the country, annihilating the
" fleets of France and Spain—I say, I must remind you of
" that last, that most impressive order which he issued to
" those brave men under his command, calling upon them
" to recollect that ' England expects every man to do his
" duty '—an order so nobly given, and so gloriously and
" triumphantly executed, that the remembrance of it can
" never be effaced from the annals of the country; and
" lastly, I must beg of you never to forget when marching
" against the enemy under those colours which I now
" place in your care—I call on you never to forget that
" they are to be stained only with your blood, to be
" surrendered only with your lives."

Colonel Arbuthnot's reply was as follows:—

" It is impossible for me, Sir, to express the
" gratification I have derived from the address you have
" just delivered to the regiment under my command,
" a gratification which I see, on looking round, has been
" shared by all. Our good fortune, Sir, has been great in
" having these colours presented to us by an officer, the

"chief part of whose life has been spent in the camp and
"the field, who by his own exertions has risen through all
"ranks to his present high station, who has so frequently
"received the thanks of his King and his country; and
"gratified as he must have been at these marks of appro-
"bation and honour, still that could not have been equal
"to the consciousness which he must have felt how
"justly he merited them, and how richly he had earned
"them.

1833.

"For me, Sir, this is a proud day, and I have every
"reason to be proud, but however great my pride may be,
"it is far and far increased when I bear in mind that
"from the day I assumed command of this regiment to
"the present period, every indvidual, whether officer, non-
"commissioned officer, or soldier, has not only exerted
"himself to meet my wishes, whatever they might be, but
"anxious as I must be for the reputation of it, everyone
"has shown even greater anxiety, if possible, to main-
"tain and uphold the high character it so justly deserves,
"and has so long obtained.

"In presenting these colours, you have imposed a sacred
"trust on us—the honour of our regiment is in our own
"hands. I am well aware, Sir, if circumstances should
"require us to act in defence of our king and country, that
"in the face of the enemy it will be more difficult for me
"to restrain their ardour than to inflame their courage,
"but should a stimulus be wanting, that stimulus would
"be—'Remember, Sir Hussey Vivian confided these
"colours to your charge!'

"The recollection of the day will never be effaced from
"the memory of any here present, for depend upon it, Sir,
"that in whatever quarter of the globe it may be our fate
"to serve, or in whatever position we may be placed, the
"21st of January, 1833, will always be remembered, and
"the name of Sir Hussey Vivian will often be mentioned
"with pride, I hope I may say with affection, and certainly
"with pleasure."

1833. The old colours were placed in the great hall of Kilmainham hospital.

The head-quarters (two companies), band, buglers, and recruits occupied Beggar's Bush barracks, the remaining companies being quartered at Georges Street, Portobello, Pigeon House Fort, and Royal barracks, until August, when the whole regiment moved into the Palatine Square Royal barracks. In September, it marched, under the command of Major McKay, to Kilkenny, where the head-quarters and four companies were stationed, detachments being sent to Thomas Town, Callon, Gore's bridge, Castlecomer, and Maryborough.

While at Kilkenny, Captain the Honourable F. G. Howard was accidently killed. He was on his way with Lieutenant Straton to visit the detachment at Castlecomer, when the horse he was driving took fright and ran away. Captain Howard in endeavouring to get out of the carriage, became entangled in the trace and was dragged for about half-a-mile; when taken up he was dead.

The regiment was twice inspected, while at Kilkenny, by Major-General Sir Edward Blakeney.

1834. In April, 1834, the 90th marched to Naas, where the head-quarters and six companies were quartered. Two companies under Major Slade proceeded to Carlow, Captains Wilson and White going with their companies to Athy and Ballinglass respectively.

The escort duties were very heavy, and one night orders were received for the regiment to march immediately to Maryborough for election duty, where it remained three weeks. On its return to Naas, it was again inspected by Sir E. Blakeney.

1835. In the spring of 1835, the regiment marched to Dublin, occupying the Richmond barracks, and subsequently, those at Beggar's Bush, sending out detachments. While in Dublin, orders were received to proceed to Ceylon for a tour of foreign service.

The regiment, in September, moved from Dublin to

Cork, sending detachments to Mill Street and Ballincollig. **1835.** On its arrival at Cork, the corps was inspected by Sir Thomas Arbuthnot, and the service companies were formed to the number of six, their total strength being about 650 men.

In October, two companies, under the command of Captain Suckling, embarked on board the ship *Valleyfield*, and sailed for Ceylon. In November, the head-quarters and remaining companies went on board the Indiaman *Sir Charles Malcolm*, and were detained in Cork harbour for three weeks, when it was discovered that the ship leaked; orders were then received to sail for Plymouth for repairs, at which place the 90th disembarked on the 8th of December.

The regiment sailed for Ceylon on the 4th of January, **1836.** touched at the Matree Islands on the 5th of May, sighted Ceylon on the 21st, and landed on Sunday the 22nd, after a voyage of nearly five months. The companies under Captain Suckling had arrived two months before, and were stationed in the fort of Colombo, the late arrivals taking up quarters on Slave Island, about a mile from the fort. Two days after the arrival of the head-quarters, the whole regiment was inspected by Lieutenant-General Sir J. Wilson, who expressed his gratification and surprise at the perfect manner in which the drill movements were performed after so protracted a voyage, and informed Colonel Arbuthnot that he would report most favourably to the Commander-in-Chief on the efficiency of the regiment.

The unhealthy climate of the island soon began to affect both officers and men, one of its first victims being Lieutenant and Adjutant J. H. Cotton, who died in July after a short illness.

In September, Captains Eld and Egerton proceeded **1837.** with their companies to Point de Galle, about which time Colonel Arbuthnot was appointed commandant of the garrison, and shortly after exchanged with Colonel **1838.** Peddie of the 72nd.

1839. The two companies from Point de Galle rejoined head-quarters in October; and in January, 1839, the whole regiment marched from Colombo to Kandy. While stationed there the men suffered very severely from ophthalmia, several losing their sight entirely, and a great number having to be invalided home.

In April, a detachment of two companies, under Captain Mann, was sent to Trincomalee; and in the following month a draft of 150 men, under Captain Bowyer, joined the regiment. Arriving in the hot season, after a long voyage, the climate told so severely upon them that in the course of three weeks after their arrival thirty-five had died and the remainder were ailing for some months.

1840. Colonel Peddie, whose failing health necessitated a change, proceeded to Newera Ellia, where he died in August, 1840, regretted by the whole regiment, which he had commanded for a time which, though short, was sufficient to make his loss keenly felt.

1841. In December, 1841, the regiment, under Colonel Singleton, K.H., who had been recently appointed to the command, marched to Colombo, where it was rejoined in
1842. March, 1842, by the detachment from Trincomalee.

1844. The 90th returned to Kandy in 1844, in which year cholera broke out at head-quarters, as well as at Trincomalee, where the usual number of detached companies were stationed; several men died at both places.

1845. Early in the following year, Lieut.-General Sir Colin Campbell inspected the regiment, and expressed himself as being much pleased with its appearance and steadiness under arms.

About November, the gratifying news was received that the relieving regiment might be shortly expected in the island. The 90th, consequently, for the last time marched to Colombo, and prepared for its departure.

1846. The 15th Foot arrived in January, 1846, when the two regiments were inspected together. Sir Colin Campbell in saying farewell to the 90th, remarked upon the severity with which the climate had dealt with it, adding that under 1846. all trials it had maintained its high character, and that he would send home a most favourable report of its efficiency to the Duke of Wellington. Prior to the departure of the 90th, Colonel Singleton exchanged with Colonel Slade of the 30th Regt. Early in February, No. 6 Company, under Captain Mann, embarked on board the *Maria Somes*, hired transport, for Trincomalee, where the two detached companies were taken up, and the course shaped for England. The officers of the 90th Light Infantry on board the *Maria Somes* were Captains Mann and Geale, Lieutenants McNeil, Walter, J. Peddie, R. Grove, Purcell, O'Gorman, and Assistant Surgeon W. Maclise.

All went well for several days, even weeks had passed, when one afternoon the ship was overtaken by a sudden tempest of the most violent character, the sails were split, and the royal and top-gallant masts snapped off. In a few moments broken spars, torn sails, rigging, and blocks were swinging in mid-air in most dangerous confusion, rendering the task of shortening the remaining sails most difficult and hazardous. Meanwhile the storm increased to a hurricane—no sails could stand against it, and the vessel rolled and laboured so much, that it was deemed expedient to cut away the mainmast by the board. Before attempting this, it was of course necessary to ease off broadside to the gale, where the vessel lay in the trough of the sea, the huge waves breaking over her; directly the mainmast was overboard, an endeavour was made to bring the ship's head up into the wind, so as, if possible, to remain hove-to; unfortunately in the attempt the rudderhead sprung, and all steering power was lost. In this dilemma, all that could be done was to lash hammocks and strips of canvass in the mizen shrouds, to assist in keeping the ship's head a little up in the wind. The storm was most furious, and from its disabled state, there was little or no hope of the ship being saved—even the crew despaired, especially when it was discovered that there

H

1846. was much water in the hold. The pumps had been worked by relays of the 90th men, but it was no longer possible for them to remain on deck—moreover, the pumps became more or less out of order. The men, women, and children were all battened down below, for fear of their being washed overboard, and their demand for drinking water became frequent and most urgent, the heat between decks being excessive. It devolved upon the subaltern officers for nearly three days and nights to hand water, which had unfortunately become impregnated with salt, down the main-hatch whenever a moment's opportunity could be seized for lifting the tarpauling and other coverings from a small portion of the hatchway. The sufferings of those below were most distressing to witness; stripped to their skin and in a violent perspiration, they crowded beneath the hatchway, each one with outstretched hands hastily plunging a basin into or towards the bucket as it was lowered.

The hurricane continued in full force, and it was supposed that the ship had been carried along into the very centre of its fury; its position was unknown, for during the three days the storm continued not a single gleam of light broke through the clouds, and of course no observation could be taken. All hands despaired of life. The crew, worn out by their unavailing efforts, came aft and mixed with the officers; only the mizen and fore-lower masts were standing, the latter with the foreyard attached, but swinging violently from side to side. The captain, wishing to preserve this spar, ordered the foreyard to be lashed, but none of the crew would make the attempt. He then most courageously went forward alone and got on to the forecastle, seized the foreyard as it swung past his head, but not having time to lash it to the mast he was carried overboard, and as the ship's head dipped violently into the sea he was lost to sight under the tremendous waves, but reappeared as the vessel heaved up, still clinging to the end of the foreyard. In this manner he swung two or three times across the bows and into the waves on either side of the ship, occasionally touching the deck with his feet, but failing, time after time, to secure either himself or the spar. At last he managed to seize a rope's-end and lashed the yard to the mast.

As the hurricane increased in strength more disasters occurred. The starboard cabin was stove in; the Government Agent, an officer of the Royal Navy, broke his arm, which was set, under most adverse circumstances, by Assistant Surgeon Maclise; the rudder was carried away, and the skylight of the saloon was burst open by a tremendous sea shipped on the poop. However, on the third day a gleam of light pierced the massive clouds and hope revived; the waves were still breaking over the wreck, but the wind, by slow degrees, moderated, and the following day was comparatively fine. The soldiers and women, who had been all this time battened down, had suffered fearfully, as nothing could be done in the way of supplying fresh air. At length one dead body was passed up, then another and another—in all sixteen—who had been suffocated or had died from exhaustion during the three days and nights this most dreadful storm had lasted. Those who had remained on deck were all suffering, more or less, from exposure and from constant wet—showing itself especially in swelled legs and feet. After the storm had subsided the decks were ventilated and washed, and those who were able had plenty of work to do, chiefly at the pumps, as there was reported to be fourteen feet of water in the hold; but the chief difficulty to contend with was the want of a rudder; however, some spars were found and bolted together and then shaped into the proper form. Then arose another difficulty—the new rudder had to be fixed in its place. An examination of the stern-post led to the discovery of the pintails and gudgeons of the old one some depth below water, but there seemed no means of getting them, and their recovery was about to be abandoned when a man of the name of Gunnion, a private in the 90th,

1846.

1846. volunteered to dive, and after many attempts, attended with great danger from the sharks, which could be seen on all sides, he succeeded in regaining the much-wanted articles. The rudder was then placed in position, and the foreyard, in saving which the captain had so boldly risked his life, was rigged as a jury mast, sail was made, and in about a fortnight's time the crippled vessel reached the Mauritius.

As soon as the history of the shipwreck was known at Port Louis the greatest possible sympathy and kindness from all persons were shown to the sufferers. The men were placed in barracks in the Fort, and for some time were excused all duties. The officers and men of the 12th Regiment, then quartered in the island, received their comrades of the 90th with open arms; indeed, nothing could have been kinder than their attention in every way. The Governor, Sir William Gomm, invited the officers for a week or ten days' stay with him at his country residence, called Réduit, where they were provided with every comfort they could require. After a stay of two months, during which time the *Maria Somes* was repaired, the three companies re-embarked and sailed for the Cape of Good Hope.

G.O. issued by Lieut.-Genl. Sir W. Gomm.

" Head-Quarters, Réduit,
" Mauritius, 25th April, 1846.

" No. 41.

" The Lieut.-General has had under his minute
" observation the several reports called for, relative to the
" disasters which have befallen the detachment 90th Light
" Infantry, consisting of three companies embarked from
" Ceylon on board the *Maria Somes*, hired transport, in
" the month of February last, for the purpose of pro-
" ceeding to England, and forced to take refuge in the
" port of this island, for repairing the damage sustained

" by the vessel from the hurricane which it encountered on
" the 27th ultimo and three following days.

" These reports have been perused with a painful and
" very lively interest so forcibly exemplifying the vicis-
" situdes to which the British soldier is exposed in the
" ordinary discharge of his duty to his Sovereign and to
" his country, calling for a display of a variety of energies
" rarely, if ever, excelled by the troops of other nations.

" Thus, while the British soldiers on the continent of
" India were pursuing a course of almost unexampled
" triumphs on the junction of the Punjaub, the gallant
" men of the 90th Light Infantry were undergoing the
" yet severer trials of constancy and endurance under
" extremest perils and distress; but the sound heart,
" undauntable energy, and a trust far higher, never
" failing, brought them out of the conflict victorious, as
" they ought to be.

" Deplorable as has been the loss of life through the
" adoption of measures had recourse to for the general
" safety, it is the opinion of competent naval authority
" on the spot, to whom the details have been referred,
" that the sacrifice under the circumstances was un-
" avoidable, but the stern necessity brought out into yet
" stronger relief the confidence placed by the men in the
" judgment, presence of mind, and watchfulness over their
" welfare by their officers; and these again gave proof by
" their example that such firm confidence was well
" reposed.

" The Lieut.-General assures Captain Mann, the officers,
" and soldiers under his command, that it will be his
" gratifying duty promptly to forward the reports before
" him for submission to his Grace the Duke of Wellington,
" to whom every record tending to elevate the character
" of the British soldier before the world is so precious.

" Officers on board :—

    " Captn. Mann.
    "   Geale.

1846.

1846.
"   Lieut. Walter.
"   Peddie.
"   Grove.
"   O'Gorman.
" Asst. Surgeon Maclise."

The head-quarters and remaining three companies, under the command of Captain Eld, embarked on board the hired transport *Mariner*, on the 16th of February, and after an easy voyage, saddened by the death of several men from the effects of their long stay in Ceylon, arrived at Simon's Bay on the 3rd of April.

On the arrival of the head-quarter companies at the Cape, they were ordered to take part in the operations against the Kaffirs who had attacked the colonists. General Sir Peregrine Maitland, Commanding-in-Chief, directed them to sail round to Algoa Bay, whence they were, on landing, to push on to the front. Graham's Town was reached on the 25th of April, on which day Mr. Norden, a merchant who had been appointed to the Colonelcy of the Yeomanry corps, was shot when gallantly leading on his men against a body of Kaffirs in a strong position in the bush, a few miles from Graham's Town. The enemy carried away the body which they placed in a conspicuous position on the following day, probably as a decoy. On the 27th a large body of the inhabitants, a few of the Cape corps, and the companies of the 90th, headed by Colonel Johnstone, the Commandant of the town, went out and brought in the mangled corpse of this brave officer.

After a day's halt, the wing of the 90th and part of the 91st marched for Fort Beaufort, escorting a large convoy of supplies. During the march the enemy hovered round, ready at any moment to dash in and seize the waggons; the opportunity, however, was never given to them, and the little party arrived safely at its destination on the 30th of April.

On the 24th of May, the 90th left Fort Beaufort, Captain Eld and 100 men occupying Fort Brown, and a

company, under Lieutenant Lecky, being posted at Koon- **1846.**
appe Drift to keep open the communications; the remainder, a mere handful, under Captain Bringhurst, moving on to Graham's Town, whence they were sent out in small parties to collect supplies.

In the beginning of June, these foraging parties were called in, and, their strength being made up to 100 men, they were sent off, under Captain Bringhurst, with Lieutenants Owen and Johnson, to Fort Peddie, viâ Trumpeter's Drift, to escort a convoy of waggons with supplies. The escort arrived at Trumpeter's Drift safely, but could not advance owing to the enemy being in force in Trumpeter's Bush. After a fortnight's halt they were ordered to proceed, and moved over the ground where a convoy, guarded by native levies, had been plundered a few weeks before. At the top of Trumpeter's Bush a troop of the 7th Dragoon Guards was on the look out for them, as it was expected every moment that the convoy would be attacked; the cavalry joined the escort, which reached Fort Peddie safely—the men of the 90th remaining there for some time.

The three companies which were on board the *Maria Somes* arrived at Graham's Town at this period, and were employed on outpost duty until the 23rd of June, when they were formed up and, with part of the 7th, 91st, Cape Mounted Rifles, Burghers, and Hottentots, took the field, under the immediate command of Sir Peregrine Maitland, and encamped at the mouth of the Fish River.

On the 6th of July, a force, under the command of Major Yarborough of the 91st, composed of 150 men of the 91st and part of the 90th, made its first march from Fish River mouth along the shore to the mouth of the Reka, where they encamped; on the 15th they arrived at the Buffalo River after a most trying march, the waggons with supplies and tents being so far behind that for four days the men had no meat, and the officers only such food as their horses could carry.

1846. For a time the division halted to enable supplies to come up, and on the 17th, the regular infantry, under General Maitland, proceeded to the Dike flats, viâ King William's Town, en route to the Amatolas to intercept the Gaikas. On the 21st of July, they encamped four miles from King William's Town, and on the 19th of August were at Fort Beresford.

In August, Colonel Slade, and Lieutenants Davies, Butler, Meredith, and Wyvill arrived at the Cape from England, and joined the regiment; the detached companies were called in, and moved by the Fish River on Block Drift, where a force, composed of the 27th, 46th, part of the 91st, and a battery of artillery, was encamped, of which Colonel Slade, on arrival, took the command. While in this permanent camp, two companies of the 90th, under Captain Bringhurst, were sent off across the Kei to harass the enemy; on their return they found the river impassable, owing to the rains having flooded it, and had, consequently, to bivouac on the bank, with scarcely any provisions and no cover, for three days, before being able to rejoin the head-quarters at Graham's Town.

About the 13th of September, the division under Sir Peregrine Maitland moved towards the mouth of the Fish River, which it reached on the 19th.

In October, the 90th, under Lieutenant-Colonel Slade, the 45th, under Lieutenant-Colonel Erskine, a troop of the 7th Dragoon Guards, and some artillery, once more moved inland, advancing on Block Drift. By the end of November, all the principal Gaika Chiefs had given in.

On the 23rd of October, at Fort Beaufort, the Swellendam Native Infantry, numbering 350 men, mutinied, and marched off in the direction of Graham's Town; they were immediately followed by Captain Ward, of the 91st Regiment, with six sappers and two artillerymen, and a 3-pounder howitzer, who hoped to stop them at a bridge outside the Fort; in this, however, he was not successful; the mutineers passed over at the double, and on three

rounds of blank being fired, they rushed up a hill near **1846.**
the bridge, and turned to defend themselves. In the
meantime, a few mutineers, who had followed behind the
gun, were attempting to pass it; Captain Ward rushed in
amongst them and seized one man, opened the pan of his
firelock, and after a struggle secured him; he also took
another, and kept both of them prisoners.

Soon after, eighty men of the 90th, who where at Fort
Beaufort on escort duty, came up to Captain Ward's
assistance, who immediately directed them to follow the
mutineers, when an order was received from Colonel
Richardson to cease the pursuit, as Mr. Beaver, a clergy-
man, and Mr. Calderwood, a missionary, had offered to
follow the insurgents and induce them to return—a difficult
task, in which they were partially successful.

January the 6th, 1847, orders were received for the **1847.**
90th to embark for England immediately. The regiment
accordingly having concentrated, marched for Graham's
Town en route to the coast, where it was hoped that
transports would be in readiness to receive it. However,
on arrival at Port Elizabeth, it was found that the
Thunderbolt, in which they were to embark, had not yet
come in. Its advent was anxiously awaited until the 3rd
of February, when the ship appeared in sight, having
on board Sir Henry Pottinger and Lieutenant-General
Berkeley. The men of the regiment were eagerly watching
her approach, imagining that the moment was at hand
when they would leave a country in which they had toiled
and suffered through a wearisome war with but little
chance of credit. Their hopes were, however, doomed to
be disappointed, for in rounding Cape Receif, the vessel
struck upon a sunken rock, and leaked so badly, that she
had to be driven ashore. There was so much water in the
ship that the furnaces were extinguished, and she only had
just sufficient steam left to drive her towards the beach.

In spite of pumps, worked day and night, where the
Thunderbolt touched ground there she remained. The

1847. water in her did not decrease, and the engineer suspected that the sea-pipe must be open. Should such be the case, until it was closed all labour must prove unavailing, and as the vessel was full of greasy opaque water, it seemed impossible for anyone to reach the engine-room. Private Gunnion, 90th Light Infantry, came forward and offered to make the attempt. After receiving precise instructions as to the situation of the pipe, he descended, and naturally lost his way in the filthy liquid, but with indomitable pluck, he went down again and again, and eventually succeeded. The pipe was open, he closed it, and the quantity of water in the ship was reduced, but the injuries she had sustained were of so serious a nature, that she had to be broken up.

The words of one who saw the 90th at this time may well be quoted.

" The appearance of the 90th on leaving the colony is
" so totally different to what it presented on its arrival
" here, that it goes far to prove the good effect of the Cape
" climate on constitutions debilitated by Indian service.
" Under every disadvantage of fatigue, privation, and
" a residence under canvass in the height of an African
" summer, with the thermometer at times 157° in the open
" air, the 90th, on their march from Graham's Town to the
" coast, presented a perfect picture of a regiment of British
" veterans.

" I saw them in my evening ride on the 5th of February,
" as they toiled up a steep hill before me, with their long
" line of waggons and dusky waggon drivers. How
" cheerful they looked! I envied them as I turned my
" horse's head back to the land of banishment and anxiety!
" I could not help uttering the words, ' happy 90th, God
" speed you!' aloud, as the last waggon passed me, and
" an old soldier with a bronzed cheek and white hair
" saluted me by way of ' thank you for your good will.'

" How little they anticipated their disappointment at
" Algoa Bay."

In a few days the *President* came into the Bay, on board 1847. of which, the regiment embarked, proceeding to Cape Town, where it was quartered, in daily expectation of leaving for home. However, affairs on the frontier again looking serious, the 90th was sent by wings in the *Rosamond* to the mouth of the Buffalo River—that commanded by Major Eld landing there on the 28th of July.

In April, Lieutenant and Adjutant Davis had been appointed superintendent of native police—a force which he rendered very efficient; in June, their conduct in the field was put to the test. The Gaika chief, Sandilla, having stolen some cattle from Fort Hare, two troops of the 7th Dragoon Guards, two companies of the 45th Regiment, and 80 of the Kaffir police, under Lieutenant Davis, were sent to demand compensation. The chief's herds were seized, but on the return of the party, it was waylaid by the enemy, and most of the beasts retaken; during the fight, the police fought bravely, and did good service against their countrymen.

An order arrived from England in July, that soldiers of the 27th, 90th, and 91st Regiments, desirous of settling in the country, or wishing to serve as non-commissioned officers in the additional companies of the Cape Mounted Riflemen, were to state their wishes to the Government; one hundred men of the 90th volunteered to remain in the country; and on the next outbreak of hostilities in 1852, they were nearly all of them murdered by the Kaffirs.

The right wing of the regiment which left for Buffalo Mouth, after the three companies, under Major Eld, had landed, was caught in a hurricane and driven into Algoa Bay, where it was detained for a day or two. On landing at Buffalo Mouth, two companies, under Captain Gale, were left there, the remainder pushing on to the Goolah heights to rejoin the left wing.

The regiment remained near the coast until January, 1848, when, after being inspected at Buffalo Mouth by

1848. Sir Harry Smith, it was sent by wings to Cape Town, whence, after a stay of a fortnight, it embarked on board the ship *General Hewett*, and sailed for England, arriving at Spithead on the 18th of April, after an absence from home of 13 years.

From Spithead the ship went round to Gravesend, where the regiment disembarked, and proceeded direct to Chatham, at which place it was joined by the depôt companies, 600 strong. At the end of May, the regiment was formed into ten companies, and shortly afterwards was inspected by Sir George Brown.

In August, the corps marched from Chatham *viâ* Maidstone to London, whence it proceeded by rail to Ashton-under-Lyne, where the head-quarters and three companies were quartered, the remaining companies being detached to Stockport, Colne, Sheffield, Bradford, and Burnley. While in this district the Chartist riots broke out in Ashton; the companies quartered there were turned out, but were not called upon to do more than patrol the streets and keep order.

Surgeon Ellson, of the regiment, died at Ashton, after a very short illness.

1849. While stationed here, the 90th was twice inspected by General Sir W. Warr.

1850. In the spring of 1850, it marched to Manchester, where it was quartered for a year, being twice inspected by Major-General Sir G. Cathcart during that time.

1851. Early in 1851, orders were received for the regiment to proceed to Buttevant, whence, after a stay of three weeks, the regiment left for Cork, where the head-quarters and two companies were stationed, the remainder being detached to Haulbowline, Spike Island, Mill Street, and Bandon. During their stay at Cork the elections came off, and the companies were out under arms for three days, performing the unpleasant duties necessary on these occasions.

While at Cork, in January, new colours were received, **1852**. the old set being placed in Kilmainham hospital.

Early in 1852, the 90th moved to Dublin, occupying the Ship Street barracks, and furnishing detachments to Oldborough House and Beggar's Bush. While here the corps was inspected by Major-General Cochrane.

In the winter of 1853, it moved into the Royal Square **1853**. barracks, which it occupied until November, 1854.

During its stay in Dublin, 28 of the non-commissioned officers were ordered to proceed to England, for the purpose of organizing a Militia Regiment which had been raised.

This year war was declared against Russia, but at the **1854**. beginning of the struggle it seemed as if the 90th was destined to have no share in it.

Up to the present time Light Infantry Regiments had enjoyed the privilege of not serving in India, an exemption which Viscount Hardinge, the Commander-in-Chief, had just abolished, sending the 43rd and 52nd Regiments out to that country, and ordering the 90th to be in readiness to proceed there early in the next year. However, upon Lord Raglan's application for reinforcements, these plans were altered, and the Perthshire Light Infantry received orders by telegram to proceed to the Crimea at once. The longed-for message arriving while the regiment was at divine service on the 12th of November.

Accordingly, on the following Sunday, it proceeded to Kingston, and embarked on board the s.s. *Europa*, arriving at Balaclava on the 3rd, and disembarking on the 5th of December.

The following officers landed with the 90th—its strength at that time being 814 non-commissioned officers and privates:—

Lieutenant-Colonels.

F. Eld. | G. S. Deverill.

1854.

Majors.
R. P. Campbell. | Duncan Campbell.

Captains.
W. P. Purnell. | R. H. P. Crawford.
T. Smith. | J. Perrin.
R. Barnston. | J. C. Guise.
P. O'Gorman.

Lieutenants.
R. Vaughton. | H. Preston.
H. H. Crealock. | W. B. Persse.
G. J. Wolseley. | J. Clerk Rattray.
J. H. Wade. | P. A. L. Phipps.
R. Magenis. | W. J. Rous.

Ensigns.
A. G. Daubeny. | L. H. L. Irby.
Hon. J. F. Pennington. | P. J. Deverill.
G. Graham.

Paymaster, Sam. Williams.
Adjutant, H. H. Crealock.
Quartermaster, D. Jackson.
Surgeon, R. Anderson.

On landing, the regiment proceeded to the front, and was attached to the second brigade of the Light Division.

The day after its arrival, it went into the trenches, and occupied the advanced rifle pits, engaging the enemy at once in a musketry duel. However, on the Russians opening fire with shot and shell, an order was sent down for the 90th to cease firing.

From this date, for many months, the regiment was occupied in wearying trench duties, in the performance of which several lives were lost, and many men were wounded.

Although many fell by the hands of their enemies, a far greater number died from disease, brought on by the severity of the weather, against which they had no protection, and from want of the common necessaries of life, it being no uncommon sight to see from four to six corpses removed from the tents in the morning for burial— Serjeant-Major Geddes, a most promising young soldier, being unfortunately among the victims.

These miseries, however, were shared by every British regiment in the camp, and were borne without a murmur by all.

On the 30th of December, Lieutenant G. J. Wolseley was posted to the right attack, as assistant engineer, in which position he remained until the termination of hostilities.

About 12 o'clock p.m. on the 22nd of March, 1855, the Russians made a sortie with 8,000 men against our advanced trenches and the French works in front of the Mamelon. Though taken at a disadvantage and opposed to superior numbers, the guard of the trenches made a splendid resistance, and drove the Russians back at the point of the bayonet, after an hour's severe fighting.

" In this attack on the rifle-pits the mortar battery was
" carried by an enormous force of the enemy, who held it
" for about 15 minutes. At the time the heavy fire between
" the French and Russians was going on, a portion of the
" 90th Regiment was employed on fatigue duty, on the
" right of the new advanced works on our right attack.
" They were in the act of returning to their posts in the
" Gordon Battery just at the moment the heavy firing on
" right had ceased, when a scattered, irregular fusillade
" commenced, in the dark, on the left of their position,
" close to the mortar battery. Captain Vaughton, who
" commanded the party of the 90th, ordered his men to
" advance along the covered way to the works. They
" moved up in double time, and found the Russians in
" complete possession of the mortar battery. The
" 90th at once opened as heavy a fire of musketry as

1855. "they could upon the enemy, who returned it, when an alarm was given that our men were firing upon the French; but the mistake was speedily discovered by the enemy's fire being poured in with more deadly effect, and the small party of the 90th suffered considerably. Then, with a loud 'hurrah,' the gallant little band sprang with the bayonet upon the enemy, who at once precipitately retired over the parapet, followed by our rifle balls, which were poured in upon them incessantly till every round in the men's pouches was expended. In order to keep up the fire, the men groped about among the dead Russians and exhausted all the cartridges they could find in the enemy's pouches.

"As an act of justice, the names of the officers and men of the party of the 90th Regiment whose conduct was distinguished in this affair should be recorded. They are—Clarke, Brittle, and Essex (sergeants); Carruthers, severely wounded, (corporal); Fare, Walsh, Nicholson (wounded), and Nash; Captain Vaughton received a severe contusion in this affair."

In April, a draft joined the head-quarters from England.

On the 10th of May, at about 1 a.m., a strong Russian force attacked the English trenches on the left of the right attack, close to the Woronzoff road. They were taken in flank by the Light Division, and utterly routed. In this affair the Russians are supposed to have lost 150 men, the loss in the Light Division being only 14 *hors de combat*—the 90th having one man wounded.

A strong draft joined the regiment in June, with the following officers—Captains Vaughan and Denison, Lieuts. Wilmer, Swift, and Sir C. Pigott.

The commanders of the allied forces decided in June to make an assault upon some outworks of Sebastopol, preceded by a heavy fire of artillery. Accordingly, on the 7th, the French advanced against the Mamelon, and a column, composed of detachments from the Light and 2nd

Divisions, moved against the battery in the Quarries, with a view to obtaining these important works before the final assault. 1855.

Lord Raglan, in his despatch dated June 9th, describes the affair as follows :—

" Before Sebastopol, June 9th, 1855.

" My Lord,

" I have the great satisfaction of informing your " Lordship that the assault which was made upon the " Quarries, in front of the Redan, from our advanced " parallel in the right attack, on the evening of the 7th " instant, was attended with perfect success, and that the " brave men who achieved this advantage, with a gallantry " and determination that does them infinite honour, main- " tained themselves on the ground they had acquired, " notwithstanding that during the night, and in the " morning of yesterday, the enemy made repeated at- " tempts to drive them out, each attempt ending in failure, " although supported by large bodies of troops and by " heavy discharges of musketry and every species of " offensive missile.

" The French on our right had shortly before moved " out of their trenches and attacked the Ouvrages Blancs " and the Mamelon. These they carried without the " smallest check, and their leading column rushed for- " ward and approached the Malakoff Tower ; but this it " had not been in contemplation to assail, and the " troops were brought back and finally established in " the enemy's works, from which the latter did not " succeed in expelling them, though the fire of musketry " and cannon which was brought to bear upon them was " tremendous.

" I never saw anything more spirited and rapid than the " advance of our allies.

" I am happy to say that the best feeling prevails

I

1855. " between the two armies, and each is proud of and
" confident in the gallantry and high military qualities
" of the other.

" I apprised your Lordship, by telegraph on the 6th,
" that our batteries re-opened that afternoon. The fire
" was kept up with the greatest energy until the day closed,
" when it was confined to vertical fire; but the next
" morning the guns resumed the work of destruction, and
" the effect was such that it was determined by General
" Pelissier and myself that the time had arrived for
" pushing our operations forward. Accordingly, soon
" after six o'clock on the evening of the 7th, the signal
" was given for the assault of the works I have enume-
" rated, and the result was most triumphant.

" The troops employed in storming the Quarries were
" composed of detachments from the Light and 2nd
" Divisions, and at night they were supported by the 62nd
" Regiment.

" The command of these troops was entrusted to Colonel
" Shirley, of the 88th, who was acting as General Officer
" of the Trenches, and he was assisted in the arrange-
" ments, and guided as to the points of attack and dis-
" tribution of the troops by Lieutenant-Colonel Tylden,
" of the Royal Engineers, the directing engineer officer
" of the right attack.

" Although nothing could be more spirited than the
" attack of the Quarries, or more creditable to every officer
" and man engaged in the operation, yet I cannot refrain
" from drawing your Lordship's especial attention to the
" energy and determination which they all displayed in
" maintaining and establishing themselves after their first
" success in them. They were repeatedly attacked during
" the night, and again soon after daylight on the 8th, and
" it was in resisting these repeated efforts on the part of
" the enemy, that a great portion of the heavy loss the
" army has to deplore was sustained.

" The mode in which Colonel Shirley conducted this

" very arduous service, and carried out his orders, entitles
" him to my highest commendation.
    " I have the honour to be,
        " etc., etc.,
            " RAGLAN."
" To the Rt. Hon. Lord Panmure,
    " Secy. at War, London."

In the list of names of officers specially mentioned by Lord Raglan are:—Lieutenant-Colonel Campbell, 90th, and Captain Wolseley, 90th, who was also recommended by Colonel Tylden.

The Commander-in-Chief in his despatch, dated June 12th, mentioned that " Major Macdonell, Rifle Brigade, " commanded a portion of that corps, and of the 41st, 47th, " 49th, 77th, and 90th Regiments, detached from the guard " of the trenches. The remainder of the 90th was in sup- " port, having just come off trench duty."

Lieutenant-Colonel Campbell, as mentioned in the foregoing despatch, was in command of the storming party at the commencement of the action, and after the Quarries were taken he assumed the command of the whole force engaged, and remained in the battery until the morning of the 8th.

The following letters fully describe Lt.-Colonel Campbell's services, for which he obtained a brevet-colonelcy, and was made a Companion of the Bath.

Lieutenant-General Simpson to Lord Panmure.

            " Before Sebastopol, July 17th, 1855.
" My Lord,
        " I have the honour to submit for your Lordship's
" information the accompanying letters from Lieutenant-
" Colonel Campbell, 90th Regiment—the one referring to
" his personal services, and the other to those of a party
" of the 55th Regiment, on the occasion of the capture of

1855. " the Quarries in front of the Redan, on the night of the
" 7th ultimo.

" With regard to Lieutenant-Colonel Campbell's own
" services, I think it right to inform your Lordship that I
" find, upon inquiry, that the charge of holding the
" Quarries on the night in question, and of repelling the
" repeated attacks of the enemy, was confided to that
" officer after he had led the assault, and was in fact a
" separate and detached command from that of Colonel
" Shirley, who acted as General of the day in the trenches
" of the right attack; the despatch of the late Field-
" Marshal Lord Raglan has already shown how admir-
" ably that duty was performed by the brave men who
" were under the direction of Lieutenant-Colonel Camp-
" bell.

" The Lieutenant-Colonel's letter, recording the good
" conduct of the party of the 55th Regiment, speaks for
" itself.

" I have, etc.,
" JAMES SIMPSON.
" Lieutenant-General Commanding."

*Lieutenant-Colonel Campbell to Lieutenant-Colonel
Brownrigg.*

" Camp, Light Division, July 13th, 1855.

" Sir,

" The despatch of the late lamented Field-Marshal
" Lord Raglan, of 9th of June, mentions that I commanded
" the storming party in the Quarries on the evening of
" the 7th June. May I beg most respectfully that you will
" bring it to the notice of Lieutenant-General Simpson,
" commanding the forces, that I not only had the honour
" of commanding the storming party, but that having been
" twice wounded in the assault, I retained the sole and
" undivided command in the Quarries, not only of the

1855.

"original attacking force and supports, but of all re-
" inforcements during the whole night, until relieved at
" 7 a.m. on the 8th. The despatches must have explained
" already that the enemy made several desperate efforts
" during the night to regain the works, and that on three
" occasions overpowering numbers succeeded in re-entering,
" but were on all occasions driven back at the point of the
" bayonet. The entire night was, indeed, one continued
" struggle for this position, the fatigue and anxiety of
" which I have never recovered from. When Lord
" Raglan's despatch was completed, I have reason to
" suppose his Lordship had not received the details, as
" my own report to Colonel Shirley, General of the
" Trenches, was unavoidably delayed in consequence of
" my wounds and not being able to write. In justice
" to myself, conscious of having performed an important
" duty to the best of my ability, and successfully, I now
" respectfully submit this statement to the Commander of
" the Forces, with the hope that he may be pleased to
" have my services, on this occasion, mentioned and
" particularised. At present, several officers have equal
" praise in the despatch who were not in the Quarries
" at all.

" I have, etc.,
" ROB. CAMPBELL, Lieutenant-Colonel,
" Commanding 90th Light Infantry."

Lord Raglan was so impressed with the value of Lieutenant-Colonel Campbell's services on the night of the 7th, that he visited him the next day, in order to be personally assured of his safety, and to express his thanks.

Captain Wolseley, whose duty it was, as assistant engineer, to accompany the assaulting column, was wounded in the thigh during the night, and on being relieved the next morning, overcome by his exertions and from loss of blood, he fell down outside the Quarries, where he was found by . . . . .

1855. The 90th from this date continued to take its share of trench duties, losing men continually. On the 30th of August, the Russian picquets made a rush at our advanced trench, upset some gabions, but were then driven back. Captain Wolseley, taking with him a large party of men, recovered most of the gabions, and was having them put in order, when a round shot flew past the end of the sap, killing two sappers and hurling him to the ground. The shot had struck a gabion which was full of stones, many of which were dashed with fearful violence against Captain Wolseley. He was just able to totter, with assistance, to the medical officer's hut in the trenches, outside of which he was laid down in a state of semi-unconciousness. His face was battered to pieces, and he was wounded in the body in several places; indeed, so severe were his injuries, that he was sent to St. George's monastery, near Balaclava, prior to being invalided home.

On the 6th of September, while a party of the regiment, under Captain Wade, was out working in front of the Redan, private Alexander, of the 90th, distinguished himself by helping to carry into the trenches Captain Buckley, of the Coldstream Guards, who had been dangerously wounded when in command of the covering party. For his gallantry, private Alexander was recommended for the Victoria Cross, to which he was subsequently gazetted.

In the meantime, the English and French batteries were hurling shot and shell on the devoted city, and in the camps, preparations were being made for the assault; the different orders were issued on the 7th, the following being those for the Light Division :—

" Division Orders,
" September 7th, 1855.

" 1.—The Redan will be assaulted after the French " have attacked the Malakoff. The Light and Second " Divisions will share this important duty, each finding " respectively the half of each party. The 2nd Brigade

"of the Light Division, with an equal number of the 2nd 1855.
"Division, will form the first body of attack, each division
"furnishing—first, a covering party of 100 men, under a
"field officer; second, a storming party carrying ladders,
"of 160 men, under a field officer (these men to be
"selected for this especial duty—they will be the first to
"storm after they have placed the ladders); third, a
"storming party of 500 men, with two field officers;
"fourth, a working party of 100 men, with a field officer.
"The support will consist of the remainder of the brigade,
"to be immediately in rear.

"2.—The covering party will consist of 100 rank and file
"the 2nd Battalion Rifle Brigade, under the command of
"Captain Thyers, and will be formed on the extreme left
"of the fifth parallel, ready to move out steadily in ex-
"tended order towards the Redan. Their duty will be to
"cover the advance of the ladder party, and keep down
"the fire from the parapet.

"3.—The first storming party of the Light Division will
"consist of 160 men of the 97th Regiment, under com-
"mand of Major Welsford. This party will carry the
"ladders and will be the first to storm; they will be
"formed in the New Boyau running from the centre of
"the fifth parallel; they will form immediately in rear of
"the covering party. They must be good men and true
"to their difficult duty, which is to arrive at the ditch of
"the Redan, and place the ladders down it, to turn
"twenty ladders for others to come down by.

"4.—The next storming party will consist of 200 of the
"97th Regiment, under the command of Lieutenant-
"Colonel the Hon. H. Hancock, and 300 of the 90th
"Regiment, under the command of Captain Grove. This
"party will be stationed in the fifth parallel, and will
"assault in columns of divisions at one place. The Light
"Division will lead the whole column of attack, which
"will be formed in divisions of twenty files, and so told off.

"5.—The supports, consisting of the 750 men of the

1855. "19th Regiment and 88th Regiment, with part of a
"brigade of the Second Division on their left, will be
"placed as they stand in brigade in the fourth parallel,
"from whence they will move into the fifth parallel as
"soon as the assault is made by those in front of them.

"6.—The working party of 100 men will be furnished
"by the 90th Regiment, under command of Captain
"Perrin, and will be placed in No. 2 and 3 left Boyau;
"they will afterwards receive their instructions from an
"officer of the Royal Engineers.

"7.—The remainder of the Light and Second Divisions
"will form a reserve—the Light Division in the right
"Boyaus, between the third and fourth parallels; the
"Second Division in the left Boyaus, between the third
"and fourth parallels.

"8.—The 1st and Highland Divisions will be formed in
"that part of the third parallel in communication with the
"French right attack, and in the middle ravine.

"9.—Two days' rations will be drawn and cooked, and
"issued to the men before 6 a.m. to-morrow.

"10.—Ten additional rounds of ammunition will be
"served out to each man on the private parades of
"regiments to-morrow morning.

"11.—The men will parade with red coats and forage
"caps; water-bottles to be quite full.

"12.—The covering party and first storming party will
"assemble at the usual place of meeting for the trenches
"at 7 a.m. The next storming party, the working party,
"the supports, and the reserve will parade, respectively,
"at the same place, at intervals of half-an-hour."

Shortly after mid-day our men rushed out of the fifth parallel and made for the salient of the Redan. As they crossed the open ground the guns from the barrack battery, and some on the right of the Redan, loaded with grape, swept away a considerable number; the remainder, however, pressed on, and passing through the abattis and across the ditch, entered the work, the Russians at once opening a heavy fire upon them from the traverses and breastworks to which they had retreated.

The rapidly-increasing fire of the enemy cruelly diminished our force; and the men, jammed into the angle of the salient and mixed up together, began to return the fire without advancing. At this period Colonel Windham, the senior officer inside the Redan, which he had entered shortly after the storming parties, seeing that without reinforcements no forward movement could be made, sent three officers, at intervals, to demand the required help; finding, however, that no fresh troops came forward he determined to go himself to Sir W. Codrington. Captain Crealock, of the 90th, happened to be near, busily engaged in getting his men into order preparatory to leading them against the breastworks, and Colonel Windham explained to him his reasons for leaving, saying "I must go to the " General for supports; now mind, let it be known, in case " I am killed, why I went away."

The Russians now in great force rushed with the bayonet upon our men, who met them firmly face to face; the odds were, however, so much against them, and they had suffered so terribly from the cross fire, that they were driven over the parapet and into the ditch at the moment Colonel Windham was returning to their assistance with the 1st Royals.

Dr. Russell, the *Times*' special correspondent, thus describes the struggle that ensued :—

" Our soldiers, taken at every disadvantage, met the " enemy with the bayonet too, and isolated combats oc- " curred, in which the brave fellows who stood their " ground had to defend themselves against three or four " adversaries at once. In this mêlée, the officers, armed " only with their swords, had but little chance; nor had " those who carried pistols much opportunity of using

1855. "them in such a close and sudden contest. They fell like
"heroes, and many a gallant soldier with them. The
"bodies of English and Russians inside the Redan,
"locked in an embrace which death could not relax, but
"had rather cemented all the closer, were found next day
"as evidences of the terrible animosity of the struggle.
"But the solid weight of the advancing mass, urged on
"and fed each moment from the rear by company after
"company, and battalion after battalion, prevailed at last
"against the isolated and disjointed band, which had
"abandoned that protection which unanimity of courage
"affords, and had lost the advantages of discipline and
"obedience. As though some giant rock advanced into the
"sea and forced back the agitated waters that buffeted it, so
"did the Russian columns press down against the spray of
"soldiery which fretted their edge with fire and steel, and
"contended in vain against their weight. The struggling
"band was forced back by the enemy, who moved on,
"crushing friend and foe beneath their solid tramp.
"Bleeding, panting, and exhausted, our men lay in heaps
"in the ditch beneath the parapet, sheltered themselves
"behind stones and in bomb craters in the external slope
"of the work, or tried to pass back to our advanced
"parallel and sap, having to run the gauntlet of a
"tremendous fire. Many of them lost their lives or were
"seriously wounded in the attempt."

By 1.48 the struggle for the Redan was over. Our men had fought and fallen with their usual gallantry, and had they been properly supported must have succeeded.

The following list of killed and wounded will show the part played by the 90th on the 8th of September:—

Captain H. Preston . . . ⎫
Lieutenant A. D. Swift . . ⎬ killed.
Ensign H. F. Wilmer. . . ⎭

Captain H. M. Vaughan . . { died of wounds received.

1855.

Captain W. B. Tinling
    J. H. Wade
Lieutenant J. C. Rattray
    P. S. Deverill
    H. H. Goodricke
    Sir C. Pigott, Bt.
} severely wounded.

Captain R. Grove
    J. Perrin
Lieutenant H. J. Haydock
    W. J. Rous
    J. J. Nunn
    N. Graham
} slightly wounded.

1 sergeant, 3 privates . . . killed.
4 sergeants, 33 privates . . missing.
13 sergeants, 119 privates . wounded.

" Lieutenant Swift penetrated the furthest of all those
" who entered the Redan, and his dead body was dis-
" covered far in advance, near the re-entering angle."

On the 10th, exploring parties pushed forward into the Redan which they found in ruins, and discovered that the Russians had evacuated the whole of the city on the south side of the harbour. Many of the houses were filled with wounded Russians who had been left behind, and in the great hospital were found some English wounded, among them Captain Vaughan of the 90th. The following letter, taken from Nolan's history of the war, describes his sufferings:—

" He was found at 8 a.m., on the 10th of September,
" sitting on the lower step of a staircase that led to the
" upper floor of the building. His leg was badly broken;
" he had nothing on him but a flannel shirt and a pair of
" socks, and when first spoken to he was delirious; he ap-
" peared to be very cold, as he was shivering. I procured
" him water, and it was distressing to see the avidity with

1855. "which he swallowed it. I procured a stretcher, and
"placed a feather bed on it, and I never left him till I
"deposited him safely in the lines of the 00th, under the
"care of Dr. Anderson, the excellent surgeon of that regi-
"ment; the first stretcher did not do, and I had it changed
"at the Redan. His mind wandered frequently, and he
"then almost always spoke in French; but by speaking
"gently to him and holding his hand, I was generally
"enabled to make him understand what he was talking
"about, and then he gave me a clear account of what had
"occurred to him. He was wounded very soon after en-
"tering the Redan. After our attack was repulsed, the
"Russian officers gave orders that he should be taken
"carefully to the rear, and while in their presence he was
"well treated, but I fear he was treated with much bru-
"tality as he was being conveyed to the rear. He
"complained that the men who were taking him dragged
"him along roughly, and that his broken limb frequently
"came in contact with gabions, stones, etc., giving him
"great pain. Upon arriving at the building where I
"found him, which was full of dead and dying, he appears
"to have been unkindly treated. His wound had not been
"dressed. He repeatedly supplicated for water, but no
"one gave him a drop. Thank God! they were not
"Englishmen. It is impossible to conceal that the gallant
"gentleman's sufferings must have been intense, but he
"had a gallant heart to meet his fate, and endure the pain
"that God thought fit to inflict upon him."

On his arrival in camp, Captain Vaughan told some of his brother officers that when he fell inside the Redan a Russian soldier was on the point of bayoneting him, when he made the Masonic sign, which, being understood by his assailant, saved his life for the time being. He died on the 11th.

Dr. Douglas Reid, one of the medical officers present at the assault, describes in a few words, much to the honour of his corps, the hours which passed between the issuing of the orders and the attack.

"The night before the attack was spent by most of us in "making those final arrangements of our affairs that are "so necessary when there exists an absolute certainty that "some must fall, probably many. One of the captains of "the 90th, Preston, who was a thoroughly religious man, "seemed to have a presentiment that he would never come "out of the attack alive, but his cheerfulness did not in "any way desert him, and he employed himself in en- "couraging and stimulating the younger officers. Two of "them had only joined a few days before and did not know "what fear or danger were. All three fell the next day.

"The morning of the attack, Saturday, the 8th of Sep- "tember, was cold, windy, and dispiriting; nevertheless, "our men were in the highest spirits, and anxiously longing "for their orders to form up on parade and march to the "scene of action. Up to this day our average morning "sick list was very heavy, so heavy that it took the medical "officers the whole morning to attend to them. On the "morning of the 8th of September, there were no sick, "that is to say, none of the men would attend at the hos- "pital that day for fear they might be ordered to remain "in camp. One young ensign, on the sick list for some "days with dysentery, went to the surgeon and reported "himself quite well; and thus, on the day of the taking of "Sebastopol, the 90th sent in a blank sick report.

"It had been arranged the previous night that all the "officers should breakfast together in the mess-hut, and "this arrangement was carried out. There was a kind of "solemnity about this gathering, but not a trace of anxiety "as to the result of the battle that was to follow so soon. "One of the most cheerful and hopeful, was Herbert "Vaughan, whose subsequent sufferings have become a "matter of history."

When it was known that the city was abandoned,

1855.

1855. General Simpson issued an after-order of which the following is part:—

"General After-order,
"Head-Quarters, September 9th,
"The Commander of the Forces congratulates the army
"on the result of the attack of yesterday.

"The brilliant assault and occupation of the Malakoff
"by our gallant allies obliged the enemy to abandon the
"works they have so long held with such bravery and de-
"termination.

"The Commander of the Forces returns his thanks to
"the general officers, and officers and men, of the Second
"and Light Divisions, who advanced and attacked with
"such gallantry the works of the Redan. He regrets,
"from the formidable nature of the flanking defences, that
"their devotion did not meet with that immediate success
"which it so well merited.

* * * * * * * * * * *

"By order,
"H. W. BARNARD, Chief of the Staff."

In his despatch, dated September the 18th, General Simpson mentions those officers whose names had been brought before him, as having distinguished themselves in the assault on the 8th, by the officers commanding their respective divisions.

90th Light Infantry.—Captain Grove, commanding; Captain Smith, Captain Vaughan, Captain Tinling, Captain Close, Captain Crealock, Captain Wade, Captain Magenis, Captain Preston, Lieutenant Graham, Lieutenant Deverill.

Sergeant-Major Cummin, Sergeant Saunderson, Sergeant Monaghan, Sergeant Smallie.

The troops were now occupied in destroying the dockyards and fortifications of the south side of Sebastopol.

The fatigue parties engaged in this work were frequently **1855.** annoyed by the fire from the forts on the northern side—no casualties, however, occurring in the 90th.

On the 15th of November, about 3 p.m., a fearful explosion shook the camp; 100,000 pounds of powder had exploded in the French siege train, setting fire to all the stores there and to the neighbouring English park. The Light Division was on the ground which it first took up in 1854, and was consequently nearest to the conflagration. Shells were bursting in every direction, and there was great danger of more explosions, happily overcome by the exertions of those who hurried to the spot. 136 Non-commissioned officers and men were killed and wounded, the 90th having one sergeant and two privates among the latter.

On the 20th of September, Crimean medals, about 10 per company, were given to the men on parade.

In the beginning of April, 1856, peace was proclaimed, **1856.** and the soldiers of the Allied and Russian armies fraternized cordially, visiting each other's camps, and meeting at the races and other entertainments which were set on foot. General Lüders, the Russian Commander-in-Chief, inspected the whole British army on the 17th—shortly after which preparations were made for the evacuation of the Crimea.

In June, the 90th—27 officers and 757 non-commissioned officers and men—embarked on board H.M.S. *Queen*, which was towed by the *Terrible* as far as Constantinople, whence she proceeded under sail for England.

The regiment landed at Portsmouth in the end of July, having lost, during its absence of eighteen months, six officers and 274 non-commissioned officers and men.

On its arrival in England, the 90th proceeded to Aldershot, where it remained until February, 1857, when it **1857.** moved to Portsmouth, being quartered in the Anglesea Barracks.

The regiment had only been a week at Portsmouth when

1857. it received orders to go to India at once. The necessary preparations were being made, when another order was received, conveying the welcome information that it was not to start until June. All now looked forward to a few months' hardly-earned rest in comfortable quarters, when, at the end of March, another official message was received directing the 90th to start immediately for China.

Seven hundred men were to go in the *Himalaya*, and three hundred in the *Transit*—two ships which had been bought into the Navy, and were officered and manned like men-of-war.

Accordingly, at the beginning of April, the *Transit* started with three companies under Major Barnston, accompanied by the following officers:—

Captains.

J. C. Guise.   L. H. L. Irby.
G. J. Wolseley.

Lieutenants.

J. S. A. Herford.   G. R. Miller.
W. H. L. Carleton.   A. Cherry.
R. D. Synge.   E. Carter.

Ensigns.

G. E. Perryn.   J. F. Haig.
L. W. Wilmer.

Assistant Surgeon, Jackson.

The head-quarters in the *Himalaya* left Portsmouth on the 16th of April, under the command of Colonel R. P. Campbell, C.B., with—

Lieutenant-Colonel, P. Purnell.
Brevet-Lt.-Colonel, T. Smith.

1857.

Captains.

J. Perrin, *M.*
W. P. Tinling, *M.*
H. Denison.
J. H. Wade.

R. H. Magenis.
J. Clerk Rattray.
P. A. L. Phipps.

Lieutenants.

N. Graham.
P. J. Deverill.
O. W. Every.
J. J. Nunn.
H. J. Haydock.
H. H. Goodricke.
C. B. Wynne.

A. A. Moultrie.
H. Bingham.
W. Knight.
W. Rennie.
E. C. Wynne.
M. Preston.

Ensigns.

H. B. Savory.
G. A. Agnew.
A. Eyre.
G. Gregg.
A. R. Chute.

G. H. Powell.
H. J. Edgell.
H. Gordon.
J. Williamson.
S. Handy.

Surgeon, A. D. Home.

Assistant Surgeons.

W. Bradshaw. | C. R. Nelson.

Paymaster, S. Williams.

Quartermaster, D. Jackson.

The *Transit*, on her way past the Needles, struck upon an anchor and knocked a hole in her side, in consequence of which she returned to Portsmouth for repairs.

The *Himalaya* reached the Cape de Verd Islands by the end of April, and while there, narrowly escaped

1857. being wrecked. The hawser which fastened the ship to the buoy snapped, and the vessel drifted towards the shore, fortunately a small brig at anchor stayed her course, and a land breeze springing up, the jib was set, and her head turned away from the land. In the meantime the *Transit* came in, leaving again before the *Himalaya*.

The latter proceeded to Simon's Bay, where she was again nearly running on to some rocks; fortunately the catastrophe was averted by timely signals from H.M.S. *Thunderer;* while here the regiment was once more united. After taking in coals and provision, the *Himalaya* proceeded on her way, and when in the straits of Sunda, was met by a vessel bearing despatches ordering the regiment to proceed to Calcutta, in consequence of the revolt of the native troops in Bengal. While on the way to Singapore, the ship ran on a mud bank and stuck fast. An American vessel, which was near when the accident occurred, anchored near the stranded transport for the night, and the next day, by her assistance, and a high tide serving, the *Himalaya* was got afloat and went on her way, arriving at Singapore about the 10th, and Calcutta about the 21st of July.

The 90th was immediately transferred to river steamers, and sent on to Chinsurah, at which place it stayed a week.

Lieutenant Deverill, one corporal, and three men were left behind at Calcutta, being too ill to proceed.

After receiving its camp equipment and light clothing, the regiment moved up the Ganges in river steamers for Allahabad, reaching Berhampore on the 1st August, where it was employed in disarming a native cavalry and a native infantry regiment. For the able manner in which he conducted this duty, Colonel Campbell was complimented by the Governor-General in Council.

The following extract gives a detailed account of the affair:—

"Berhampore, August 2nd. 1857.

"The steamers *Mirzapore* and *Calcutta*, with Her
"Majesty's 90th Light Infantry, arrived here at 2 p.m.
"yesterday, much to the rejoicing of the residents, who
"all flocked to the vessels.

"Great apprehensions were entertained that the troops
"here, the 63rd Native Infantry and 11th Irregular Cavalry
"would rise on the night previous, and this feeling appears
"to have extended to the bazaar people, who report that
"the conduct of the troops was boastful and insolent when
"referring to the British power to coerce them to resign
"their arms. All doubt on this score has now been
"allayed, and they have received ample proof of the
"utter inability of Sepoys to stand their ground when
"confronted with our European soldiers.

"Colonel Campbell, C.B., in command of the 90th,
"issued orders, immediately on arrival of the steamers, for
"the regiment to disembark under arms at 4 o'clock, and
"I believe it was arranged with the principals here—
"Colonel Hannyngton commanding the station, and
"Captain Alexander, of the Irregulars—that the troops
"should be ordered out on general parade. The infantry
"lines faced the *ghat*, the steamers were anchored about
"a mile distant, with the parade ground, a fine *maidan*,
"between. The cavalry lines are some two miles behind
"the infantry.

"The entire regiment of Her Majesty's 90th had dis-
"embarked, and were in full march towards the infantry
"lines by half-past 4 o'clock, under a very heavy shower
"of rain, which, however, did not appear to discomfort
"the men much, who were in great spirits at the prospect
"of a collision with the *jet blacs* of the murderers of
"defenceless women and children. On approaching the
"lines, the Native Infantry were observed to have been
"arranged in a square, and Her Majesty's 90th divided off
"into three columns, so as to intercept any attempts at a

1857. " retreat. After the reading of the Government order, the
" command to pile arms was given, and responded to
" without demur. Many of the muskets on inspection
" were found to be loaded. I must here mention that two
" brass light field-pieces had been sent out to the lines,
" manned by sailors from the Government steamer *Jumna*,
" which has been lying here for some four days. The
" muskets of the disarmed Sepoys having been taken
" possession of by a company of the 90th, the regiment
" then marched on in the direction of the cavalry lines,
" from which the Irregulars were seen to advance. On
" approaching to within a distance of about 300 yards from
" the European regiment, they dismounted, and, on a
" nearer approach, were surrounded by the 90th. Their
" commander, Captain Alexander, then communicated his
" instructions from Government for their being disarmed,
" when there was a very apparent stir among them, and
" two attempts made to remount their horses, a good
" number gaining their seats; but a flank of the 90th
" advancing towards them, and the rest being so arranged
" as to cut off their retreat, they were got into order again ;
" some of the men were actually seen to load, but, whether
" from the want of unanimity, or more probably the dread
" of the splendid body of men confronting them, their
" intentions, whatever they may have been, were not
" carried into effect.

" On the order being given to deliver up their arms and
" accoutrements, many of the men absolutely flung their
" pistols, belts, etc., into the air; and on the whole,
" although they did deliver up their arms, they manifested
" the utmost dissatisfaction. They had, however, to endure
" a still greater surprise, and one which they were evidently
" not prepared for, and that was the seizure of their horses,
" which, being their own property, they thought would not
" be taken from them. The latter were taken off to the
" hospital yard, round which, and several other pucka
" buildings, there is the enclosure of a pucka wall. The

"200 men of Her Majesty's 35th, stationed here, all this 1857.
"time were engaged in disarming the guards at their
"different posts. Thus ended the amusements of the
"evening. I must not omit, however, that while the
"Colonel and officers of the 90th, with their men, were all
"out during the rain, and up to nearly 9 o'clock at night,
"and had the entire job of placing the arms and horses
"within the enclosure above referred to, many of the
"station staff and native regimental officers walked off
"quietly to their mess; indeed, much might be said, in
"no way flattering to them, if a comparison were to be
"drawn between them and the orderly and soldier-like
"bearing and conduct of the European regiment.

"It is pleasing to record the fact that all the men of
"this splendid regiment are in capital health and spirits,
"and no sickness whatever on board. The steamers
"although crowded, are well ventilated; everything in
"fact is good but the commissariat arrangements, which,
"as usual, are infamous—the bread being the very worst
"that can be imagined, and the biscuits no better—the
"latter positively black and maggoty.

* * * * * * * * * * *

"The Colonel of the 90th despatched 200 men this
"morning at 11 o'clock to search for all arms in the
"bazaar."

On the 5th August, Maj.-Gen. Sir J. Outram, K.C.B., was appointed to the command of the Dinapore and Cawnpore divisions of the army.

In the meantime, General Havelock, with a mere handful of men, was attempting to relieve the beleaguered garrison of Lucknow. He, however, though victorious in every fight with the rebels, was unable to make headway from want of troops, and by the 16th of August, had returned to Cawnpore, where he eagerly awaited reinforcements. The 90th now proceeded up the river, and was

1857. nearing Benares, when orders were received recalling it to Dinapore, in consequence of the flight of the 5th Irregular Cavalry from Bangulpore.

Sir James Outram, in a letter to the Governor-General, dated 19th August, 1857, writes:—" On arriving near " Patna, the night before last, I learnt that the panic had " extended to Dinapore, and that the 90th Regiment, " which had passed up the river four days before, had " been recalled. I immediately despatched an express to " prohibit the return of the regiment, but unfortunately it " did not reach in time to stop the return vessels, which " came back yesterday evening, and, I regret to say, with " cholera on board 'a doctor had died. This has necessi- " tated landing the men, in order to cleanse and purify the " vessels, which cannot be ready for their reception before " to-morrow evening.

" The delay thus caused in the advance of this regiment, " and the disease likely to be engendered by long con- " finement on board crowded boats during the present " extreme heat, are the more provoking as there is in " reality not the slightest cause for alarm here. So " satisfied am I on this subject, that I have ordered a " detachment of 100 men of the 90th Regiment, which " had been kept back here, to join the regiment."

* * * * * * * * * *

The Doctor mentioned in the letter was Assistant Surgeon Nelson.

Sir James Outram had formed the plan of landing with the 5th and 90th Regiments at Benares, and from that place to advance by Jaunpore, between the Sye and Goomtee, until opposite Pertabghar or Roy Bareilly, where he was to be joined by such troops as could be spared from Cawnpore. The whole column would then advance on Lucknow.

General Havelock's force was, however, so reduced by sickness, and losses in the field, that he made urgent appeals to the Commander-in-Chief for help. Consequently, Sir James Outram received the following telegram.

The Commander-in-Chief to Sir James Outram.

" 2nd August, 1857, 11.45 p.m.
" I am rejoiced to hear of your arrival at
" Dinapore.
" The force under General Havelock is reduced by
" casualties on service and by cholera—which has been
" and still rages in his camp—to 700 men in the field,
" exclusive of detachments which guard the intrenchment,
" and keep open the communications with Allahabad.
" He is threatened by a force of some 5,000 men, with
" twenty or thirty guns, from Gwalior, besides the Oude
" force. He says, he ' is ready to fight anything, but the
" above are great odds, and a battle lost here would do the
" interest of the State infinite damage; I solicit reinforce-
" ments.' His applications for assistance have been
" frequent, and deeming his situation to demand im-
" mediate aid, I ordered the 90th Regiment to be sent to
" him with all possible speed, as also the detachment of
" the 5th Regiment, which was on board the *Benares*
" steamer, if it could be spared. Pray send the 90th at
" once to his aid. I will write to you to-morrow."

Sir J. Outram to the Commander-in-Chief (Sir Colin Campbell.)

" Telegraphic.
" Ghazeepore, 25th Aug., 1857, 10 p.m.
" Received your message of the 22nd instant
" this evening.
" In accordance with these orders the 90th Regiment,
" complete strength 765 minus 3 companies coming from

1857. "Calcutta, and such portion of the 5th as I have collected, will be sent on by steamer to Allahabad, and thence pushed on by quickest means practicable. This prevents my carrying out my intended advance to the relief of Lucknow from Jaunpore or Roy Bareilly, as proposed in my letter to the Governor-General from Dinapore, dated 20th instant, no other European troops being available; but the necessity for reinforcing General Havelock seems imperative.

"By a letter from Cawnpore, dated the 19th instant, I learn that General Havelock's moveable column consists of 1,100 Europeans and 250 Sikhs, exclusive of 300 Europeans holding Cawnpore, under General Neill.

"The 90th, the detachment of the 5th, and Eyre's battery left Buxar yesterday in three steamers and three flats, and I hope may overtake me at Benares the day after to-morrow."

General Outram and a detachment of 90 men of the 90th arrived at Allahabad on the 1st of September, and made preparations for the onward march of the remainder of the troops who arrived on the 3rd and 4th; a detachment 611 strong, with Major Eyre's battery, starting for Cawnpore on the 5th. The 90th Light Infantry, 679 men (leaving 68 sick), followed in the evening of the same day, and hoped to be with General Havelock on the 12th.

However, on arrival at Ke Poonwa on the 6th, it was found that the regiment, having been cooped up on shipboard for five months, was unequal to doing the forced marches proposed for it, a very large proportion being knocked up by this first march of 14 miles. Favourable accounts of the Lucknow garrison having been received, it was determined to take the ordinary 10 marches to Cawnpore. Three men of the 90th died at Synee on the 8th, and a large number were on the sick list. On the 11th, the column halted at Thurriaroon, arriving at Cawnpore late on the 15th.

1857.

Division Order by Major-General Sir James Outram, K.C.B., commanding the Dinapore and Cawnpore Divisions of the army.

"Camp, Cawnpore, 16th September, 1857.

"1.—All Cawnpore divisional reports to be made for "the information of Major-General Sir James Outram, "K.C.B., commanding.

"2.—The force selected by Brigadier-General Havelock, "which will march to relieve the garrison of Lucknow, will "be constituted and composed as follows :—

"*Infantry.*

"1st Brigade.—Her Majesty's 5th Fusiliers, Her "Majesty's 84th Regiment and detachment 64th Foot "attached, 1st Madras Fusiliers; Brigadier-General J. G. "S. Neill commanding, nominating his own Brigade "staff.

"2nd Brigade.—Her Majesty's 78th Highlanders, Her "Majesty's 90th Light Infantry, Ferozepore Regiment; "Brigadier Hamilton commanding, nominating his own "Brigade staff.

"*Artillery.*

"3rd Brigade.—Captain Maude's Battery, Captain "Olpherts' Battery, Brevet-Major Eyre's Battery; Major "Cooper to command, nominating his own staff.

"Cavalry.—Volunteer Cavalry, 12th Irregular Cavalry; "Captain Barrow to command.

"Engineer Department.—Captain Crommelin, Chief "Engineer; Lieutenants Limond and Judge, Engineers; "Captain Oakes, 8th Native Infantry, Assistant Field "Engineer.

"Brigadier-General Havelock, C.B., to command the "force."

1857. "The important duty of relieving the garrison of Lucknow had been first entrusted to Brigadier-General Havelock, C.B., and Major-General Outram feels that it is due to that distinguished officer, and to the strenuous and noble exertions which he has already made to effect that object, that to him should accrue the honour of the achievement.

"Major-General Outram is confident that this great end, for which Brigadier-General Havelock and his brave troops have so long and so gloriously fought, will now, under the blessing of Providence, be accomplished.

"The Major-General, therefore, in gratitude for and admiration of the brilliant deeds of arms achieved by Brigadier-General Havelock and his gallant troops, will cheerfully waive his rank in favour of that officer on this occasion, and will accompany the force to Lucknow in his civil capacity as Chief Commissioner of Oude, tendering his military services to Brigadier-General Havelock as a volunteer.

"On the relief of Lucknow, the Major-General will resume his position at the head of the forces."

Field Force After-order by Brigadier-General Havelock.

"Cawnpore, 16th September, 1857.

"Brigadier-General Havelock, in making known to the column the kind and generous determination of Major-General Sir James Outram, K.C.B., to leave to him the task of relieving Lucknow and rescuing its gallant and enduring garrison, has only to express his hope that the troops will strive by their exemplary and gallant conduct in the field to justify the confidence thus reposed in them."

The above orders so clearly mark the characters of the Generals under whom the 90th had now the honour to serve, that they could not be omitted in these records.

From the 16th to the 18th of September, the troops, 1857. under the able direction of Captain Crommelin and his Lieutenants, were employed in throwing bridges across the Ganges opposite Cawnpore, and early on the 19th the two brigades crossed the river and entered Oude, camping on the left bank of the river, while the commissariat and heavy artillery were being brought over.

The enemy offered a very slight opposition to the passage, and on the 21st the Division moved forward to Mungulwur, where the enemy was in position with six guns. They were quickly driven from this place by the infantry and Captain Olpherts' battery, and being pushed from the cover of the houses and gardens, were soon in full flight, followed by General Outram and the volunteer cavalry, who pursued them as far as Busheergunje.

On the 22nd, after a march of 15 miles, the column arrived at Bunnee bridge, over the river Sye. The bridge was found intact, owing to the hasty flight of the enemy, who were found on the 22nd strongly posted at the Alum Bagh, a large enclosed garden about two miles from Lucknow. The rebels had six guns with them, which were well served for a short time; the first shell from which mortally wounded Major Perrin and Lieutenants Graham and Preston, of the 90th. When the enemy's guns had been silenced by Captain Olpherts' battery, the whole force advanced, the 78th and 90th moving forward in line. A short stand was made by the Sepoys, near the garden, out of which they were soon driven by the infantry, who followed them nearly to the canal. The troops were then withdrawn, and occupied the Alum Bagh for the night, bivouacking under a heavy artillery fire from the enemy.

On the 24th, the baggage of the column, under a guard of the 90th, whilst making its way to the front, was approached by some of the 12th Native Irregular Cavalry. At first Lieutenant Nunn, who commanded the party, looked upon them with suspicion, and was in the act of giving directions to his scattered men to prepare for attack, when the cavalry leader called out, in English, "It's all right; we are friends!" This speech, and the knowledge that part of the 12th still remained true to us, reassured Nunn. Hardly had the horsemen come close up when they commenced cutting down the escort right and left. They killed Nunn and a great many men, and having done this they galloped off. Poor Nunn's body was found hacked to pieces; it bore a good many cuts upon it, and there was one especially which went through the crown down towards the left side, and must have cleft the skull.

Private Alexander, who had been gazetted to, but had not as yet received, the Victoria Cross, for gallant conduct in the Crimea, was killed on this occasion.

On the 25th, the outlying picquets were called in, and the Alum Bagh, in which all the sick and wounded had been placed, was garrisoned by them. The remainder of the division proceeded on its gloriously desperate task of relieving the Residency.

The brigades moved off separately; the 1st suffered severely from the heavy fire of musketry from some houses and gardens which lined the road; the enemy was gallantly attacked and driven from these, and retired across the canal. Both brigades met at the Char Bagh, on the canal, the bridge over which was swept by a battery of four guns, and the houses on all sides were loopholed. Captain Maude's battery having in vain tried to silence these guns, it was found necessary for the infantry to advance; accordingly, the bank of the canal having been lined by a portion of the 1st Brigade, the 1st Madras Fusiliers stormed and took the battery.

After crossing the bridge, the 90th was ordered by General Havelock to take two guns which were posted at the end of a narrow lane on the right of the column. Two companies, under Captains Wade and Magenis, left the road and entered the defile, which was swept by the fire from the guns and by the musketry of the enemy, who filled the houses on either side. Led by Colonel Campbell 1857. (whose life was saved by his prayer-book, in which a bullet lodged), and accompanied by Colonel Purnell and Lieutenant and Adjutant Rennie, the 90th men dashed forward, and after a brief but desperate struggle captured the guns, up to which Ensigns Gordon and Chute carried the colours. The prize was not obtained, however, without serious loss, for Lieutenant Moultrie and Colour-Sergeants Sanderson and Cole were mortally wounded, and Lieutenant Knight and many others were put *hors de combat*. As soon as the guns were in our possession, Captain Olpherts, R.A., now Lieut.-General Olpherts, V.C., C.B., who had accompanied the advance, went back and brought up some limbers, removing the guns—on which he scratched with his sword the number of the 90th Regiment—under a heavy fire from the loopholed houses.

After this, the regiment was separated into two parties, exclusive of the rear guard under Captain Clerk Rattray and Lieutenant H. H. Goodricke, which repulsed numerous attacks made upon it by cavalry and infantry.

The main body of the force pushed its way along a road lying between the canal and the city, until it debouched on the Dilkoosha road, near the 32nd hospital, thence it followed the road to the Sekundur Bagh, and keeping along it, at length entered a walled passage in front of the Mootee Munzil Palace. From the canal bridge their progress was comparatively unmolested until they approached this position, when they became exposed to a heavy fire of grape from four guns posted at the gate of the Kaiser Bagh, as well as of musketry from the "Khoosheyd Munzil" or 32nd mess house, which was strongly occupied by the enemy. While here, messages were received from the 78th Highlanders reporting that they were hard pressed; the column halted for a short time and then moved on in the direction of the Chuttur Munzil and Furhut Buksh Palaces, leaving the 90th with two of the heavy guns at the Mootee Munzil, to assist the

78th, which had come up with the main body by the road leading to the Kaiser Bagh.

The two Generals having determined to force their way to the Residency through the streets, moved on, as above mentioned, accompanied by the 78th and Brasyer's Sikhs, and, after a desperate struggle, succeeded in reaching the Bailey guard gate.

The party of the 90th, under Colonel Campbell, did not reach the entrenchment that night—with them were the doolies conveying the wounded and the heavy guns, which could not be left behind. As soon as the enemy knew of their position, taking advantage of the surrounding buildings, they closely invested the party and kept up a heavy fire upon them the whole of the 26th. While in this dangerous position, Colour-Sergeant Brittle, of Captain Phipp's company of the 90th, behaved with devoted gallantry. He sheltered himself behind a pillar of the gateway, and though exposed to a heavy fire, stood coolly picking off the enemy's gunners. He was unfortunately killed by a grape shot which struck him in the chest. Reinforcements were sent to them, under Colonel Napier, guided by Lieutenant Moorsom, of the 52nd Light Infantry, and at 3 o'clock on the morning of the 27th, the column moved quietly out and succeeded in reaching the Residency with but little loss.

Colonel Campbell was wounded on the 26th, and was carried by his servant, private Smith, along the bank of the Goomtee to the Residency.

The removal of the wounded on the 26th was attended with most calamitous results. General Outram had given orders that they should be guided to the entrenchment by one well acquainted with the place. Accordingly, Mr. Thornhill, a young civilian gallantly undertook to be their guide. Unfortunately, Mr. Thornhill missed his way and led the doolie-bearers into a small enclosed square, where a murderous fire arrested their progress. A few doolies were forced on under fire and got away, but many were left in the square, and some which had not entered the enclosure, retired and regained the right path by the river, which was the route along which Colonel Campbell had been carried. Dr. Bradshaw, of the 90th, who was sent back by Dr. Home, also of the 90th, was wounded severely.

Dr. Home, who remained with the deserted doolies, gives the following account of the affair, for his share in which he received the Victoria Cross.

"While the leading columns of the force, with Generals
" Outram and Havelock, had pushed on to the Residency,
" the rear-guard of Her Majesty's 90th Regiment, with
" the doolies containing all the wounded, remained during
" the night of the 25th of September in the passage in
" front of the Mootee Munzil Palace. Here, on the morn-
" ing of the 26th, Colonel Campbell, Her Majesty's 90th,
" came and told me that he had made arrangements for
" sending the wounded to the Residency. Supposing me
" to be the senior medical officer present, he directed me
" to take charge of them thither. He said that Mr. J. B.
" Thornhill, Civil Service, would guide us, and told me
" that we should have to cross about forty yards of dan-
" gerous ground just after we left the gate of the passage,
" and about 300 yards more of like exposure farther on,
" after leaving the shelter of a masonry house then in
" front of us, but that, when these were got over, we should
" be in perfect safety. Major Simmonds, of the 5th
" Fusiliers, with about 150 men, he said, would escort us.
" We accordingly collected the doolies, and made a rush
" for Martin's House. From the instant that we left the
" gate, we were exposed to a heavy fire from a battery of
" the enemy's across the river; and while waiting there,
" their round shot tore through the walls of the house in
" every direction. After half-an-hour, when we had re-
" formed the doolies into some order, we again moved on,
" Major Simmonds' party keeping ahead to clear the
" road. We ran on as quickly as we could across a
" nullah, about three feet deep in water, through which we

1857. " waded, and there a number of the doolie bearers and of
" the wounded were killed by the enemy's grape. We
" thence continued our course along a high wall, which
" afforded us shelter.

" After this I fancy that Thornhill lost his way, for he
" led us into an oblong square lined on each side with
" sheds. On entering this square a heavy musketry fire
" was poured upon us by the enemy, who were posted
" behind walls and upon the roofs of the sheds, on the
" right or river side, and within a short distance of us.
" We rushed on through the square as quickly as we could,
" and sheltering ourselves as much as possible under the
" arched sheds, passed through an arched gateway on the
" left side, exposed to a dreadful fire in front and rear.
" The enemy were crowded in a corner house, forming the
" angle of a street running opposite to this archway, and
" fired upon us within a few paces, so that their bullets
" would tear through several men. Here, our men fell
" thickly, and all the doolies were deserted. A number
" of doolie-bearers had been killed, and the rest were
" dispersed, and hiding in every direction. One or two of
" the doolies ran the gauntlet, and got through.

" Mr. Thornhill having now discovered his mistake
" had become greatly excited, and begged me to turn the
" doolies back; but this was no longer possible. Dr.
" Bradshaw and my apothecary went back, and got the
" rear-bearers to take their doolies up, and then returned
" and went along the river bank, and got safe into the
" Residency. These rear doolies were mostly those which
" had not yet been brought into the square. In rushing
" back through the archway to try and turn the doolies
" back, Thornhill was shot through the arm, and almost
" immediately after a second shot grazed his temple. Our
" position at this time was the following :—Between thirty
" and forty doolies were scattered in the street, in the
" square, and in the sheds on either side; the bearers who
" remained unwounded were dispersed, and hiding every-

"where. Dismounted troopers of the enemy were enter-
"ing the square, armed with swords, and three sides of it
"were surrounded by the enemy's musketeers and riflemen,
"pouring into us a deadly fire. I did not like to leave
"the doolies, and remained, though the case appeared
"desperate.

"Seeing, presently, some stragglers of the escort, I
"joined myself to them, and we entered an open doorway
"in a house which formed the right side of the archway.
"There were present, including myself, nine sound men,
"two wounded officers, Captain Andrew Becher, of the
"40th N. I., and Swanson, 78th, and three wounded men—
"total fourteen. At this time we were completely cut off
"—this was about ten o'clock. The mutineers, having
"discovered where we were, were flocking round, and
"kept up a constant fire upon the doorway. The only
"thing which checked them was the intrepidity of private
"McManus, of the 5th Fusiliers, who kept outside the
"doorway, sheltering himself behind a pillar, and ma-
"naging to screen himself under that slight cover, from
"which he kept up, for half-an-hour, a constant fire on the
"assailants. He killed numbers of them, and the fear of
"his intrepidity was so great, that he had, at last, often
"only to raise his piece to cause all the enemy to stoop,
"and leave their loopholes. They now got a great acces-
"sion to their numbers, and the noise they made was fearful.
"They kept reviling us; and indeed, we were so close,
"that continually words passed between them and Captain
"Becher. The assailants kept pressing continually closer,
"and were then not more than twenty yards from us.
"They kept on saying, 'Why do you not come out into
"the street?' and their leader called on his men to rush
"on us, saying that there were but three of us in the
"house. To undeceive them, we gave a loud cheer—
"wounded and all joining. We barricaded the doorway,
"partly with lumber which we found in the house, partly
"with sandbags, to obtain which, we stripped the dead

1857. " natives, close about the door, of their waistcloths; the
" bodies of these natives about the doorway also offered
" an impediment to their making a rush upon us. From
" their position at this time, the mutineers could fire freely
" on our doolies in the square.

" One of our number, private Ryan, Madras Fusiliers,
" was in a sad way about the fate of Captain Arnold, of
" his regiment, who was lying wounded in one of the
" doolies near. He called for a volunteer to assist him in
" removing the wounded officer. Private McManus, 5th
" Fusiliers, instantly came forward, though wounded in
" the foot. We removed our barricade, and the two
" rushed across the gateway through the terrible mus-
" ketry fire and into the square, when they tried to lift the
" doolie, but found it beyond their strength. They then
" took Captain Arnold out of the doolie and carried him
" through the same heavy firing into the house. The
" ground was torn by musket balls about them, but they
" effected their return in safety, though Captain Arnold
" received a second wound through the thigh, while in
" their arms. A wounded soldier was also brought in
" in this way, and he also, poor fellow, received two mortal
" wounds while being carried in—the men who carried
" them miraculously escaping.

" Our situation at this time seemed to ourselves far from
" desperate; we thought that by holding out for an hour
" or two, we were sure to be relieved by the rear guard
" when it marched up to the Residency. In fact, we were
" expecting them every moment. We, therefore, kept up
" a very steady fire from the doorway and from the
" window that looked into the square. An hour passed
" away, and three of our men had received wounds, which
" disabled them from firing.

" The conduct of private Hollowell, of the 78th, was
" most splendid—cheering the men, keeping up their
" courage, and doing everything to prevent them giving
" way, himself all the time firing most steadily, and con-

PLAN.

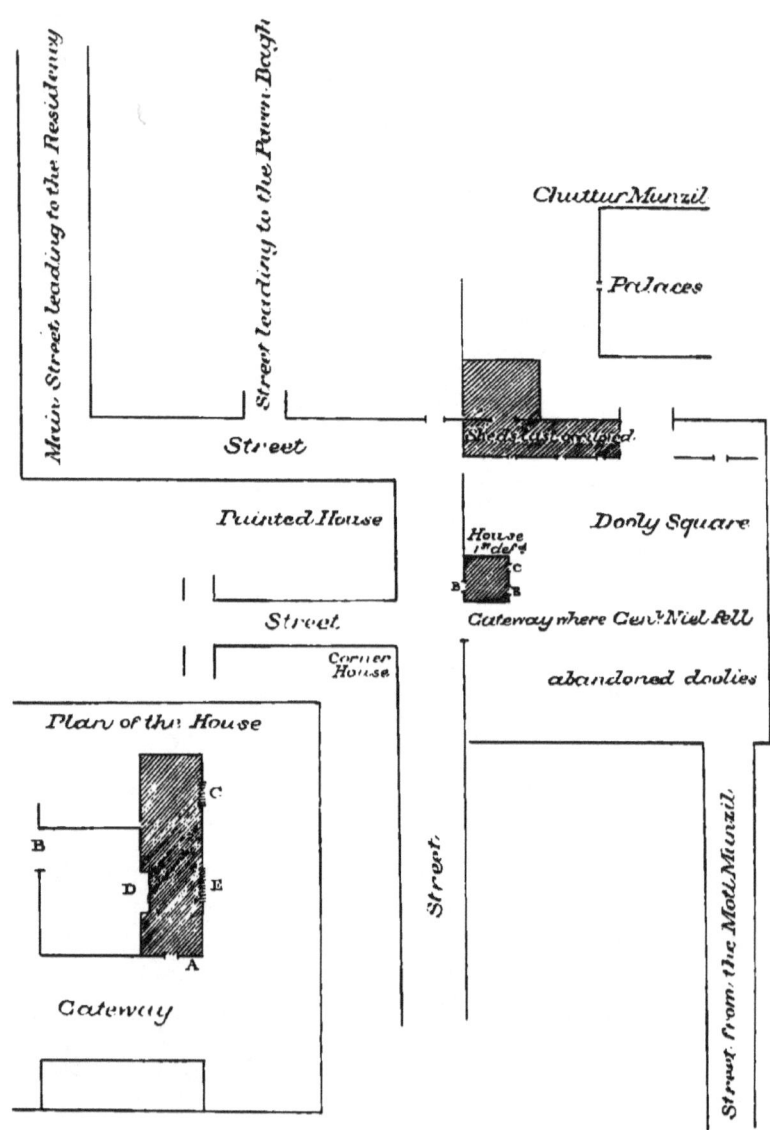

A. Door by which the Refugees entered
B. Door into the Street
C. Door into the Square
D. Plastered Venetian Window
E. Venetian Window into Square

N.B. The shaded part is that occupied by our men.

"stantly with effect. At length he killed their leader.
" The assailants, it must be explained, showed themselves
" only at intervals, when they would come forward as if
" resolved to make a rush; but Hollowell always managed
" to kill one at this critical moment, which stopped them.
" At length, he, as above said, killed their leader. He
" was quite an old man, dressed in white, with a red
" 'cummurbund,' and armed with sword and shield. Soon
" after this, the noise in the street quite ceased. An occa-
" sional shot was fired at us, but the street seemed to have
" been deserted. Just before the leader fell, the assailants
" stealthily pushed the door open at B, and fired into us
" through the plastered Venetian window at D; but, most
" providentially, without effect. Stationing myself at that
" window, and looking through the hole blown through it
" by the musket shot, I was enabled to shoot with my
" revolver, through the body, a man who came to repeat
" the fire. He staggered, and fell dead in the doorway.
" At the same time, Hollowell shot another man, en-
" deavouring to drag this one away.

" We now broke through this plaster which closed up
" the window, and got into the outer room. From the
" door we could see that the streets were quite deserted,
" and there was no noise whatever. The bodies of several
" of our soldiers were lying, without their heads, in the
" streets. About a quarter-of-an-hour elapsed, during which
" not a shot was fired on either side; when, suddenly,
" one of the men called our attention to a dull rolling
" noise in the street, which seemed to indicate that the
" enemy were bringing down a gun against us. I soon
" after saw some persons pushing a screen on wheels
" towards us, against which, at the distance of a few yards,
" a minié rifle had no effect. This screen they pushed up
" against the door B. We now retreated into the original
" room. The enemy now mounted on the roof, scraped
" through the plaster, and threw quantities of lighted
" straw down into the room. Soon the smoke became
" intolerable, and the building itself got on fire.

1857. "Thus situated, we knew not what to do. Numerous
"plans were suggested and abandoned. At last we raised
"the three most helpless among the wounded, and drag-
"ging them after us, rushed from the back door C, which
"led into the square. We had only about ten yards to
"run, when we got into the shed on the north side of the
"square. Here we found some dead and dying Sepoys.
"In making this passage, Lieutenant Swanson, of the
"78th, received a second wound, of which he died; and
"one of the wounded men was again wounded. We were
"now, including myself, six men capable of using arms,
"and four more of the wounded men capable of standing
"sentry. One end of this arched shed had a passage
"broken into it, and we were suddenly roused by two
"shots fired at us through this. After this, we put one
"man to guard this entrance, and his presence there was
"enough to keep the assailants off. The fire of the enemy
"at this moment recommenced upon us through the door-
"ways and numerous loopholes in the walls. From our
"first position in the house at the archway, we had in a
"great measure protected the doolies, but now the enemy
"were able to come through the archway, and reaching
"the doolies, commenced massacring the wounded. We
"were powerless to prevent this. The enemy crept up to
"them along the sheds, keeping the curtains of the doolies
"between us and them, and thus we did not see them
"actually doing this deed of butchery. They used swords.
"Had we seen them, however, we could have done nothing.
"One wounded officer, Lieutenant Knight, of the 90th
"Regiment, was lying in a doolie. A Sowar came up
"and was about to kill him. Knight sprung out of the
"other side of the doolie, and had instantly fifty shots
"fired at him, two of which struck him in the leg, making
"three wounds; but despite of his wounds, he succeeded
"in distancing his pursuers who followed after him, and
"he joined the rear guard shot through the legs in
"three places. The enemy now dug holes in the roof of
"the shed, and fired down on us. To avoid this, we broke

"through a mud wall into a court-yard, on the north side
"of the shed, where we providentially found two pots of
"water.

"At this time hope was gone. We saw plainly that we
"should not be succoured, and despaired, but broke
"through into the court-yard, just to escape the imminent
"death which threatened us by the fire from the roof.
"The wounded with us were calling out to us to shoot
"them, for we heard the cries of the poor wretches across
"the square, who were being inhumanly butchered.
"About thirty yards from the court-yard was the rear of a
"large building. Myself and another man crept forward
"cautiously and noiselessly to this wall. We found, about
"eight feet from the ground, an arched opening. Climbing
"on his shoulders, I managed to get inside this building
"and found a spacious court-yard, looking into a garden,
"and, as I thought, a place to which we had been directed
"by Providence for our defence and preservation. The
"walls were thick, the doorways few. I advanced a few
"feet into this building, but dared go no further. I
"beckoned to the rest to come, but there being some hesi-
"tation we were discovered by the Sepoys on the roof,
"and fired upon. We now retreated back again into the
"first shed, where the enemy had pierced the roof, carrying
"with us the water.

"It was now nearly dark, and we made our preparations
"for relief of sentries. Nine men were told off in three
"reliefs, giving three sentries, and we clustered close round
"the doorway. It soon became dark, and the scene
"baffles description. Here we were in the shed. Lying
"near us were dead men of the enemy; a dead horse,
"shot that morning—dead and living huddled together,
"and our own men wounded, some of them delirious.
"The enemy on the roof over our heads, pacing back-
"wards and forwards, their footfalls being distinctly
"audible, and enemies all around us. All hope of relief
"had long left us, and we were merely, as we thought,

1857. "clinging together in desperation. The intolerable thirst
"and the over-strained excitement of the whole day began
"about this time to overpower me, and I should not have
"cared, at some moments, to have been put out of
"suspense by death. Again the hope of life would return.
"The enemy now set fire to several of the doolies. We
"heard the moans of the unhappy dying men within them,
"but dared not communicate to one another that the
"horrid sounds had reached us.

"After our return to the shed, the enemy altogether
"ceased to fire at us. Our own ammunition would
"hardly afford more than seven rounds to six men, and
"we wholly abstained from firing. In this condition we
"passed the night, frequently jumping up in alarm that
"the enemy was approaching, and then sinking to sleep
"from exhaustion.

"About 2 a.m., we heard a heavy firing close to us, and
"a great rush of the enemy over our heads. We now felt
"certain that our situation was known, and that the firing
"proceeded from a party sent to our relief. To describe
"the revulsion of feeling is impossible. We raised a cry
"of 'Europeans! Europeans!!' and then united to give
"one loud cheer, and shouted with our might 'Charge
"them! Charge them!! Keep on your right.'

"The firing suddenly ceased. After waiting a few
"minutes, we gave ourselves up to despair. A little after,
"rousing ourselves, we consulted as to what we should do.
"I proposed to the men either to force our way back to
"the rear-guard, or forward to the Residency. They
"agreed, but on creeping forward, under shadow of the
"building, I found a large fire burning in the arch-
"way, and great numbers of men clustered about it.
"Escape, that way, was utterly impossible, whilst by the
"way by which we had come, we had to rush through the
"men who had just successfully repelled our own soldiers.
"To escape and carry away the wounded was hopeless.
"We resigned ourselves completely to our fate. A little

" after day-break, we were roused by distant firing. 1857.
" This time it had no effect upon us. It, however,
" approached nearer and nearer, when Ryan, suddenly
" jumping up, shouted 'Oh boys! them's our own chaps!'
" We then all jumped up and united in a cheer, and kept
" shouting to keep on their right. At the same time we
" fired at the loop-holes, from which the enemy were
" firing. In about three minutes we saw Captain Moorsom
" appear at the entrance hole of the shed, and, beckoning
" to him, he entered, and then by his admirable arrange-
" ments we were all brought off safely, and soon after
" reached the palace with the rear-guard of the 90th
" Regiment."

Colonel Napier, of the Bengal Engineers, (now Lord Napier of Magdala) who led the troops sent to the assistance of the 90th, at the Mootee Munzil, forwarded the following report of the affair to General Outram, on the 16th of October, 1857 :—

Colonel R. Napier, Military Secretary, etc., to Major-General Sir James Outram, G.C.B., commanding the Forces.

" Lucknow, 16th October, 1857.
" On the 25th ultimo, Colonel Campbell reported
" to you that he, with a small party of the 90th, not ex-
" ceeding 100 men and almost all the wounded, the heavy
" guns, and a large number of ammunition waggons, were
" in the walled passage in front of the Mootee Mehal
" Palace, which position he should be obliged to hold for
" the night, as he was invested by the enemy, and could
" not advance without reinforcements.
" On the morning of the 26th, a detachment of 250 men,
" under command of Major Simmonds, 5th Fusiliers, and
" part of the Ferozepore regiment, under Captain Brasyer,
" were sent by your orders to reinforce Colonel Campbell,
" under the guidance of Captain Moorsom.

1857. "They had judiciously occupied a house and garden between Colonel Campbell's position and the palace; but as they were unable to move from their position, I received orders to proceed to their assistance with a further reinforcement of 100 men of Her Majesty's 78th Highlanders, under Colonel Stisted, two guns of Captain Olpherts' battery, and Captain Hardinge's Sowars.

"Captain Olpherts strongly objected to his guns being taken, and on considering the reason that he offered, I took it upon myself to dispense with them, merely taking spare bullocks. Captain Olpherts accompanied me as a volunteer. As I had reason to believe that I could open a communication through the palace, which would bring me near the position of the guns, I took Mr. Kavanagh, an intelligent civilian acquainted with the locality, examined the palace as far as it was practicable, and obtained sufficient knowledge of it to form my plan of operations.

"I then led the party by one of the side outlets of the palace along the river bank to Major Simmonds' position under a smart fire from the enemy, from which, however, we received little damage.

* * * * * * * * * *

"At 3 a.m., the whole force proceeded undiscovered through the enemy's posts, until the leading division had reached the palace, and the heavy guns and waggons were safely parked in the garden which I had reconnoitred on the preceding day. The enemy were aroused too late to prevent the operation, but made an attack on the rear-guard, which was ineffective.

"I remained with Colonel Purnell to secure the position thus gained with trifling loss. A large body of Sepoys was discovered in a walled garden connected with that which contained our heavy guns, by men of H.M's 90th, 5th Fusiliers, and 32nd, who gallantly charged in, led by Colonel Purnell, 90th, and Captain McCabe, 32nd,

" and almost annihilated the Sepoys, securing the garden
" itself as the rear of our position. Measures were imme-
" diately taken to open a road for the guns through the
" palace, and by the 1st instant, every gun and waggon
" was safely lodged in the entrenchment.

" It now remains for me to bring to your favourable
" notice the officers commanding corps and detachments—
" Colonel Stisted, 78th; Captain Brasyer, Sikhs; Captain
" Lowe, 32nd. The late lamented Major Simmonds gave
" me very valuable aid.

" To Colonel Purnell's lot fell the more difficult duty of
" commanding the rear guard and of securing the position
" when gained."

* * * * * * * * * * *

In a subsequent report dated Novr. 20th, Colonel Napier again refers to the operations on the 27th of September and the following days :—

" On the morning of the 27th ultimo, the escort with
" the heavy train occupied the range of palaces called
" the Chuttur Munzil and Fureed Buksh.

* * * * * * * * * * *

" The position was too extensive for our force, nearly
" all of which was occupied in guarding it; but it was
" susceptible of no reduction, so that most desirable as
" it was that we should have occupied some of the exterior
" buildings as flanking defences, we were unable to do so,
" but were obliged to confine ourselves to the palaces and
" gardens, and to erect precautionary defences against any
" means of annoyance the enemy could devise. Lieut.-
" Colonel Purnell, of Her Majesty's 90th, being in com-
" mand of the rear guard on the 27th, I requested him to
" assume command of the palace garden and buildings
" adjacent to it. On the 28th, the palace buildings ex-
" tending in the direction of the Khas bazaar were explored
" by Captain Moorsom, who, with a party of fifty men of

1857.

1857. "the 90th, and 5th Fusiliers, gallantly drove the enemy
"out at the point of the bayonet, killing a considerable
"number, with the loss of one man of Her Majesty's 90th.
"Captain Moorsom then placed a picquet in a house com-
"manding the Khas and Cheena bazaars. On the 3rd
"instant, the enemy sprang a mine under the garden wall,
"which merely shook it without bringing it down. On
"the 5th, they exploded a second mine, which effected a
"considerable breach, and appeared in some force with
"the intention of making an assault; but on the head of
"the column showing itself on the breach, a well-directed
"fire from Her Majesty's 90th caused it to retreat pre-
"cipitately, and with considerable loss. The enemy also
"burned down one of the gateways of the garden, making
"a second practicable breach, at which they occasionally
"appeared to fire a shot or two. Lieut.-Colonel Purnell
"had retrenched both these breaches, which it became
"evident that the enemy had no real intention of assault-
"ing; but they exposed the garden to a severe musketry
"fire from commanding buildings on the right, called the
"Hirun Khana; it, therefore, became necessary to open
"trenches of communication, which were commenced by
"Colonel Purnell and his officers. On the 6th, the enemy
"blew up the picquet overlooking the Cheena and Khas
"bazaars, causing us a loss of three men, and in the con-
"fusion that ensued, penetrated in considerable numbers
"into the palace, where many of them were destroyed.
"They are said to have lost 450 men! the remainder were
"driven back, but continued to occupy a part of the
"palace buildings which had been in our possession; of
"these, the nearest to us was a mosque commanded by
"our buildings, but giving several easy means of access
"to our position. On the 8th, the enemy attacked from
"the mosque our nearest picquets, but were repulsed with
"loss. In order to prevent a repetition of this annoyance,
"I examined carefully in company with Lieut.-Colonel
"Purnell and Captain Moorsom, the buildings connecting

" us with those of the enemy, and we succeeded in pene-
" trating to a vault under their position, where, screened
" by the security, we could see the enemy closely sur-
" rounding the entrance, and hear them in considerable
" numbers overhead. A charge of two barrels of powder
" was lodged in the vault, and was fired by Lieutenant
" Russell, of the Bengal Engineers. The effect was com-
" plete, many of the enemy were blown up, and their
" position greatly injured, whilst we obtained a command
" over the streets leading to the Khas and Cheena bazaars
" better and more secure from molestation than our previous
" one. This post was immediately and securely barricaded
" by Captain Crommelin, of the Engineers, who this day
" resumed his duties as chief engineer, and the value
" of his services was immediately apparent. Though our
" position was improved by this explosion, the possession
" of the mosque was absolutely necessary to our security.
" I accordingly determined to recapture it, and on ex-
" pressing my wishes to Lieut.-Colonel Purnell, that officer
" himself accompanied me with a small party of the 90th
" and Madras Fusiliers. The enemy, fifty or sixty in
" number, were surprised and rapidly driven out with
" very trifling loss on our side, and the position imme-
" diately barricaded and secured by Captain Crommelin;
" it has ever since formed a good connection between
" the picquets of the advance garden and the quarters of
" Brasyer's Sikhs, and all attempts of the enemy to molest
" it have been ineffective. It falls within Captain Crom-
" melin's province to report in detail the various operations
" by which our difficult position, in close contact with the
" city, occupied by a numerous and persevering enemy,
" has been defended and protected.

" I beg to bring to the notice of Major-General Have-
" lock, the excellent services performed by Lieutenant-
" Colonel Purnell, who has commanded in the advance
" garden and its outposts since their occupation. Much of
" the trench work, by which it was rendered unassailable,

"has been executed by his men, and under his superin-
"tendence, directed by the engineer department. On all
"occasions he has given the cordial and able co-operation
"of a most brave and accomplished officer. Captain
"Grant, of the Madras Fusiliers, has commanded the post
"of the mosque from the 11th of October to the 2nd
"November, when he was severely wounded. He main-
"tained the post under a constant and close musketry fire
"and repeated attacks by mining, with cool courage and
"judgment; both these qualities were required to avoid
"real, and to disregard the imaginary, dangers of mines,
"and Captain Grant has displayed them in an eminent
"degree.

"The daring and intelligent Captain Moorsom has been
"engaged in most of the above operations, and has given
"very valuable assistance. Captains Rattray and Wade
"(90th) have shown themselves excellent commanders of
"outposts.

"R. NAPIER, Colonel,
"Military Secretary, etc."

The advanced position taken by the 90th Light Infantry, was held by it until the arrival of the relieving army, under Sir Colin Campbell.

For some few days after the relief of the Residency by Sir Henry Havelock, it was not known whether the relieving force would remain to augment the garrison, or whether, a new garrison being left to hold the place, the former defenders, women, and children would return to Cawnpore.

Sir James Outram, under the impression that there was a great scarcity of food in the entrenchment, even before the arrival of the forces now under his command, considered that it was absolutely necessary to retire a certain proportion of the troops, leaving sufficient to keep the mutineers in check, and maintain a position in the capital of Oude.

His intentions, conveyed in a telegram to the Com- 1857. mander-in-Chief, were to strengthen the garrison by adding to it the 90th Light Infantry, and, considering the loss incurred in getting into the Residency, to leave the women and children, the sick and wounded, to their care, and to retire on Cawnpore, where he would organise a force for the final relief and capture of Lucknow.

After a few days' delay, however, it was discovered that sufficient grain, etc., existed to provision the force for time enough to allow of troops being sent to their assistance, and, accordingly, the two Generals agreed to remain and share the blockade.

At this time, viz., the end of September, commenced one continued round of harassing duties. Surrounded by hordes of enemies who, by their incessant attacks, allowed the gallant few who so successfully held them at bay, not a moment's rest, and daily forced to witness the sufferings of the many helpless ones in their charge, no wonder that offensive operations, such as sorties, were hailed with delight, not only as a break to the monotony, but as a means of retribution.

On the 2nd of October, when the idea of withdrawing part of the force was still held, a party of the 78th and 90th, under the command of Major Haliburton, of the former regiment, received order to open a communication through the city to the Alum Bagh. Captain Wade, of the 90th, led the advance, and marched as far as the house of Nawab Moontaz-ood-doolah, where he was stopped by the heavy fire from a mosque close by. As neither the strength nor position of the enemy could be ascertained from this point, Captain Wade, attended by Mr. Kavanagh, crossed the street further up, under a severe fire, and having reconnoitred as far as they prudently could, returned with the information that further advance was almost impossible. The project of forcing a way back to the Alum Bagh was now abandoned.

In the attack made on the buildings held by the 90th, on

1857. the 6th, Captains Denison, Bingham, and Phipps were severely wounded, the first mentioned dying a few days after; and on the 13th of November, the 90th had further to deplore the death of Colonel Campbell, who had been wounded on the 26th of September—a strict disciplinarian, he had won the admiration of all under his command by his gallantry, and his worth was so well known, that, in a despatch, dated the 22nd of December, the Governor General says:—

" He now has to lament the death of Colonel Campbell, " Her Majesty's 90th Light Infantry, than whom the " Queen's service possessed no more gallant or promising " officer."

Sir Colin Campbell, with the troops destined to crush the rebellion in Oude, arrived at the Alum Bagh on the 12th of November, and on the 13th, by means of a semaphore, signified to the garrison his intention of moving on the Dilkoosha next day. Preparations were accordingly made to meet him half-way by those whom he came to relieve; and on the 16th, the Hirun Khana, the engine house, and the King's stables were assaulted and taken.

The attack on the engine house was entrusted to the 90th Light Infantry, with what success may be gathered from the accompanying report of the engineer officer appointed to guide them.

Lieut. D. Limond, Engineers, to Captain Crommelin, Chief Engineer, Oude Field Force.

" Lucknow, 21st November, 1857.

" According to orders, Lieutenant Chalmers, " Assistant Field Engineer, and myself, accompanied the " detachment of the 90th Light Infantry, on the attack " upon the engine house; keeping to the left on passing " that building, we found the rebels evacuating the same, " and followed them up to the most advanced building, the " Overseer's house, which I at once directed to be bar-

" ricaded. The enemy opened on it with guns from the 1857.
" Kaiser Bagh, and the house was then abandoned and
" burnt by Colonel Purnell's orders. The east wall of the
" Barahduree enclosure was at once loopholed, and the
" windows to the south blocked up with sand bags. Dur-
" ing the night a battery for three light guns was con-
" structed at the southern extremity of the lane, between
" the King's stables and Barahduree enclosure. The
" doors and windows of the engine-house, facing the river,
" were also barricaded. During the night, a trench-
" covered communication was opened to the advanced
" garden, none being necessary between the engine house
" and King's stables."

Major General Havelock, in his despatch to Sir James
Outram, dated 16th Nov., 1857, refers to Colonel Purnell's
service in the following words :—
"I must commend all the officers in charge of detach-
" ments, but most prominently Lieutenant-Colonel Pur-
" nell, 90th Light Infantry, whose conduct throughout the
" affair evinced the most distinguished gallantry, united
" to imperturbable coolness, and the soundest judgment."

The detachment of the 78th, under Captain Lockhart,
was equally successful in its attack on the King's stables,
which buildings, when once in our possession, were handed
over to the charge of Colonel Purnell's detachment of the
90th. The regiment was thus placed the nearest to the
approaching troops, and on the 17th, met the men of the
three companies which had left England under Major
Barnston.

The whole regiment being now reunited, the reasons for
its separation must be given before detailing the glorious
work which it had before it.

After leaving the Cape, a few days after the *Himalaya*,
the *Transit* ran due east until within a few days' sail of
Australia, when her course was turned towards the north.

1857. Rough weather was now experienced, and very shortly afterwards, the ship was caught in a cyclone. The main-yard snapped in two, every sail was torn to ribbons, and the ship very much strained, so much so, that a rent, twenty-four feet long, was discovered in her side, through which the water poured in such quantities that five hundred tons were pumped out in one day. It became a matter of speculation how long the ship would hold out. Providentially, the storm abating, the leak was kept under, and the vessel was nearing Singapore, when, on the 10th of July, it ran upon a coral reef and remained fixed.

Thanks to the presence of mind of Major Barnston, and the admirable discipline of the men, but little confusion ensued. An officer of the 90th, Lieutenant Herford, who was on board, gives the following account of what happened after the ship struck.

" It was an anxious moment, but we had all our work to
" do. Some of us were sent down to remain with the men,
" in order to keep them quiet, while others superintended
" the bringing up of provisions, and securing as much
" fresh water as possible. The boats were hoisted out,
" and the baggage brought on deck; the water soon filled
" the mess-room and came over the stern of the poop.
" Between us and the land, about a mile and a half
" distant, was a long low reef, and on this it was de-
" termined to disembark the troops first, that we might
" get clear of the ship with all good speed—as, indeed, no
" one among us could say at what moment she might not
" go down altogether. The men behaved admirably—as
" quietly and as orderly as if on parade, and the boats
" were quickly filled and went to and fro from the reef
" until all the troops were landed—those under my care
" being the last party which left for the reef, with the
" exception of the officers in command."

* * * * * * * * * *

" It is difficult to describe the seaweed-covered rock,
" rising out of the sea, upon which knots of shipwrecked

"soldiers and officers stood, anxiously looking at the
"wreck, feeling thankful to have escaped from the sinking
"ship. The reef consisted of two peaks rising from a
"long lozenge-shaped surface, which, on our first landing,
"extended a little above the water's edge; but as 'time
"and tide wait for no man,' we were soon threatened to
"be overtaken by the latter.

"Higher and higher it mounted, until the summit of the
"peaks alone remained above water and became two
"islands. On board the ship we had all had to work hard,
"and had come off in something less than *demi-toilette*.
"Exposed to a tropical sun in the middle of the day,
"allowed barely a mouthful of fresh water, not knowing
"whether we could easily procure more on shore, how
"long the hours seemed before the return of the boats
"from the mainland! We had had space enough and to
"spare on first reaching the reef, but were now becoming
"closely packed, and felt not quite comfortable at the idea
"of being left a prey to sharks in that Eastern sea, if by
"chance the boats were not to return in time to relieve us
"from our position. Five hours were passed by some of
"us on the reef, under the burning sun, and only those
"who have been in a similar plight can understand our
"joy on finding ourselves again on *terra firma* on the
"Island of Banca."

The island is under the protection of the Dutch, whose representatives, on this occasion, behaved with great kindness to the shipwrecked soldiers. On the 18th, Her Majesty's gun-boat *Dove* arrived from Singapore, with the news of the outbreak of the Indian mutiny, and was followed in a few days by H.M.S. *Actæon*, in which the companies of the 90th embarked, and reached Singapore on the 23rd of July.

On the 29th, H.M.S. *Shannon*, commanded by Captain Peel, came in, and the detachment received orders to embark the next day in her and the *Pearl*, Captain Sotheby, to proceed to India.

1857. The march from the temporary barracks to the ship was made in a deluge of rain. Lieutenant Herford says:—
" We were very glad to reach the *Pearl* at last, where we
" were very well received. The sailors were extremely
" kind to our men, immediately supplying them with dry
" clothes, and giving them everything they had in the way
" of provisions, so that we soon saw our soldiers clad as
" sailors, in blue frocks and caps, looking comfortable and
" contented. Nor were the officers more backward in their
" treatment of us. They made us go into their cabins,
" and fitted us out of their own wardrobes, and the
" Captain very kindly asked five of us into his cabin, and
" begged us to make it our home as long as we should be
" on board. All our detachment was on board the *Pearl*,
" with the exception of Captain Guise and his company,
" which had embarked in the *Shannon*. This ship was
" also conveying Lord Elgin to Calcutta, and sailed at
" the same time as ourselves."

A voyage of a few days brought both ships to Calcutta, and the troops, embarking in river steamers the day after their arrival, proceeded to Chinsurah, where they remained until the 28th of August, as arrangements had to be made for refitting the detachment, which had lost everything in the wreck of the *Transit*.

On the 28th of August, Captain Wolseley's company of the 90th proceeded by rail to Raneegunge—the remainder following on the 29th and 30th; and on arrival at the end of their first day's journey, bullock-waggons were found waiting to take them on, by the means of which the party reached Benares on the 10th of September. The next day it started for Allahabad, by the same conveyance it had before used, arriving there about the 13th. Futtehpore was reached on the 3rd of October, and Major Barnston was directed to hold the place.

The following telegrams show the movements of the detachment:—

The Officer commanding at Allahabad to the Chief of the Staff, Calcutta. 1857.

(Telegraphic).

"Allahabad, 3rd October, 1857, 11.30 a.m.

"When I telegraphed to you, Major Barnston, "thirteen officers, and 296 men (90th) were at Futtehpore; "ninety-five men more proceed to join, and ought to reach "Futtehpore on the 6th. I have since heard that Major "Barnston and 150 men have been withdrawn by the "officer commanding at Cawnpore, who states he has to "send a company to Lucknow. On this I cautioned the "officer commanding at Cawnpore not to meddle with "the Futtehpore post, except under Commander-in-Chief's "or General Outram's orders. I don't know on what "authority he withdrew the men from Futtehpore. One "railway engine runs for forty miles on the Cawnpore "road.

"etc., etc., etc."

The Chief of the Staff, Calcutta, to the Officer commanding at Cawnpore.

(Telegraphic,.

"Calcutta, 3rd October, 1857.

"I have just received a report that Major "Barnston, with 140 men of the 90th Foot, has been "ordered up to Cawnpore from Futtehpore, thereby "seriously weakening the latter post beyond Sir James "Outram's original intention. You are to let me know "by telegraph, for the information of His Excellency, by "whose authority the movement has been made."

The Officer commanding at Cawnpore to the Chief of the Staff, Calcutta.

(Telegraphic).

"Cawnpore, 6th October, 11 a.m.

"In answer to your message of the 3rd instant, "Major Barnston had my orders only to send up 150 men,

1857. " with due proportion of officers. Finding on its arrival
" here he had himself come up, I immediately ordered him
" back to resume his command; he left this accordingly
" the same night. General Outram left instructions to
" bring up troops from Futtehpore in the event of their
" being required; and as I had to send forward a large
" detachment of 252 infantry, two 9-pounders, with one
" sergeant, one naik, six gunners (European), and six
" trained Sikhs, I found it necessary to bring up the
" detachment (90th) to Cawnpore."

The Chief of the Staff to Major Barnston, Futtehpore.
(Telegraphic).

" Calcutta, 7th October, 1857.
" His Excellency having been under the impres-
" sion that the party of Her Majesty's 10th Regiment,
" lately under your command, was going on to Lucknow
" immediately, changed his mind respecting you, and
" directed that you should accompany it; but as it now
" appears that such was not the case, other troops having
" gone forward, you are to remain at Futtehpore, and
" command the latter post. If the detachment of Her
" Majesty's 90th Regiment, now at Cawnpore, leaves for
" Oude, you must get to it. His Excellency has ordered
" two guns, equipped with bullocks, to be sent from Alla-
" habad to Futtehpore. Communicate the last order
" respecting yourself to Colonel Wilson by telegraph.
" Inform me by telegraph what precautions have been
" taken for strengthening the post at Futtehpore, and
" whether, in your opinion, two 9-pounder guns are enough
" for it; also, what provisions are laid in."

Early in October, the companies of the 90th were at
Cawnpore, and on the 17th had their first engagement
with the enemy. News having been received that the
rebels were in force at Sheo Rajpore, some miles from
Bithoor, Brigadier Wilson, taking with him a field battery,

a few native horse, and detachments of the Madras Fusiliers, the 64th and 90th Regiments, moved in their direction.

An officer who took part in this expedition gives the following account of it:—

"Some 650 infantry, a battery of artillery, and a few
"Sowars, of the garrison of Cawnpore, marched on the
"morning of the 18th inst. towards a village called Sheo
"Rajpore, distant hence some sixteen miles, where it was
"reported a large force of rebels had collected, with the
"fiend Nana at its head. We moved off at one o'clock
"a.m., and after several halts, we got as far as Bithoor,
"where we rested, and breakfasted on hard biscuit and
"rum and water. At about twelve o'clock we again
"moved off, under a broiling sun, and after accomplishing
"five or six miles, intelligence was received that the
"enemy were in a grove of trees, not half-a-mile a-head,
"with two guns in position—a 24-pounder and a 9-pounder.
"We had not moved on much further when it was thought
"prudent to deploy our small force on each side of the
"road, but this move we were rather late in putting into
"effect, for the detachment of the 90th Light Infantry,
"which was in the rear, had just commenced to move off
"the road, when the enemy's guns opened fire, and told
"terribly on the fated 90th. The first shell burst imme-
"diately before this detachment, killing two and wounding
"two or three others. Our guns shortly afterwards com-
"menced, but our shot fell far short, and we had to
"advance closer up, so as to get in range, and it is well
"we did, for the shot of the enemy came pretty quick, but
"now passed harmlessly over our heads, except one or two
"shells which exploded immediately above us, but did us
"no injury. After exchanging twenty or thirty rounds
"the enemy's guns were charged—I should have said
"position, as the guns were already silenced and being
"limbered up. No sooner was this effected than the
"cowardly rascals made off, leaving behind two waggons

1857. " which could not be moved, owing to some of the horses
" being knocked over by our shot. The enemy, however,
" cut the traces, etc., of the animals, and fairly bolted.
" They left behind them three country carts laden with
" ammunition, and these also fell into our hands. Though
" our movement was quiet and quickly done, yet the rebels
" knew of and had prepared for our coming. The action
" altogether did not last an hour, but in this short space of
" time we had two killed and six wounded. The two
" former and five of the latter belonged to the 90th Light
" Infantry, and the other wounded man is one of the
" Madras Fusiliers, who was struck in the arm. Of the
" five wounded of the 90th, no less than four had to
" undergo amputation, one from the shoulder, one from
" the thigh, and two from the arm."

On the 19th, the force was occupied in destroying Bithoor, the residence of the Nana, returning to Cawnpore on the 20th, and the day after, Major Barnston, with a force of 500 men, including those of his own regiment, started with a convoy of provisions for the Alum Bagh. When about eight miles from its destination, the rear guard of the column, Captain Wolseley's company, was attacked by the enemy's cavalry; they were received with a volley, which staggered them, and on the main body falling back they made off.

The convoy now moved forward to within about a mile and a half of the Alum Bagh, when it was again attacked. A large body of the enemy was advancing on the right. Captain Irby and the Madrasees drove the infantry back, and the baggage and carts were closed up, Lieutenant Herford being left to cover the guns, which were halted and placed in position to command the plain. Some cavalry was now observed advancing at a gallop, with the intention of cutting off the baggage, but Captain Moir's guns played upon them with such effect that they retired with loss, and allowed the waggons to proceed without further molestation.

The detachment was ordered, after having rested for a 1857. day or two, to return to Cawnpore. As the enemy had, however, appeared in very great numbers, and had become more daring than usual, Lieutenant-Colonel McIntyre, of the 78th, directed the party to remain with him, an order which shortly after received the sanction of the Commander-in-Chief.

On the 26th of October, Colonel Greathed arrived at Cawnpore with the field force from Delhi, when Brigadier-General Grant assumed command of the column, and moved in the direction of Lucknow, crossing the Ganges on the 30th of October. The advanced guard of this force was expected at the Alum Bagh on the 2nd of November, but it was not until the 4th that it made its appearance. On the 9th Sir Colin Campbell moved to Buntara, and on the 12th he marched to the Alum Bagh, driving the enemy from their position and from the fort of Jellalabad.

The next day the companies of the 90th marched out and joined the 4th Brigade, under the command of Brigadier Sir Adrian Hope. The brigade was formed of the 53rd, 93rd, and a battalion of about 600 men, made up of companies of the 90th, 84th, and Madras Fusiliers, under the command of Major Barnston. About 9 a.m. on the 14th November, the army moved forward, under the command of Sir Colin Campbell, who, finding that the enemy, expecting him to advance by the same road as General Havelock, had not strengthened the south side of the Martinière, determined to reduce it by artillery fire, and enter the city from that point. Operations were commenced by battering the Dilkoosha Palace, which was carried without much resistance, after an hour's firing. The Martinière was then occupied by the detachment of the 90th, which was shortly after directed to encamp in a grove near a mud wall, behind which the enemy was in position. The men were about to dine when a heavy musketry fire denoted that the rebels were attempting, in force, to retake the position. The 90th companies were

1857. sent to the support of the 93rd, and advanced, under a terrible fire from some guns posted on the opposite side of the canal; these they were ordered to take, and, changing direction, moved against them, but on arrival at the canal it was found impassable, the enemy having dammed it up. Darkness was now coming on, and as Sir Colin Campbell intended holding the line of the canal for the night, Captain Wolseley received orders to picquet his company on the spot—the remainder of the troops retiring.

The following day the force remained stationary, waiting for a supply of ammunition—Major Barnston's detachment being on picquet, under a heavy fire of musketry the whole time.

The advance was resumed on the 16th, the Commander-in-Chief leaving all his baggage at the Dilkoosha, in charge of H.M's 8th Regiment. At 12 o'clock, Major Barnston's battalion started, and, having crossed the canal, turned to the right, coming at once under the fire of the enemy. "Major Barnston pressed on, and reached
" some houses on the edge of an open space, across which
" ran a road, now commanded by the guns of the rebels.
" Captain Wolseley was directed to double across this
" opening—a run of about 300 yards—and occupy some
" ruined houses on the other side; this he did amid a
" perfect shower of shot and bullets. After keeping up a
" musketry duel from behind the remains of some walls
" scarcely breast high, he advanced with the intention of
" driving out the enemy.

" Marching rapidly along a narrow lane, Captain
" Wolseley's company was leading into the town, with
" some of the 9th Lancers in front, though the horses
" began to kick and plunge under the heavy fire to which
" they were subjected. The enemy retired, keeping up a
" hot fusillade, and as they gave ground the guns were
" brought forward. Captain Wolseley, by his example
" animated his men, and himself assisted in dragging the
" guns to the front through the sand, which lay ankle

"deep. Sergeant Newman rendered himself conspicuous
"by his gallantry, and another of the sergeants of the
"same company, who had been wounded by a musket ball
"which carried away his upper lip, passing clean through
"his face, refused to leave, and remained till the close of
"the action.

"Captain Wolseley was now ordered to protect the flank
"of Captain Blunt's troop of Horse Artillery, and, passing
"the enclosure of the Sekundur Bagh, advanced to a line
"of huts, the remains of the native lines, where he
"remained for the rest of the day, protecting the flank of
"the forces engaged in taking the Shah Nujeef, and
"fighting from house to house.

"In the meantime the remainder of Major Barnston's
"battalion had, in company with other regiments, moved
"against the Sekundur Bagh, from which the rebels kept
"up a withering fire. The front entrance having been
"forced by the 93rd, the 53rd, 4th Punjaub Infantry,
"and the detachments of the 90th followed. When once
"our troops were inside, the enemy made but little re-
"sistance, and prayed for mercy. Their cries, however,
"were unheeded by men who had but lately left the scene
"of the massacre at Cawnpore, and few escaped to tell the
"awful vengeance taken for that foul deed.

"From the Sekundur Bagh, Sir Colin Campbell led
"Major Barnston's regiment of detachments against the
"Shah Nujeef. Behind a parapet, raised on the massive
"terrace of this tomb, the enemy were clustered, and
"poured a frightful fire on a company of the 90th, which
"got up within fifteen yards of the main building. They
"could discover, however, no entrance, and both subalterns
"Lieutenant E. C. Wynne and Ensign H. Powell, who
"commanded it having been wounded, the men were
"directed to move behind some neighbouring huts. As
"Major Barnston was bringing up the rest of his
"regiment, some of our guns were got into posi-
"tion, and opened on the Shah Nujeef, from which

1857. " one of the first shots fired wounded Major Barnston
" desperately.

" The place was now battered by guns, 18-pounders, for
" two hours, and then Brigadier Hope was ordered to take
" it with the 93rd Highlanders. Finding, however, that
" no breach had been effected, Captain Peel, R.N., brought
" up one of his heavy guns, and opened fire within a few
" yards of the building. A breach was made in the outer
" wall, but there was yet an inner one, and the enemy still
" kept up a fearful fire from the raised platform; but seeing
" the determination of their assailants, and alarmed by
" the progress of the attack, they began to leave the place,
" which was carried with a rush by the Highlanders.

" On the morning of the 17th, operations were resumed,
" Sir Colin Campbell was engaged in pressing back the
" enemy, so as to give the desired space for further ope-
" rations, and communications were opened between the
" left rear of the barracks and the canal. Captain Peel
" brought up his guns about noon, and kept up a heavy
" fire on the Mess-house. After the building had been
" battered about three hours, Sir Colin determined to storm,
" and Captain Wolseley was directed to hold himself in
" readiness for that duty.

" The Commander-in-Chief informed Captain Wolseley
" that he would be supported by a company of Sikhs, and
" the detachment of his regiment, which was now led by
" Captain Guise. His instructions were, that, in the event
" of the drawbridge being up, and his not being able to
" effect an entrance, he was to leave his men under cover,
" and return and report to him.

" The storming party started, and under a hot fire
" from the neighbouring buildings arrived under the
" garden wall, over which their leader, Captain Wolseley,
" clambered in company with a bugler. In the garden were
" several of the enemy, who fired upon him and then fled.
" On finding that the drawbridge was down, he ordered
" the bugler to sound the advance, and entered the build-

"ing, on the roof of which he raised the British standard. Every gun which the rebels could bring forward was brought to bear on the Mess-house, and the fire was so heavy, that the party had to retire under cover. Captain Irby now came up with his company, and was directed by Captain Wolseley to take some houses on the left, while he proceeded to attack those on the right, the fire being heavy from both directions. Captain Irby succeeded in occupying the Tara Kotee, which he held against all attempts to dislodge him.

"The Motee Mahul Palace was now the only obstacle to a meeting between the besieged and those who came to their relief. The building was strongly garrisoned, but nothing daunted, Captain Wolseley led his company against it, and finding that the entrances were built up, sent part of his men back to fetch crowbars and picks, and during their absence, keeping his men well under cover, he endeavoured to subdue the fire from the loop-holes. When the men were returning with the tools, private Andrews left his shelter to point out the way; he had no sooner, however, entered the street, when he was shot down. Captain Wolseley, whose servant Andrews had been, sprang forward and carried him off, the man receiving another severe wound as he was being removed.

"While the men were knocking a hole in the wall of the palace, Mr. Kavanagh came up to the party and informed Captain Wolseley that he knew of an entrance at another part of the enclosure. The two proceeded on their search, which was unsuccessful, the enemy having built up every crevice, and on their return, they found that an opening had been made in the wall barely large enough for a man to crawl through. However, small as it was, and undismayed at the probability of the enemy being ready to receive him, Ensign Haig proceeded to force himself through—his captain arriving in time to witness his gallantry.

"The men now rapidly enlarged the hole, and the

"whole party entered, Ensign Haig being found unhurt.
"Entering the palace from the courtyard, they had just
"won, they proceeded to drive the Pandies from room to
"room, and finally out of the building into the Goomtee—
"firing on them with terrible effect.

"The Motee Mahul being in our possession, the gallant
"little band who had wrested it from overwhelming numbers
"proceeded on its way to the Residency, meeting en route
"the head-quarters of the regiment. Thus, after months
"of separation, the companies of the 90th Light Infantry
"met once more, surrounded on all sides by signs of their
"devotion and success.

"The Commander-in-Chief now determined to withdraw
"from the city, which he had won after so much hard
"fighting, and to retire on Cawnpore. This decision was
"at first ill-received, as it was thought that by giving up
"Lucknow, the British prestige would be ruined. Subse-
"quent revisits have proved that Sir Colin Campbell's
"retrograde movement had been well considered, and was
"the right thing to do; consequently, on the 18th, a con-
"verging artillery fire was brought to bear on the Kaiser
"Bagh, with a view to mask the preparations being made
"for the withdrawal. A covered way was made from the
"Residency to beyond the Sekundur Bagh, at which the
"whole of the troops worked hard throughout the day; in
"the evening, Major Barnston's detachment of the 90th
"was sent out on picquet near the Shah Nujeef.

"The next day the ladies, women, and children, and the
"sick and wounded, numbering in all about 2,000, left the
"Residency, escorted by 600 men under Captain Tinling
"of the 90th. They passed through the Bailey Guard,
"the Fureed Buskh, and the Chuttur Munzil, and crossing
"the line of fire from the Kaiser Bagh, went on by the
"Martinière and the Motee Mahul to the Sekundur Bagh,
"where Sir Colin Campbell was waiting to receive them.
"During the night they moved on to the Dilkoosha, the
"treasure and guns following slowly. Thanks to the

" admirable arrangements, the enemy knew nothing of
" what was going on, and though they continued to fire at
" the line of buildings in our possession, made no attempt
" to prevent the retreat. The garrison was withdrawn on
" the night of the 22nd, the picquets of the 90th remaining
" at their posts until General Hope's brigade had left the
" Motee Mahul, when they retired, forming the rear guard
" of the column.

" On the 23rd, the 90th detachment, which had not as
" yet rejoined the head-quarters of the regiment, taking
" post in front of the Martinière, covered the onward
" march of the non-effectives and baggage, and on the
" following day, as they were about to leave his brigade,
" General Hope addressed the officers and men on parade,
" complimenting them on their behaviour, and thanking
" them for the assistance they had afforded him. At the
" same time, the following General Order by the Com-
" mander-in-Chief was read :—

" Head-Quarters, La Martinière, Lucknow,
" 23rd Novr., 1857.

" The Commander-in-Chief has reason to be
" thankful to the force he conducted for the relief of the
" garrison of Lucknow.

" Hastily assembled, fatigued by forced marches, but
" animated by a common feeling of determination to ac-
" complish the duty before them, all ranks of this force
" have compensated for their small number in the execu-
" tion of a most difficult duty by unceasing exertions.

" From the morning of the 16th till last night, the
" whole force has been one outlying picquet, never out
" of fire, and covering an immense extent of ground, to
" permit the garrison to retire scathless, and in safety,
" covered by the whole of the relieving force.

" The ground was won by fighting, as hard as it ever
" fell to the lot of the Commander-in-Chief to witness, it
" being necessary to bring up the same men over and over

1857. "again to fresh attacks; and it is with the greatest grati-
"fication his Excellency declares that he never saw men
"behave better.

"The storming of Sekundur Bagh and Shah Nujeef has
"never been surpassed in daring, and the success of it was
"most brilliant and complete.

"The movement of retreat of last night, by which the
"final rescue of the garrison was effected, was a model of
"discipline and exactness. The consequence was that
"the enemy was completely deceived, and the force retired
"by a narrow tortuous lane, the only line of retreat open,
"in the face of 50,000 enemies, without molestation.

"The Commander-in-Chief offers his sincere thanks to
"Major-General Sir James Outram, G.C.B., for the
"happy manner in which he planned and carried out
"his arrangements for the evacuation of the Residency
"of Lucknow.

"By order of his Excellency the Commander-in-Chief.
    "(Signed)   W. MAYHEW, Major,
        "Deputy Adjutant-General of the Army."

On the 18th and 25th of November, Sir Colin Campbell forwarded the following despatches to the Governor-General:—

"Head-Quarters, Shah Nujeef, Lucknow,
            "18th Novr., 1857.
"My Lord,
    "I have the honour to apprise your Lordship that
"I left Cawnpore on the 9th November, and joined the
"troops under the command of Brigadier-General Hope
"Grant, C.B., the same day at Camp Buntara, about six
"miles from Alum Bagh.

"There being a few detachments on the road, I deemed
"it expedient to wait till the 12th before commencing my
"advance.

"On that day I marched early for Alum Bagh, with the

"following troops:—Naval Brigade, eight heavy guns;
"Bengal Horse Artillery, ten guns; Bengal Horse field
"battery, six guns; heavy field battery Royal Artillery;
"detachments Bengal and Punjaub Sappers and Miners;
"H.M.'s 9th Lancers; detachments 1st, 2nd, and 5th
"Punjaub Cavalry and Hodson's Horse; H.M.'s 8th, 53rd,
"75th, and 93rd Regiments of Infantry; 2nd and 4th
"Punjaub Infantry. Probable total—700 cavalry, 2,700
"infantry.

"The advance guard was attacked by two guns and a
"body of about 2,000 infantry. After a smart skirmish,
"the guns were taken, Lieut. Gough, commanding
"Hodson's Irregular Horse, having distinguished himself
"very much in a brilliant charge, by which this object
"was effected.

"The camp was pitched on that evening at Alum Bagh.
"This place I found to be annoyed to a certain extent by
"guns placed in different positions in the neighbourhood.

"I caused the post to be cleared of lumber and cattle,
"and placed all my tents in it.

"I made my arrangements for marching without bag-
"gage when I should reach the park of Dilkoosha, and
"the men were directed to have three days' food in their
"havresacks. I changed the garrison at Alum Bagh,
"taking fresh men from it, and leaving H.M.'s 75th Regi-
"ment there, which had been so much harassed by its late
"exertions.

"On the 14th, I expected a further reinforcement of 600
"or 700 men, who joined my rear guard, after my march
"had commenced, in the morning of that day.

"As I approached the park of Dilkoosha, the leading
"troops were met by a long line of musketry fire.

"The advance guard was quickly reinforced by a field
"battery and more infantry, composed of companies of
"H.M.'s 5th, 64th, and 78th Foot, under command of
"Lieutenant-Colonel Hamilton, H.M.'s 78th Highlanders,
"supported by the 8th Foot. After a running fight of

1857. " about two hours, in which our loss was very incon-
" siderable, the enemy was driven down the hill to the
" Martinière, across the garden and park of the Martinière,
" and far beyond the canal.

" His loss was trifling, owing to the suddenness of the
" retreat.

" The Dilkoosha and Martinière were both occupied;
" Brigadier Hope's brigade being then brought up and
" arranged in position in the wood of the Martinière, at
" the end opposite the canal, being flanked to the left
" by Capt. Bourchier's field battery, and two of Captain
" Peel's heavy guns.

" Shortly after these arrangements had been made, the
" enemy drew out a good many people, and attacked our
" position in front.

" He was quickly driven off, some of our troops crossing
" the canal in pursuit.

" On this occasion, the 53rd, 93rd, and a body of the
" 4th Punjaub Sikhs distinguished themselves. Two very
" promising young officers lost their lives—Lieutenant
" Mayne, Bengal Horse Artillery, Quarter-Master-Gene-
" ral's Department, and Captain Wheatcroft, Carabineers,
" doing duty with H.M.'s 9th Lancers.

" All the troops behaved very well.

" With the exception of my tents, all my heavy baggage,
" including provisions for fourteen days for my own force
" and that in Lucknow, accompanied me on my march
" across the country to Dilkoosha, covered by a strong
" rear guard, under Lieutenant-Colonel Ewart, of H.M.'s
" 93rd Highlanders. This officer distinguished himself
" very much in this difficult command, his artillery, under
" Captain Blunt, Bengal Horse Artillery, assisted by the
" Royal Artillery, under Colonel Crawford, R.A., having
" been in action for the greater part of the day. The
" rear guard did not close up to the column until late
" next day, the enemy having hung on it until dark on
" the 14th.

"Every description of baggage having been left at
"Dilkoosha, which was occupied by H.M.'s 8th Regi-
"ment, I advanced direct on Sekundur Bagh early on
"the 16th.

"This place is a high-walled enclosure of strong
"masonry, of 120 yards square, and was carefully loop-
"holed all round. It was held very strongly by the
"enemy. Opposite to it was a village, at a distance of
"100 yards, which was also loopholed, and filled with
"men.

"On the head of the column advancing up the lane to
"the left of the Sekundur Bagh, fire was opened on us.
"The infantry of the advance guard was quickly thrown
"into skirmishing order to line a bank to the right.

"The guns were pushed rapidly onwards, viz., Captain
"Blunt's troop, Bengal Horse Artillery, and Captain
"Travers's Royal Artillery heavy field battery.

"The troop passed at a gallop through a cross fire from
"the village and the Sekundur Bagh, and opened fire
"within easy musketry range in a most daring manner.

"As soon as they could be pushed up a stiff bank, two
"18-pounder guns, under Captain Travers, were also
"brought to bear on the building.

"Whilst this was being effected, the leading brigade of
"infantry, under Brigadier the Honourable Adrian Hope,
"coming rapidly into action, caused the loopholed village
"to be abandoned, the whole fire of the brigade being
"then directed on the Sekundur Bagh.

"After a time a large body of the enemy, who were
"holding ground to the left of our advance, were driven by
"parties of the 53rd and 93rd—two of Captain Blunt's
"guns aiding the movement.

"The Highlanders pursued their advantage and seized
"the barracks, and immediately converted it into a mili-
"tary post—the 53rd stretching in a long line of skir-
"mishers in the open plain, and driving the enemy before
"them.

1857. "The attack on the Sekundur Bagh had now been
"proceeding for about an hour and a half, when it was
"determined to take the place by storm through a small
"opening that had been made. This was done in the
"most brilliant manner by the remainder of the High-
"landers, and the 53rd, and 4th Punjab Infantry, supported
"by a battalion of detachments under Major Barnston.

"There never was a bolder feat of arms, and the loss
"inflicted on the enemy, after the entrance of the Sekundur
"Bagh was effected, was immense—more than 2,000 of the
"enemy were afterwards carried out.

"The officers who led these regiments were Lieutenant-
"Colonel Leith Hay, H.M's 93rd Highlanders, Lieutenant-
"Colonel Gordon, H.M's 93rd Highlanders, Captain Wal-
"ton, H.M's 53rd Foot, Lieutenant Paul, 4th Punjab Infantry
"(since dead,, and Major Barnston, H.M's 90th Foot.

"Captain Peel's royal naval siege train then went to
"the front, and advanced towards the Shah Nujeef to-
"gether with the field battery and some mortars—the
"village to the left having been cleared by Brigadier
"Hope and Lieutenant-Colonel Gordon.

"The Shah Nujjeef is a domed mosque, with a garden,
"of which the most had been made by the enemy. The
"wall of the enclosure of the mosque was loopholed with
"great care. The entrance to it had been covered by a
"regular work in masonry, and the top of the building
"was crowned with a parapet. From this, and from the
"defences in the garden, an unceasing fire of musketry
"was kept up from the commencement of the attack.

"This position was defended with great resolution
"against a heavy cannonade of three hours. It was then
"stormed in the boldest manner by the 93rd Highlanders,
"under Brigadier Hope, supported by a battalion of
"detachments under Major Barnston, who was, I regret to
"say, severely wounded—Captain Peel leading up his
"heavy guns, with extraordinary gallantry, within a few
"yards of the building to batter the massive stone walls.

" The withering fire of the Highlanders effectually covered 1857.
" the naval brigade from great loss, but it was an action
" unexampled in war—Captain Peel behaved very much
" as if he had been laying the *Shannon* alongside an
" enemy's frigate.

" This brought the day's operation to a close.

" On the next day communications were opened from the
" left rear of the barracks to the canal, after overcoming
" considerable difficulty. Captain Peel kept up a steady
" cannonade on the building called the Mess-house. This
" building, of considerable size, was defended by a ditch
" of about twelve feet broad, and scarped with masonry,
" and before that a loopholed mud wall. I determined to
" use the guns as much as possible in taking it.

" About 3 p.m., when it was considered that men might
" be sent to storm it without much risk, it was taken by a
" company of the 90th Foot, under Captain Wolseley, and
" a picquet of H.M's 53rd, under Captain Hopkins, sup-
" ported by Major Barnston's battalion of detachments,
" under Captain Guise, H.M's 90th Foot and some of the
" Punjab Infantry, under Lieutenant Powlett. The Mess-
" house was carried immediately with a rush.

" The troops then pressed forward with great vigour,
" and lined the wall separating the Mess-house from the
" Motee Mahul, which consists of a wide enclosure, and
" many buildings. The enemy here made a last stand
" which was overcome after an hour, openings having
" been broken in the wall, through which the troops
" poured with a body of sappers, and accomplished our
" communications with the Residency.

" I had the inexpressible satisfaction shortly afterwards
" of greeting Sir James Outram and Sir Henry Havelock,
" who came out to meet me before the action was at
" an end.

" The relief of the besieged garrison had been ac-
" complished.

" The troops, including all ranks of officers and men,

"had worked strenuously, and persevered boldly in follow-
"ing up the advantages gained in the various attacks.
"Every man in the force had exerted himself to the
"utmost, and now met with his reward.

"It should not be forgotten that these exertions did not
"date merely from the day that I joined the camp, the
"various bodies of which the relieving force was com-
"posed, having made the longest forced marches from
"various directions to enable the Government of India to
"save the garrison of Lucknow—some from Agra, some
"from Allahabad—all had alike undergone the same
"fatigues in pressing forward for the attainment of this
"great object. Of their conduct in the field of battle
"the facts narrated in this despatch are sufficient evi-
"dence, which I will not weaken by any eulogy of mine.

"I desire now to direct the attention of your Lordship
"to the merits of the officers who have served under my
"orders on this occasion.

* * * * * * * * * *

"Major Barnston, H.M.'s 90th Regiment, commanding
"2nd battalion of detachments (dangerously wounded),
"and Captain Guise, H.M.'s 90th Regiment, who succeeded
"Major Barnston in his command."

* * * * * * * * * *

"Head-Quarters, Camp, Alum Bagh,
"25th November, 1857.

"My Lord,

"In continuation of my report of the 18th, I have
"the honour to apprise your Lordship that the left rear of
"my position was finally secured on the night of the 17th
"instant, by the building called 'Bank's House' having
"been seized by a party of the 2nd Punjaub Infantry
"(Sikhs) specially employed for that purpose.

* * * * * * * * * *

"During the next three days I continued to hold the
"whole of the country from the Dilkoosha to the gates of

"the Residency, the left flank having been secured in the
"manner above mentioned, with a view to extricating the
"garrison, without exposing it to the chance of even a
"stray musket-shot.

"From the first all the arrangements have been con-
"ducted towards this end. The whole of the force under
"my immediate command being one outlying picquet,
"every man remained on duty, and was constantly subject
"to annoyance from the enemy's fire; but such was the
"vigilance and intelligence of the force, and so heartily
"did all ranks co-operate to support me, that I was
"enabled to conduct this affair to a happy issue, exactly
"in the manner originally proposed.

"Upon the 20th, fire was opened on the Kaiser Bagh,
"which gradually increased in importance until it assumed
"the character of regular breaching and bombardment.

"The Kaiser Bagh was breached in three places by
"Captain Peel, R.N., and I have been told that the enemy
"suffered much loss within its precincts. Having thus led
"the enemy to believe that immediate assault was con-
"templated, orders were issued for the retreat of the
"garrison, through the lines of our picquets, at midnight
"on the 22nd.

"The ladies and families, the wounded, the treasure, the
"guns it was thought worth while to keep, the ordnance
"store, the grain still possessed by the commissariat of the
"garrison, and the state prisoners had all been previously
"removed.

"Sir James Outram had received orders to burst the
"guns which it was thought undesirable to take away,
"and he was finally directed silently to evacuate the
"Residency of Lucknow at the hour indicated.

"The dispositions to cover their retreat and to resist the
"enemy, should he pursue, were ably carried out by
"Brigadier Hon. Adrian Hope, but I am happy to say the
"enemy was completely deceived, and he did not attempt
"to follow. On the contrary, he began firing on our old

"positions many hours after we had left them. The movement of retreat was admirably executed, and was a perfect lesson in such combinations.

"Each exterior line came, gradually retiring, through its supports, till at length nothing remained but the last line of infantry and guns, with which I was myself to crush the enemy if he had dared to follow up the picquets.

"The only line of retreat lay through a long tortuous lane, and all these precautions were absolutely necessary to ensure the safety of the force.

"It was my endeavour that nothing should be left to chance, and the conduct of the officers in exactly carrying out their instructions was beyond all praise.

"During these operations, from the 16th instant, the remnant of Brigadier Greathed's brigade closed in the rear, and now again formed the rear guard as we retired to Dilkoosha.

"Dilkoosha was reached at 4 a.m. on the 23rd instant by the whole force.

"I moved with General Grant's division to the Alum Bagh on the afternoon of the 24th, leaving Sir James Outram's division in position at Dilkoosha, to prevent molestation of the immense convoy of the women and wounded which it was necessary to transport with us.

"Sir James Outram closed up this day without annoyance from the enemy.

"I have, etc.,
"C. CAMPBELL, General,
"Commander-in-Chief."

The 90th Light Infantry was now attached to General Outram's division, which was to hold a position at the Alum Bagh, with a view to keeping in check the rebel army until such time as it could be finally dispersed, and on the 27th of September, the Commander-in-Chief, with General Grant's division, escorting the wounded, women, and children, retired on Cawnpore, which he reached in 1857. time to save it from the clutches of the Gwalior Contingent.

The force under the command of Sir James Outram was composed of the remains of H.M's. 5th, 78th, 84th, and 90th Regiments, and Brasyer's Sikhs ; a battery of Royal Artillery, under Captain Maude, and one of Bengal Artillery, under Captain Olpherts, several guns of position, a battalion of Military Train acting as cavalry with some of the 42nd Native Irregulars; the whole amounting to 4,442 men.

About 1,500 yards in front of the camp was the Alum Bagh, held as an outpost, on the right front the fort of Jellalabad, some villages to the left, and outposts in villages on the right and left rear ; a strong detachment was also posted at Bunnee Bridge.

Daily attacks were made by the enemy on the different outposts of this extended position, but they refrained from any assault in force until late in December, on the 10th of which month, news was received of the defeat of the Gwalior troops at Cawnpore, and it then became known to the 90th and other regiments, that their baggage, documents, etc., had been seized by the rebels in their partial successes prior to the arrival of the Commander-in-Chief. On the 11th, a convoy was sent to Cawnpore, escorted by 275 men, including 50 of the 90th. It returned with a supply of provisions, etc., in time to take part in an attack made on the rebels on the 22nd, which is thus described :—

Major-General Sir J. Outram, G.C.B., commanding troops in Oude, to the Deputy Adjutant-General of the Army.

" Camp before Lucknow, 23rd December, 1857.
" I have the honour to report, for the information
" of his Excellency the Commander-in-Chief, that I had
" yesterday an affair with the enemy at a village called

1857. "Guilee, three miles hence, situated a little to the right of the road to Dilkoosha.

"I had been informed two days previously by my spies, that the enemy contemplated surrounding my position, in order to cut off supplies, stop all foraging expeditions, and to intercept my communication with Bunnee. With this object, they despatched a force to Guilee, which took up a position between that village and Budroop, which places are about a mile distant from each other.

"On the evening of the 21st instant, I learnt that the rebels had been reinforced, and that their strength amounted to about 4,000 infantry, 400 cavalry, and 8 field guns (since ascertained to have been only 4; all of which were captured).

"Having ascertained that a space of about half-a-mile intervened between their position and the gardens skirting the canal and the Dilkoosha, I moved out at 5 a.m., in the hope of surprising them at daybreak, and intercepting their retreat to the city, with a force detailed in the accompanying divisional order, which I have this day issued, and to which I beg to refer his Excellency for all details, and for the terms in which I express my appreciation of the conduct of the troops on the occasion.

"The main body of the enemy being on the march considerably in advance, retreated to the city by a detour to the left, out of our reach, and concealed by intervening topes of trees, on hearing the attack on their rear; but the loss of four horse-artillery guns, much ammunition, besides elephants and baggage, and some fifty or sixty men slain, will, I think, deter the enemy from again venturing beyond their defensive works, or at any rate from attempting, for some time to come, to carry out their plan of surrounding this camp within a too limited circumference; and I have great hopes that the success of this expedition will be productive of good effect in restoring confidence to the neighbouring inhabitants."

Extracts from the Division Order issued by Major-General Sir James Outram, G.C.B.

" Camp, Alum Bagh, 23rd December, 1857.
" 1.—Major-General Sir James Outram has much pleasure
" in recording in division orders his satisfaction with the
" conduct of the officers and men under the command of
" Brigadier Stisted, engaged yesterday in the skirmish at
" Guilee, in which four guns and twelve waggons filled
" with ammunition were captured.
" 2.—The right column, under the command of Lieu-
" tenant-Colonel Purnell, Her Majesty's 90th Regiment,
" consisting of detachments of the 78th and 90th Regiments
" and of the Ferozepore Regiment of Sikhs, excited his
" admiration by the gallant way in which, with a cheer,
" they dashed at a strong position held by the enemy,
" and from which they were met by a heavy fire. Regard-
" less of the overwhelming numbers, and of the six guns
" reported to be posted there, the suddenness of the attack,
" and the spirited way in which it was executed, resulted
" in the immediate flight of the enemy, with hardly a
" casualty on our side."

* * * * * * * * * *

On the 23rd of December, Captain Wolseley went to Cawnpore with his company, and on arrival, to his deep sorrow, which was shared by every officer and private in the regiment, heard that Major Barnston had died from the effects of the wounds received at the storming of the Shah Nujeef. " By the death of Major Barnston, many " lost their best friend—society, a true gentleman—and the " service, one of its brightest ornaments."

News was now daily received of the preparations being made by the rebels for a grand attack, which, however, seemed to progress but slowly, for it was not until the 11th of January, 1858, that General Outram obtained decided

1858. information of an attack which was to be made on the following morning. In consequence of reports that Mansoob Ali was collecting men and receiving reinforcements from Lucknow, with a view to cut the communications, and hearing also that an escort of 450 infantry, 4 guns, and 80 cavalry had been sent with a convoy to Cawnpore, the rebels, doubtless encouraged by this reduction of the force, advanced against the left front of the camp in masses amounting to about 30,000 men. As soon as their movements were decidedly in advance, the brigades—the right mustering 713, and the left 733 Europeans and 100 men of the regiment of Ferozepore—were formed in front of their lines.

The attack on the left front and flank was covered by a large body of skirmishers, who advanced steadily until they came within range of the guns at the Alum Bagh, and those of the advanced batteries on the left front and centre, the fire from which was so severe, that the enemy gave way.

Major Olpherts drove off a large body of infantry and cavalry which was endeavouring to penetrate to the rear, driving them back towards the city, and doing much execution by the fire of his guns on their masses at 500 yards. The Jellalabad outpost was threatened at the same time that another attack was made on the left front and flank; both attempts were successfully repulsed, notwithstanding the enormous numbers brought to bear against these points. About noon, the enemy advanced upon the Alum Bagh, and again brought forward their guns against the Jellalabad picquet, but, unable to stand against the heavy fire of artillery and musketry brought to bear upon them, they retired, and by 4 o'clock p.m., the whole of the enemy had disappeared and retired to the city, or to their original positions in the gardens and villages in front.

General Outram in his despatch dated the 12th of January, 1858, says:—

" Nothing could exceed the eagerness of the troops to **1858.**
" come in contact with the rebels, nor their disappointment
" at their precipitate flight to the cover of their works the
" moment the guns opened, and our line of skirmishers
" advanced.

" The artillery made excellent practice on the masses of
" the enemy, and in reply to the fire from their batteries,
" which was maintained on our outposts and Alum Bagh
" with little intermission.

" The steadiness of the troops, and the promptitude with
" which my orders were carried out by my officers, gives
" me every assurance that the enemy's attack, if it had
" been as formidable as their forces were numerous, would
" have been as signally defeated."

The signal failure of their attempts to force the Alum Bagh position seemed to have had but little effect upon the rebels, who renewed the contest on the 16th with a similar result.

Major-General Sir J. Outram, G.C.B., commanding in Oude, to General Mansfield, Chief of the Staff of the Army in the East Indies.

" Camp, Alum Bagh, 17th January, 1858.

" I have the honour to report, for the information
" of his Excellency the Commander-in-Chief, that the
" enemy made an attack on my position yesterday, similar
" to that reported in my letter of the 12th instant, except
" that, though they did not show in such general strength,
" their attack was more bold than before. In the morning
" they made a sudden attack on the Jellalabad picquet,
" and were received with a heavy fire, which drove them
" back immediately, leaving on the ground their leader,
" a Hindoo devotee representing Hunnoman, who was
" advancing bravely at their head, and several killed and
" wounded, whom they were unable to carry off. As they

1858. "were seen removing many bodies, their loss must have been severe. Two 9-pounders, under Captain Moir, were sent down to support the picquet, and completed the expulsion of the enemy from the cover in its front.

"Much credit is also due to Lieutenant Wynne, of Her Majesty's 90th, who commanded the Jellalabad picquet.

"Also to Lieutenant-Colonel Smith (90th), commanding the post; and Captain Maude, commanding the artillery at Alum Bagh.

"To Captain Rattray (90th), commanding the infantry; Lieutenant Gully, commanding the battery of No. 1 advanced outpost on the left; and to the officers and men of their posts for their vigilance and alertness in checking and punishing the enemy at every opportunity.

"H. W. NORMAN, Major,
"Deputy Adjutant-General of the Army."

Major-General Sir J. Outram, G.C.B., to the Deputy Adjutant-General of the Army.

"Camp, Alum Bagh, February 17th, 1858.

"The events that have occurred since my last report, dated the 17th ultimo, have been of no great importance. The enemy have received information of the continual passage of troops and stores along the Cawnpore road, and evince a nervous restlessness which betrays itself in constant assemblies of large bodies of men, both cavalry and infantry, and demonstrations of attacks, which a few rounds from our nearest guns have in general put an immediate end to. Although these threatened attacks have cost us but very few casualties, they are excessively harassing to the troops, whom I am obliged constantly to turn out and keep under arms.

"On the 15th instant, a strong body of horsemen, supported by infantry, were observed moving towards our left rear. As a convoy was on the road, and a most

" violent dust storm favourable for them to approach it
" unobserved was blowing, I ordered out two of Captain
" Olpherts' horsed guns and a troop of the Military Train
" to observe their movements. And on a further report of
" the enemy's increasing strength being made, I supported
" them with the rest of the battery, the remainder of the
" Military Train, a detachment of Wale's Horse, and Her
" Majesty's 90th Light Infantry.

" In the meanwhile, a portion of the enemy's cavalry
" and infantry, escorting a person in a palanquin, having
" advanced well into the open, Captain Olpherts' two guns
" and the troop of the Military Train galloped to the front
" and opened on them with grape, killing and wounding
" several and dispersing the remainder. I have since been
" informed that it was the Moulvie himself who headed
" this party, and that he was severely wounded.

" On the 16th instant, the enemy filled their trenches
" with as many men as they could hold, and assembled in
" vast numbers under the topes in their rear, while at the
" same time a body of cavalry and infantry was detached
" to threaten our left flank. During the morning they
" made repeated demonstrations of advancing to attack,
" but their courage apparently as often failed them, and
" they almost immediately returned to their position.
" About 5.30, they suddenly issued in clouds of skirmishers
" from their trenches, advancing for some distance towards
" our batteries posted on the left and centre of our line,
" and after opening a smart fire of musketry on the out-
" posts of the left front village they advanced towards it
" in large bodies. They were repulsed by the picquet,
" consisting of two hundred of the 90th Light Infantry,
" under command of Lieutenant-Colonel Smith, of that
" regiment, after losing a good many men.

* * * * * * * * * * *

" I have, etc.,
" J. OUTRAM, Major-General,
" Commanding 1st Division."

1858.

1858.   The preparations of the Commander-in-Chief were now nearly complete, and the news of his intended advance roused the mutineers once more into action. Determined to crush the little army which had so long held them at bay, they advanced against the camp on the morning of the 21st, their approach being, as usual, heralded by a heavy, but comparatively harmless, fire from every available gun.

"Camp, Alum Bagh, 21st February, 1858.

"I have the honour to report that this morning
" the enemy attacked my position, and with the usual
" result.

" Having filled all their trenches with as many men as
" they would hold, and placed large masses of infantry in
" the topes all along our front in support of them, they
" commenced a simultaneous movement round about our
" flanks, at the same time threatening the whole length of
" our position, and attacking the north-east corner of the
" Alum Bagh, and also the picquet and fort of Jellalabad,
" against which they brought four guns.

" I immediately, on perceiving their intention, rein-
" forced the posts of Alum Bagh and Jellalabad, which
" easily repulsed the attacks made on them and inflicted
" much loss on the assailants, who had advanced, under
" cover of long grass and underwood, within grape shot
" range of both these posts.

" I have the pleasure to state that, as on all former
" occasions, the conduct of the troops engaged, both
" officers and men, was admirable.

" Majors Tinling, 90th Light Infantry, and Nicholson,
" Royal Engineers, commanded respectively at Alum
" Bagh and Jellalabad, and defended their posts with much
" spirit. Major Nicholson particularly praises the energy
" with which Lieutenant Ford, of the Royal Artillery,
" opposed the fire of the enemy's four guns with the only
" gun that could be brought to bear on them.

"Our loss amounted to nine wounded.

"I have, etc.,
"J. OUTRAM, Major-General,
"Commanding 1st Division."

Had the enemy's forces, amounting to above 120,000 men, been led by Chiefs whose knowledge of war was equal to their perseverance, the small body of troops under General Outram would have had but little chance of holding, unaided, the extended position it was forced by circumstances to take up. Again and again the Sepoys came forward, proving by their heavy losses on each occasion that it was not bravery that was wanting to ensure success, retiring, however, each time with a dearly-bought conviction of the immense superiority of those they so frequently endeavoured to overcome. Therefore, when, during the whole of the 25th, they assaulted from all quarters the weak defences so gallantly held, it was probably with a foreboding of further defeat, which was most thoroughly realised.

In the morning, the main body of the rebels advanced against the right, in the direction of the Jellalabad picquet, where they were met by a counter attack led by General Outram, which was completely successful, "and "speedily converted their retreat into a rout," two of their guns being captured by the military train. At 1 p.m., the foe had vanished, but about 4 p.m. they moved out again, on this occasion directing their principal efforts against our left, and showing more determination than they had hitherto done. They repeatedly advanced within grape and musket range, and must have suffered severely, but they kept up their fire during the night, probably with the object of covering the parties engaged in moving their dead. Our loss, in all, amounted to five men killed, and thirty-five officers and men wounded.

General Outram, states that "the conduct of the troops "throughout the entire day and night was excellent at

1858. "every point, and merits the highest commendation." Indeed, so much was he impressed with the behaviour of the 1st Division on this and previous occasions, that, imagining he had not done the troops sufficient credit in his reports, he forwarded to the Commander-in-Chief a despatch, in which he pointed out the many difficulties with which they had had to contend, and the devotion with which they had been overcome.

Major-General Sir J. Outram, G.C.B., Commanding First Division, to the Deputy Adjutant-General of the Army.

" Camp, Alum Bagh,
" 28th February, 1858.

" 1.—My separate despatches have, from time to time, " apprised his Excellency the Commander-in-Chief of the " several affairs we have had with the enemy, and of my " sense of the services which have been rendered on these " occasions by the officers and men under my command.

" 2.—But I am desirous of expressing to his Excellency " in a more connected form, the very deep obligations " under which they have placed me throughout the whole " period we have been associated together—obligations " which I am certain his Excellency and the Government " of India will feel to be theirs also; and I trust it will not " be deemed presumptuous or superfluous if, on the eve of " more active operations, which may probably involve a " severance of the ties that now unite us, I venture to " submit to his Excellency's favourable notice, the admir- " able conduct of a force, which though it has been " strictly enjoined by his Excellency to limit itself to " defensive operations, and though its casualties have been " few, has held an important position, and by its steadi- " ness and bravery, rendered, what I venture to hope will " be regarded as, a very valuable service to the state.

" 3.—Circumstances demanded that, on the relief of

"Lucknow, his Excellency should withdraw his army to other districts, certainly for months, possibly for the greater part of a year. But it was deemed of paramount importance that a military footing should be retained in Oude during his Excellency's absence, however protracted that might prove; and to the division which it has been my honour and good fortune to command was allotted the task of maintaining, for an indefinite period, the honour of the British arms, and of representing the authority of the British Government in this province.

"4.—It was considered advisable, both on political and strategic grounds, that we should remain in close proximity to the Capital. The position assigned us was within a mile-and-a-half of the suburbs of Lucknow. Our advanced posts were within gunshot range of the outworks of a vast city, swarming with hosts of mutinous Sepoys, with Nujeebs—the undisciplined but well-armed soldier of the rebel Government, with many thousand city 'budmashes'—the armed and turbulent scum of a population of 700,000 souls, and with numerous bands of feudal retainers of the Chieftains and great Zemindars of Oude, whose normal state for the last fifty years has been one of warfare.

"5.—The enemy thus ranged against us, and certain to receive large accessions from the Sepoys dispersed in other parts by the victorious forces of his Excellency, had the resources of the entire province at their disposal, while our supplies had to be derived periodically from Cawnpore—a distance of 45 miles; they were known to be well furnished in artillery, and to be strong in cavalry, an arm in which we were ourselves lamentably deficient; and they were animated by every motive of hostility and vengeance that could be supplied to men conscious of having irretrievably committed themselves by the inflammatory exhortations of Hindoo and Mahomedan fanatics of reputed sanctity, and by the scornful taunts

1858. " to which they were subjected by the spirited mother of
" the boy-king.

" 6.—Such was the position assigned to the 1st Division
" on the 27th of November last; and to enable it to
" perform the duties that must devolve on it, his Excel-
" lency increased its strength to 4,422 men of all arms—
" Europeans and Natives.

Corps.	Details.	
	Europeans.	Natives.
Artillery	332	108
Cavalry.		
Military Train	221	—
Volunteer Cavalry	67	—
12th Irregular Cavalry	3	40
Oude Irregular Cavalry	1	37
Infantry.		
5th Fusiliers	526	—
84th Foot	431	—
75th Foot	335	—
78th Highlanders	439	—
90th Light Infantry	591	—
1st Madras Fusiliers	411	—
Ferozepore Regiment	5	295
Madras Sappers	4	110
27th Madras Native Infantry . . .	9	457
Total . .	3,375	1,047
Grand total, Europeans and Natives	4,422	

" But his Excellency is aware that, of this nominal force,
" a detachment, 540 strong (subsequently reinforced by
" 100 Europeans), was ordered to be kept at Bunnee, 12
" miles off, where, though of service in keeping open our
" rear, and preserving the bridge over which the army had
" to return when advancing to the reduction of Lucknow,
" they were obviously of little use to this division in the

"special duty assigned to it of holding the plain of **1858.**
"Alum Bagh.

"7.—Our original force was, therefore, in reality considerably less than 4,000 of all ranks. Of these the forts of Alum Bagh and Jellalabad absorbed about 600 men, brigade and camp duties 450 more; and thus, after deducting sick and wounded, there remained of all arms and ranks (European and native) little more than 2,000 available for action during the absence of the convoys (averaging 450 men) which we had fortnightly to send to Cawnpore. These were on the road for about two-thirds of each month, and of their departure and return the enemy were, of course, as well informed as ourselves.

"8.—The military topography of the locality, and our grazing exigencies, rendered it impossible to reduce the circumference of our camp and its outworks to less than 10 miles and 1,200 yards. And on our small force there devolved the duty not only of defending this large and incompact position against a foe who could have brought large bodies of troops to bear against us simultaneously at several distant points, but of supplying foraging parties, and of being prepared to move out beyond our limits to meet the enemy whenever, by his attempts to cut off our communications, to menace Bunnee or Cawnpore, or by other hostile demonstrations, he might render such an operation necessary.

"9.—Between the 27th of November and the 12th of February, his Excellency had, at great inconvenience to himself, sent us reinforcements, European and native, to the extent of 1,216 men, together with several pieces of ordnance, and on the 12th and 13th February he furnished us with a body of sappers and miners, amounting to about 1,200 men. Of these 700 were undrilled, yet they were most acceptable and may be considered an equivalent for the 75th Regiment, of which we were deprived on the following day. On the 22nd, our strength was further increased by the 1st Bengal Fusiliers,

1858. "numbering 587 of all ranks, and on the 24th we were
"additionally reinforced by two squadrons of dragoons,
"a troop of horse artillery, and Hodson's Horse.

"10.—But, in bringing the claims of this division to his
"Excellency's consideration, I think it but fair to remind
"him that when, on the 22nd December, we moved out to
"surprise a strong force of the enemy, threatening to cut
"off our communications, our reinforcements amounted to
"only 340 details and recruits; that when, on the 12th
"January, we repulsed 30,000 of the enemy our reinforce-
"ments aggregated less than 600; and that the Sikh
"Cavalry, with the accompanying European details, which
"reached us, with the return convoy, on the 16th January,
"only arrived in time to see us again inflict on the foe a
"still heavier repulse.

"11.—Although the successes which the division has
"achieved whenever it has come into contact with the
"enemy were purchased at the very trifling loss of a few
"casualties on our side on each occasion, the troops are, I
"consider, not less deserving of credit for the unflinching
"front with which they have withstood and held in check
"an enemy numbering such odds.

"12.—That their gallant demeanour was the cause of
"our remaining comparatively unmolested I have no
"doubt; for, though we have only had five engagements
"of sufficient importance to be reported to his Excellency,
"the enemy has frequently, and of late with increasing
"frequency, appeared in force, with the evident intention
"of simultaneously assaulting us at different points, but,
"on finding us prepared to receive him, he has deemed it
"prudent to relinquish his designs, and remained satisfied
"with replying from a distance to the accurate fire of our
"artillery, from which it could easily be seen he sustained
"considerable loss.

"13.—These manifestations have not only been more
"numerous, but have been characterised by a greater
"boldness within the last fortnight—a fact susceptible of

"easy explanation. The vast and daily augmenting "accumulation of stores of all kinds lately forwarded to "this camp, in view of the impending operations, have "greatly excited the alarm of the enemy, and it has "become obvious to him that by the dispersion of this "division and the destruction of our material he can alone "hope to avert, or even delay, the terrible retribution that "awaits him at the hands of the Commander-in-Chief.

"14.—It is almost superfluous to say that where men "have behaved so well in the field as the troops of the "1st Division they must have been in a high state of "discipline. Such has, indeed, been the case; and their "admirable conduct must be held all the more praise-"worthy when we consider the extreme exposure and "discomfort the whole of them have had to endure from "the loss of their warm clothing and our deficiency of "tentage, and that most of them had already sustained "much privation during the seven weeks they were "besieged in Lucknow.

"15.—This gratifying state of matters, as his Excellency "will readily imagine, has been in no small degree due to "the kindness, care, and attention which the officers of all "arms and ranks have bestowed on their men, and to the "earnest anxiety with which they have endeavoured at all "times to promote their comfort and provide for their "amusement.

"16.—From first to last, all alike, officers and men, have "acquitted themselves most admirably; and I cannot, "therefore, refrain from this recapitulation of the services "of my comrades—and that before the commencement of "the approaching operations, lest it may be out of my "power to testify hereafter to their devotion, discipline, "and bravery.

"17.—I am certain that neither his Excellency nor their "country will forget the heroic troops whom it has been "my proud privilege to command, and to his Excellency's "kind consideration I now commend them. In doing so

1858. " I must crave permission to depart from the usual for-
" mality of making special recommendations, for I feel
" that to do so would involve injustice to all those officers
" whose names might be omitted. As a matter of course,
" I am under the very deepest obligations to the com-
" mandants of brigades, regiments, detachments, and
" outposts, and to the members of the divisional, brigade,
" and personal staff for the zealous, earnest, and most
" valuable aid they have rendered me on all occasions.
" But, I feel that my obligations are equally great to every
" officer in the force, for every officer has exerted himself as
" if the safety and reputation of the force depended
" exclusively on his individual exertions.

* * * * * * * * * * *

" I have, etc.,
" J. OUTRAM, Major-General,
" Commanding 1st Division."

On the 28th of February, the Commander-in-Chief moved to Buntara, about four miles from Alum Bagh, where Sir Edward Lugard's Division was encamped—the divisions under Sir Hope Grant and Brigadier-General Walpole joining him the next day. The army, which was now hourly drawing nearer and nearer to the doomed city, numbered in all about 26,000 men, and was organized as follows:—

Artillery division, under Major-General Sir Archdale Wilson, K.C.B.—six troops of Horse Artillery, ten companies of Foot Artillery, and the Naval Brigade, under Captain W. Peel, C.B.; two companies of Royal Engineers, Bengal Sappers and Miners, Punjaub Sappers and Miners, and corps of Pioneers.

Cavalry Division, under Brigadier-General Hope Grant— 9th Lancers, 2nd Dragoon Guards, 7th Hussars, 2nd Punjaub Cavalry, detachment 5th Light Cavalry, 2nd Battalion Military Train, Hodson's Horse, etc.

First Infantry Division, under Lieutenant-General Sir

James Outram, G.C.B., consisting of the Alum Bagh garrison.

1858.

Second Infantry Division, under Major-General Lugard—34th Regiment, 53rd Regiment, 42nd Highlanders, 93rd Highlanders, 4th Punjaub Rifles.

Third Infantry Division, under Brigadier-General Walpole—23rd Regiment, 79th Highlanders, 1st Bengal Fusiliers, two battalions Rifle Brigade, 2nd Punjaub Infantry.

Fourth Infantry Division, under Brigadier-General Franks.

Sir Colin Campbell, with the second Infantry Division, and a strong force of artillery and cavalry, advanced on Dilkoosha, on the 2nd of March, "and seized that position " after a skirmish, in which a gun was taken from the " enemy." The Third Infantry Division and the remainder of the Siege Train closed up on the Dilkoosha position during the 3rd and 4th, the right of the line then resting on Bibiapore and the Goomtee, the left being towards the Alum Bagh. Three infantry regiments were now withdrawn from the Alum Bagh, one of them being the 90th Light Infantry, which was brigaded with the 42nd, 93rd, and 4th Punjaub Rifles, under the Hon. Adrian Hope.

General Franks, with his division, came into direct communication with the main body of the army on the 5th, and on the same day the Goomtee was bridged near Bibiapore.

On the 6th, General Outram, with a strong force of all arms, including the Third Infantry Division, crossed to the left bank of the Goomtee, for the purpose of operating against the eastern side of the city, and of closing some of the great avenues of supply leading into the town. "The " plan of attack which had been conceived was now de-" veloped, and Sir J. Outram was directed to push his " advance up the left bank of the Goomtee, while the " troops in the position of Dilkoosha remained at rest till " it should have become apparent that the first line of the

1858. " enemy's works, or the rampart running along the canal
" and abutting on the Goomtee, had been turned.

" The works may be briefly described as follows :—

" The series of courts and buildings called the Kaiser
" Bagh, considered as a citadel by the rebels, was shut in
" by three lines of defence towards the Goomtee, of which
" the line of the canal was the outer one.

" The second line circled round the large buildings
" called the Mess-house and the Motee Mahul, and the first
" or interior one was the principal rampart of the Kaiser
" Bagh.

" The rear of the enclosures of the latter being closed
" in by the city, through which approach would have been
" dangerous to an assailant.

" These lines were flanked by numerous bastions, and
" rested at one end on the Goomtee, and at the other on
" the great buildings of the street called the Huzrut
" Gunge, all of which were strongly fortified, and flanked
" the street in every direction."

Sir James Outram was fruitlessly attacked on the 7th ; and on the 9th, he seized the Chukker Walla Kotee, or Yellow House, the key of the enemy's position ; the Martinière being stormed and taken at the same time by General Hope's brigade. The 90th was left in possession of the place during the night, and the next day three companies were sent out on picquet, the remainder of the regiment, with the 53rd, moving forward in the evening to occupy a building near the Sekundur Bagh, which was taken early on the 11th—the Begum Kotee falling into our hands on the same day.

The enemy's first line of defences was now in our possession, and " thenceforward the chief engineer pushed
" his approach with the greatest judgment through the
" enclosures, by the aid of the Sappers and of heavy guns,
" the troops immediately occupying the ground as he ad-
" vanced, and the mortars being moved from one position

" to another as ground was won on which they could be **1858.**
" placed."

Throughout the 12th and 13th, the Imaumbara and the Kaiser Bagh were heavily bombarded, the Commander-in-Chief having determined to assault the buildings as soon as practicable breaches were made. Accordingly, early on the 14th, the Imaumbara was taken by the 10th Foot and the Ferozepore Regiment of Sikhs, who pressing forward in pursuit of the flying foe entered the Kaizer Bagh by one entrance, while six companies of the 90th rushed in by another.

" Supports were quickly thrown in (the remaining com-
" panies of the 90th and the 53rd Regiments), and all the
" well-known ground of former defence and attack—the
" Mess-house, the Tara Khotie, the Motee Mahul, and
" the Chuttur Munzil—was rapidly occupied by the troops,
" while the engineers devoted their attention to securing
" the position towards the south and west. The day was
" one of long and continued exertion, and every one felt
" that, although much remained to be done before the
" final expulsion of the rebels, the most difficult part of
" the undertaking had been overcome.

" The 15th, was employed in securing what had been
" taken, removing powder, destroying mines, and fixing
" mortars for the further bombardment of the positions
" still held by the enemy on the line of our advance up
" the right bank of the Goomtee, and in the heart of
" the city.

" Brigadier-General Sir J. Hope Grant, K.C.B., was
" sent out with cavalry on one side towards Seetapore to
" intercept fugitives, while Brigadier Campbell, marched
" with like orders in the direction of Sundeela, on a
" similar duty. They returned on the 17th to their former
" positions.

" On the 16th instant, Sir James Outram, with the 5th
" Brigade, under Brigadier Douglas, supported by two
" other regiments, Her Majesty's 20th and the regiment

1858. " of Ferozepore, having crossed over the Goomtee by a
" bridge of casks opposite the Sekundur Bagh, advanced,
" according to order, through the Chuttur Munzil to take
" the Residency.

" During the first movements of this operation, a move-
" ment of the enemy in retreat across the stone bridge
" became apparent.

" Sir James was ordered to press forward, and he was
" able, almost without opposition, not only to take the
" iron bridge in reverse, which was the principal object,
" but also to advance for more than a mile and occupy the
" Muchhee Bhowun and great Imaumbara.

" In short, the city was ours.

" Brigadier-General Walpole's picquets on the left were
" attacked by the retreating enemy, who was, as usual,
" heavily repulsed.

" On the 19th, a combined movement was organised.

" Sir James Outram moved forward directly on the
" Moosa Bagh, the last position of the enemy on the line
" of the Goomtee.

" Sir J. Hope Grant cannonaded the latter from the left
" bank, while Brigadier Campbell moving right round the
" western side from the Alum Bagh, prevented retreat in
" that direction.

" The rout was now complete, and great loss was
" inflicted on the enemy by all these columns.

" On the 21st, Sir Edward Lugard was directed to attack
" a stronghold held by the Moulvie in the heart of the
" city. This he occupied after a sharp contest, and it now
" became possible to invite the return of the inhabitants,
" and to rescue the city from the horrors of this prolonged
" contest."

Lucknow was taken, and by its capture the last hope of the rebels was crushed. There was no longer any point, strong in itself, round which their defeated and disheartened hordes could gather; they were forced to disperse and await in distant parts of the country the further punishment which was so soon to follow. **1858.**

The struggle being virtually at an end, Sir James Outram applied to be relieved of his duties as Chief Commissioner in Oude, and on the 3rd of April, he handed over his office to Mr. Robert Montgomery. Before leaving the army, he wrote to Colonel Purnell as follows :—

"Lucknow, 29th March, 1858.

"My dear Colonel,

"In my various despatches I have endeavoured
"to express my sense of the obligations under which I lie
"to yourself and the glorious 90th, but I was in hopes of
"doing so in still stronger terms in my farewell order to
"the 1st Division. I find, however, that my official order
"must be of too general a nature to admit of specifying
"individual officers or corps. I must be content, therefore,
"to address a few words to you personally, my gallant,
"and, if you will permit me to call you so, 'dear' friend,
"and I avail myself of a temporary lull in the tempest of
"official work which plays around me to say how much I
"am indebted to you for the earnest, hearty, and valuable
"aid you have ever rendered to me, and how much I
"admire you as a soldier, and esteem you as a man.

"Wherever I may be, I shall ever retain the dear, brave
"old 90th in affectionate and admiring remembrance, and
"think with pleasure of the happy and not uneventful
"days I have spent with them on the march, in battle,
"and in quarters—and thinking of them, there must ever
"be present to my mind their noble commander. God
"bless you, my dear Purnell; that you and yours, and in
"'yours, I include every officer and man in the regiment,
"may be ever prosperous and happy in all your under-
"takings, is the sincere and earnest prayer of your and
"their affectionate friend,

"J. OUTRAM."

"COLONEL PURNELL,

"Commanding 90th Regiment."

1858. A division, composed of Olpherts' and D'Aguilar's troops of horse artillery, Gibbon's and Carton's field batteries of artillery, four garrison batteries, one company of engineers, and three companies of Punjaub pioneers, 2nd Dragoon Guards, Lahore Light Horse, 1st or Wales' Regiment of Sikh cavalry, and Hodson's Horse, Her Majesty's 20th, 23rd, 38th, 53rd, 90th, and 97th Regiments, 1st Madras Fusiliers, Head-quarters, 27th Madras Native Infantry, and 5th Punjaubees, was placed under command of Sir Hope Grant, and left to garrison the city, while flying columns were formed from the remainder of the troops and sent out in pursuit of the mutineers.

In April, the 90th left their camp at the Dilkoosha, and moved into quarters in the Zoor-Buksh Palace, near the Kaiser Bagh. While stationed in Lucknow, Captain Wolseley was appointed Deputy Assistant Quarter-Master-General of the division, and on the 11th, he proceeded with a column of 3,000 men against Baree, a village 25 miles distant from Lucknow.

An escort being required at this time, 250 men of the 90th were told off for the duty; to make up this number, five companies had to be sent, the strength of the regiment being so much reduced. About the middle of April, small pox broke out, carrying off Lieutenant Carleton and several of the men.

On the 23rd, the 90th Light Infantry moved out from Lucknow and joined the column, taking the place of the 1st Bengal Fusiliers, which now moved in the direction of Roy Bareilly, where the enemy was supposed to have assembled 10,000 men for the purpose of attacking Oonao. The force marched at once for Nawabgunj, hoping to surprise the enemy, who, however, unfortunately, being warned in time, retired from Oonao on Poorwah, which was reached by General Sir Hope Grant's column on the 1st of May. As it was necessary to destroy a strong fort which had just been evacuated by the rebels, the troops remained at Poorwah for a few days, resuming their march on the 4th, when they moved in the direction of Parthan, where another fort existed, arriving there on the 7th, the necessary demolitions being carried out by the engineers on the following day. 1858.

News of the vicinity of the rebels was continually being brought in, and the direction of the march was almost as frequently being altered. The column was now moving across country, and rapidly approaching the Ganges; on the 10th, the village of Dhoondea Keira was reached, the place was burnt, and the neighbouring fort blown up, the march being resumed on the 11th. Early on the 12th, the force encamped on the same spot to which it had marched a night or two previously, the enemy having doubled and placed himself in rear, imagining in all probability that his ruse would not be noticed. A rest of only a few hours was all that was obtained; for, finding that the foe was but a few miles off, General Grant determined to move after him; accordingly, at 3 p.m., the wearied troops again set out, but soon "the intense heat began to tell upon the " column; men were sun-struck and fell in all directions. " Many of the trees, on each side of the way, had groups " of soldiers lying under them who could not move a step " further." The enemy was found in a strong position near the village of Sirsee, and opened fire about 5 o'clock. General Grant formed his column with the cavalry and horse artillery covering his right flank, and attacked at once with his usual boldness. The rebels, numbering about 16,000 men, almost surrounded the British force, but the cavalry and horse artillery kept the right flank clear, while the rifles, Sikhs, and 90th drove them away from the left flank with such determination that they broke and fled into the jungle. Towards the end of the engagement, an attempt was made to cut off the baggage which had been left in the rear in charge of a small guard, which performed its duty so well that nothing was taken.

The force now returned to Lucknow where it arrived on the 21st, worn out by the severity of service on which it had been engaged. A heavy loss had been inflicted on

1858. the rebels and another victory had been won, but it had cost dear, for out of 3,500 men 32 had died of sun-stroke and 500 were sick, the loss of the 90th being 4 dead and 75 sick.

A few days after his return to Lucknow, Sir Hope Grant heard that Bene Madhoo was threatening the Cawnpore road with a large force, and, being anxious to catch this energetic chief, he went off after him with part of his division on the 25th, leaving a brigade, formed of the 38th, 90th, 3rd Battalion Rifle Brigade, part of the Bays, and some heavy guns, to form a standing camp, under the command of Colonel Purnell of the 90th. On the 27th, Lieutenant Gordon, of the 90th, died from the effects of the climate; he was the 13th officer lost to the regiment since its arrival in India. Their names are:—killed, Lieutenants Graham, Nunn, and Moultrie; Colonel Campbell, C.B., Major Barnston, Brevet-Major Perrin, Captain Denison, and Lieutenant Preston, died from wounds; Ensigns Knox and Chute, Lieutenants Gordon and Carleton, and Assistant-Surgeon Nelson had fallen sick and died.

The brigade remained inactive until the 11th of June when it was broken up, the 3rd battalion Rifle Brigade and the Bays proceeding to join Brigadier Horsford's force.

On the following day, orders were received for 300 men of the 90th to join General Grant at Chinhut, to which place he had moved on hearing of the appearance at Nawabgunj Bara Banki of the forces he had been vainly endeavouring to overtake since the 25th ult.

The remainder of the regiment followed this detachment to Chinhut, where it remained in charge of the camp and baggage. " General Grant's expedition had been a " perfect success. He had found the enemy at Nawabgunj " occupying a good position, and having a nullah in their " front. He had taken them quite unawares and attacked " them at daylight; by 8 o'clock, about 600 of the enemy " were killed and nine guns were taken."

Further exertions were, however, required before the 1858. numerous bands, scattered all over the country, could be dealt with, and but short time was therefore allowed to the troops for rest. On the 20th, news was received that Maun Singh, one of the leaders of the rebellion in its earlier days, now that he had declared in favour of the British rule, was besieged by his former friends at a place called Shahgunj, whither General Grant proceeded on the 21st—the 90th, Bengal Fusiliers, Ferozepore Regiment, a troop of horse artillery, and 400 cavalry, moving up from Chinhut to relieve the division. As usual, the enemy fled at his approach, but were followed up and driven across the Goomtee at Sultanpore by Brigadier Horsford, who remained on the opposite bank until joined by General Grant on the 22nd of August. The greater part of the troops crossed the river on rafts between the 25th and 27th; and on the 29th, the rebels, numbering about 20,000 men, with a powerful artillery, were attacked and driven from the strong position they had taken up.

In the meantime, Colonel Purnell's brigade, though stationary, was not idle. Bands of rebels were constantly threatening the villages and police stations in the neighbourhood, keeping the troops in a state of suspense, and necessitating the despatch of detachments to the aid of the menaced posts. On the 26th of August, 160 men of the 90th, with some cavalry, moved off during the night, in the direction of a village near the fort of Bhetai, hoping to surprise the enemy, but they, unfortunately, had been warned of the approach of the troops in time to enable them to get safely into the fort, which was too strong to be attacked with any hope of success by the mere handful sent against it, which accordingly withdrew. The cold season had now commenced and preparations were being made for taking the field, the isolated brigade at Nawabgunj acting as a containing force. Fortunately, Colonel Purnell, the Brigadier, was capable of turning to advantage the experience he had

1858. gained under the noble Outram in the camp before Lucknow, and, though the forces under his command numbered but 1,500 men, he was able to hold at bay the thousands who filled the jungles by which his position was surrounded.

On the 1st of November, the Queen's Proclamation was read by the Commissioner, crowds of natives coming into the camp from the surrounding villages for the purpose of hearing it. The ceremony passed off quietly, notwithstanding that the mutineers at Bhetai sent in word to say that they were coming also, and would do more than listen. Orders were received on the 7th for a detachment to be sent to a point eleven miles along the Fyzabad road, where it was to halt and endeavour to intercept a body of the enemy, who were expected to pass near there on their way to join the Begum on the other side of the Gogra. The detachment, consisting of the 90th, the Bays, the Sikh Cavalry, and eight guns, set out during the night, and arrived at their destination some hours before daylight, where they waited patiently for the Sepoys, who, however, had received information of their position and never came near them. The party returned to camp the following day thoroughly disgusted by these continued disappointments.

The good effects of the Queen's Proclamation were daily becoming more and more evident. Forts which would have taken time, and would have cost many valuable lives to subdue, were being quietly given up—their garrisons, for the most part, returning to their former avocations. Some few leaders, whose misdeeds forbade them hope for pardon from the English, and others, fewer still, who yet upheld the boy-king of Oude, wandered over the country, their forces becoming weaker hourly as the futility of their resistance became more apparent to their followers. Powerless to do more than keep up a spirit of dissatisfaction in the districts through which they passed, they nevertheless imposed upon the British troops the harassing duty of following them. In the middle of November,

Bene Madhoo, the most active and daring among them, **1858.** contrived to evade the separate columns which had been despatched after him, and moved in the direction of the Begum, who was still at the head of considerable forces. With a view to cut off a part of the retreating army, which was expected to cross the river Goomtee at a ghât near Saftegunj, Colonel Purnell's brigade moved up to that place, thereby closing the approaches to the river. While waiting for Bene Madhoo, who, knowing perfectly well that his retreat was cut off, remained at a respectful distance, news was brought to the Brigadier that the Sepoys in the Bhetai jungle were about to attack his standing camp; he was, therefore, forced to return to Nawabgunj for its protection. Of course, hardly had he quitted Saftegunj, when Bene Madhoo, whose intelligence department was perfect, crossed safely over the river with the majority of those who had been infesting Central Oude.

By the prompt return of Colonel Purnell, the camp was saved, and, to the delight of all in his brigade, the time of wearisome inaction passed in its defence was brought to a close on the 5th Decr., by the arrival at Nawabgunj of the Commander-in-Chief, with eight regiments. Intimidated by his approach with so large a force, the enemy abandoned the large tract of jungle in the vicinity, leaving four hundred men only in the fort of Bhetai.

On the 6th, the division under Lord Clyde (Sir Colin Campbell) moved forward, the 90th accompanying it, to Byram Ghât, near the banks of the Gogra, where it halted for a day. On the 8th, the Commander-in-Chief resumed his march, taking with him all but a brigade, composed of the 23rd, 90th, a regiment of Ghoorkas, and the Lahore Light Horse, which was left, under the command of Colonel Purnell, in charge of the heavy guns and to protect the construction of a bridge of boats for their passage across the river, which at this point is about a mile in breadth. On the opposite bank was a village, held by the rebels, which it would have been necessary to take under very

P

1858. difficult circumstances, had not its defenders, probably hearing of the advance of Lord Clyde, thought it advisable to retire, whereupon the 23rd Regiment was sent across to occupy it. All boats of sufficient size had been destroyed by the enemy, and it was some days before any could be brought from up or down the stream; however, by the 17th, the formation of the bridge was rapidly progressing. Intelligence now came in that Lord Clyde was marching on Baraitch, and that General Grant was advancing towards Toolsipore, and at the same time the 90th received orders to march in a north-west direction, in order to clear the country of any bands of Sepoys lurking about, and to protect the people who were pulling down the various forts.

During the march, which otherwise was without interest, numbers of Sepoys came in to offer submission, and on one occasion forty Sowars, who had belonged to the 11th Irregular Cavalry, gave up their arms, and followed into camp, as prisoners, two of the native horsemen who accompanied the regiment. On Christmas Day, the 90th arrived at Jehangirabad, situated on the banks of a small stream, running into the Chowka Nuddee, where it remained until the 23rd of February, 1860, when it received orders to return to Nawabgunj, arriving there on the 26th.

The war was virtually at an end, and the Great Indian Mutiny, now an event of the past, was to be remembered by those who had crushed it with feelings of honest exultation, and by those who had brought it about with sentiments of the most abject terror. The 90th Light Infantry had had the good fortune to be actively employed throughout the struggle, and the soldiers of all ranks who had the honour to belong to this distinguished corps, were proud in the knowlege that they had not only done their duty, but had done it so well as to merit the approbation of the noble Outram—one of those chiefs whose lives, as well as deeds, are the glory of their country.

Since the arrival of the regiment in India in July, 1857, until February, 1859, the numbers who had died of wounds or sickness or had been killed in action amounted to 14 officers and 312 non-commissioned officers and men.

While quartered at Seetapore, two movable columns were sent out under the command of Majors Guise and Tinling, the whole regiment moving into permanent barracks on their return. Shortly after, it was inspected by Major-General Sir R. Walpole, and on the 21st of December, 1860, by his Excellency General Sir Hugh Rose, G.C.B., Commander-in-Chief.

On the 15th of February, 1861, the 90th marched from Seetapore, under the command of Colonel Smith, C.B., and arrived at Allahabad on the 26th of March. In May, the pleasing news was received that the officers, non-commissioned officers, and privates of the regiment, who had entered Lucknow, or who had been left in the Alum Bagh position on the 25th of September, 1857, with Major-General Sir Henry Havelock, had been granted one year additional service towards good-conduct pay and pension on discharge per Horse Guard's letter dated 11th April, 1861, No. 21 '90th Foot, 29'. The General Order, dated Horse Guards, 24th March, 1862, No. 810 'additional service, Lucknow, 1862', confirming the same, was received in May, 1862.

In the first year of its stay in Allahabad, the regiment lost, by death, the services of Colonel Thomas Smith, C.B. On the 11th of December, 1862, the head-quarters, and Nos. 2 and 3 companies, under Colonel Guise, V.C., who had succeeded to the command, proceeded by rail to Agra, being followed the next day by Nos. 4, 5, 8, and 9 companies, which arrived on the 13th, the remaining companies joining on the 16th. The regiment remained in camp until the morning of the 18th of December, when it commenced its march for Meerut, where it arrived on the 31st.

The regiment marched from Meerut, *en route* to Lahore,

P 2

1863. on the 1st December, 1863, and arrived at Meean Meer on the 6th of January, 1864, at which station it was ordered to remain, the war on the north-west frontier having been
1864. brought to a close. While quartered at Meean Meer, Lieutenant Despréaux J. Boileau died, to the deep sorrow of the whole corps. On the 17th of November, the 90th, under the command of Lieutenant-Colonel Clerk Rattray, marched from Meean Meer and arrived at Peshawur on the 21st of December, 1864, whence, after a sojourn of a
1865. year, it proceeded to Nowshera on the 11th December, 1865.
1866. In January, 1866, the tribes on the Euzofzāie frontier having refused to pay their tribute, a large force of native troops from the Peshawur Brigade, a battery of artillery, and the left wing of the 90th Light Infantry, under Major H. W. Palmer, were ordered to cross the Cabul river at Nowshera, and marching *viâ* Hoti Murdan, to invade the disaffected districts. The whole force, under the command of Brigadier-General H. T. Dunsford, C.B., marched to Hoti Murdan on the 16th of January, and pushing forward on the following day, reached the foot of the Swat hills.

The villages, which were found to be deserted, were at once destroyed, when the malcontents, overawed by the strength of the force opposed to them, sent messengers to the deputy commissioner promising to pay up all arrears. The object of the expedition having been attained, fortunately without bloodshed, the troops returned to their different stations, the 90th detachment arriving at Nowshera on the 26th of January.

1867. The regiment left Nowshera on the 15th of January, 1867, and arrived at Subathoo on the 2nd of March. Soon after its arrival, an outbreak of cholera necessitated the removal of the companies into detached camps, but in spite of the precautions taken to check the disease and the untiring efforts of the medical officers, Doctors Boyd, Thomson, and Turner, fifty men, women, and children fell victims to the scourge.

On the 20th of November, 1868, the 90th marched from 1868. Subathoo, and proceeded to Delhi, whence it moved by train to Jubbulpore, continuing its journey by bullock-cart to Kamptee, where it arrived on the 31st of December.

The regiment consisting of twenty-two officers, and 445 1869. non-commissioned officers, rank and file, marched from Kamptee on the 27th of September, 1869, to Nagpore, whence it proceeded by rail to Bombay, where it embarked on board H.M.S. *Jumna* on the 30th of September, and sailed for England on the following day. On arrival at Suez, the 90th disembarked, and crossed the isthmus by rail, re-embarking on board H.M.S. *Serapis* at Alexandria, in which ship, it arrived at Portsmouth on the 3rd of November, after an absence, on foreign service, of nearly thirteen years.

At Portsmouth, the regiment was transferred to H.M.S. *Orontes*, in which it was joined by twelve officers and 141 non-commissioned officers and men belonging to the dépôt companies from Winchester.

On the 4th, the journey was resumed, and the regiment proceeded to Edinburgh, arriving in Leith roads on the 7th. On the 9th, it disembarked at Granton and marched to Edinburgh Castle, where it was quartered, one company being detached to Greenlaw.

The following was the establishment of the regiment:—

Lieutenant-Colonel	1
Majors	2
Captains	10
Lieutenants	14
Ensigns	6
Staff	5
Sergeants	49
Buglers	20
Corporals	40
Privates	520
Total	667

1870. Two companies were sent, on detachment, to Dundee on the 29th March, 1870, their quarters in the castle being occupied by the dépôt companies of the 32nd Light Infantry.

On the 1st of May, the establishment of the regiment was reduced to the following strength:—

Lieutenant-Colonel	1
Majors	2
Captains	10
Lieutenants	10
Ensigns	4
Staff	3
Sergeants	49
Buglers	20
Corporals	40
Privates	460
Total	599

and on the 1st of September the strength was raised by the addition of two hundred privates—a reduction of one hundred privates being again made in February, 1871.

While quartered in Edinburgh, the regiment acquired a new set of colours, the old set being retained until a fitting place for their reception could be decided on.

1871. On the 6th of June, 1871, the head-quarters of the regiment, consisting of four companies, with the dépôt 32nd Light Infantry attached, moved from Edinburgh to Glasgow, and were quartered in the Gallowgate Barracks; three companies, under command of a field-officer, were detached to Stirling Castle, two companies to Ayr, and one to Dundee.

1872. On the 27th of June, 1872, the old colours of the regiment, which had been carried through the Crimean and Indian Mutiny campaigns, were placed over the monument, erected in the East Church, Perth, by the officers of the 90th, to the memory of their comrades who fell in the Crimean war. The regiment was represented on this occasion by Majors Palmer and Wood, V.C., Captains Rogers, V.C., Rennie, V.C., Perryn, Hackett, Murray, Ward, and Campbell; Lieutenants Lawrence, Hervey, Stevens, Lethbridge, Laye, Sandham, and Eyre; Sergeant-Major Newman; Quarter-Master Sergeant Hitcham; Sergeant Instructor-in-Musketry Wishart; Bugle-Major Bullard; Colour-Sergeants McPartland, Duckworth, Cousins, Kershaw, McKerrow, Peters, Brown, Smith, Woodbridge, and Gill. On arrival at the Perth railway station, the 90th officers were received by Lord-Provost Pullar, and General Campbell, and a guard of honour of the Royal Perthshire Rifles. The officers of the 90th, Lieutenants Lawrence and Eyre, bearing the colours, were escorted from the station, preceded by the band of the militia, by the magistrates and the officers and men of the Royal Perthshire Militia. On arrival at the East Church the colours were placed over the monument, and Major Palmer, turning to the Lord-Provost, said:—

1872.

"My Lord-Provost,—In the name of the Perthshire
"Light Infantry, I beg to tender our hearty thanks to
"you and to the council for your kindness in granting
"a home to the remnants of the old colours of the regi-
"ment. They were presented to the corps in 1852, and
"have been borne by them throughout the Crimean and
"Indian mutiny campaigns, and over the monument
"erected to those who fell during the former war is a
"fitting resting-place for them. We can assure you that
"we all feel this church is most appropriate to receive
"them, because we trust that in future the communi-
"cation which has existed between the regiment and this
"city and county will be thoroughly established. We,
"therefore, confidently and gratefully commit them to
"your charge and care, as well as to the care of the
"minister and kirk-session of the East Church of Perth."

1872. The Lord-Provost, in replying, said :—

"Major Palmer and Officers of the 90th Regiment,—As chief magistrate of this city, I have great pleasure in accepting these flags which you have now erected there. I think they will be cherished with great care by the citizens of Perth for many days to come—probably when we have all passed away. I have no doubt they will be looked upon as relics worth retaining. Some of us very well recollect of the early days of Lord Lynedoch, when he first took the field at the head of this regiment, and most of us have read, in our early days, or perhaps a little afterwards, of the gallant deeds of that corps. I can assure you that there is no regiment of the line that stands so high in the estimation of the citizens of Perth and county as the 90th Regiment does. We cannot forget the gallant services of Lord Lynedoch, as well as the officers and soldiers who followed him. We know well enough it was difficult to obtain soldiers at that time. When we look on the Peninsular war, and the gallant deeds done at that time, we cannot but remember Lord Lynedoch and his men with gratitude, for they did a great work for their country in that day. I have great pleasure in accepting these relics on behalf of the citizens of Perth."

The scroll on the monument is engraved with the following words :—

"In memory of their Comrades, who fell during the Crimean war, 1854-1855, and as a tribute to their gallantry this monument is erected by the Officers of H.M. 90th Light Infantry, Perthshire Volunteers, A.D. MDCCCLVII."

On the lower part of the monument is the following inscription :—

" Captain H. Payne Crawford, died of fever at Scutari, 1872.
" 24th February, 1855, aged 31 years; Captain Herbert
" M. Vaughan, died in camp before Sevastopol,
" 12th September, 1855; Captain Henry Preston, aged 28
" years; Lieutenant Arthur D. Swift, aged 21 years;
" Lieutenant Hugh F. Wilmer, aged 18 years—who were
" killed in the British attack on the Redan, 8th September,
" 1855; also two hundred and seventy-four non-com-
" missioned officers and privates, who fell in the gallant
" discharge of their duty to their Queen and country."

On two brass plates affixed to the base of the monument the subjoined inscription has been engraved:—

" The colours, emblazoned with the honours gained by
" the 90th Perthshire Light Infantry, at Mandora, in
" Egypt, at Martinique, Guadaloupe, Sevastopol, and
" Lucknow, were presented to the Regiment on the 6th
" August, 1852, carried through the Crimean and Indian
" Mutiny campaigns, and their remnants finally here
" deposited, 27th June, 1872."

The 90th left Glasgow on the 22nd of July, and proceeding to Greenock, embarked on board H.M.S. *Orontes* for passage to Portsmouth, where it arrived on the 26th. It disembarked on the following morning and moved by rail to Aldershot, where it was encamped at Gun Hill, previous to taking part in the autumn manœuvres.

In accordance with General-Order 32, 1873, the 90th 1873. was linked with the 73rd (Perthshire) Regiment, and attached to the 60th sub-district from the 1st April, 1873, their brigade dépôt being stationed at Hamilton in the county of Lanark.

On the 5th of April, permission was granted for the regiment to wear the arms of the city of Perth on the appointments.

The 90th, on the 6th of September, moved by rail to Dover where it was quartered in the South front barracks.

1873. The continued disturbances on the West coast of Africa having ended in the open hostility of the king of Ashanti, the most powerful of the native potentates in that part of Africa, it was determined to send out a force to co-operate with the friendly tribes, and crush the power of their turbulent neighbour. The command of the expedition was given to Colonel Sir Garnet Wolseley, K.C.M.G., h.p., late 90th, who accepted the proffered services of Lieutenant-Colonel Wood, V.C., and Lieutenant Eyre, both of the 90th, and left England with them and other officers, in the s.s. *Ambriz*, on the 12th of September. On arrival at Cape Coast, Lieutenant-Colonel Wood was ordered to raise a regiment of friendly natives, of which Lieutenant Eyre was appointed adjutant. The services rendered by this corps were most valuable and were fully appreciated by Sir Garnet Wolseley.

In October, the Ashantis, to the number of about 40,000, were hovering near the coast, and greatly impeded the raising of recruits and carriers. Under these circumstances Sir Garnet Wolseley determined to attack and destroy the villages of Essaman, Amquana, and Ampenee, and after making his arrangements with the secrecy necessary to prevent the flight of the enemy, on the 14th, started from Elmina, with about 180 marines, 330 natives, one 7-pounder gun, and one rocket-tube and rockets—the whole force being under the command of Lieutenant-Colonel Wood, 90th Light Infantry. Essaman was taken, after a hard fight, and destroyed; the other villages were found deserted, and were set on fire.

In this action Lieutenant Eyre's determined and intrepid bearing was the subject of universal remark. In order to cover the flank of the column, which moved on the narrow path, he penetrated through dense bush with a few West Indian soldiers, and continued his arduous dangerous task till he dropt down, overcome with fatigue.

Sir Garnet Wolseley, in his despatch, dated Octr. 15th, 1873, referring to the action at Essaman, states:—

"I have to add that Lieutenant-Colonel Wood, V.C., **1873**. whose despatch I enclose, carried out the operations intrusted to him to my entire satisfaction.

"(Signed) G. J. WOLSELEY."

The reply to the above-mentioned despatch from the Secretary of State for War was as follows:—

"War Office, Pall Mall, Nov. 18th, 1873.
"Sir,
"I have received your despatch, No. 42/73 M.S., dated Cape Coast Castle, October 15th, 1873, together with the enclosed report of Lieutenant-Colonel Wood, V.C., giving a detailed account of the action of the 14th October. . . . . . . I have had the honour of laying this despatch and the enclosure before the Queen, and have received Her Majesty's commands to convey to you, and to Lieutenant-Colonel Wood, who, under your general direction, was in immediate command, Her Majesty's approbation of the able and gallant conduct of the officers, non-commissioned officers, and men, on that occasion. I observe, with great satisfaction, the terms in which you speak of the services rendered by Lieutenant-Colonel Wood, V.C.

"(Signed) ED. CARDWELL."

On the 14th of January, 1874, Colonel Wood's regiment **1874**. crossed the river Prah, and on the 19th, was brigaded with Russell's regiment and part of the 2nd West India Regiment, under the command of Colonel McLeod.

On the 20th, the remainder of the army crossed the river, and advanced through the thickly wooded country in the direction of Amoaful, where, on the 31st, was fought the severest action of the campaign. In this battle Lieutenant Colonel Wood commanded the right column, and was heavily engaged with the enemy when he fell, struck by a slug on the chest above the heart.

1874. *From Major-General Sir Garnet Wolseley to the Secretary of State for War:—*

"Head-Quarters, Amoaful,
"February 1st, 1874.

"Sir,

". . . . . . My whole force divided into four columns. . . . . . Right column, Lieutenant-Colonel H. E. Wood, V.C., Naval Brigade—left wing, Wood's regiment, Rait's artillery, two rocket detachments, Royal Engineer's detachment. . . . . . Up to 1.30 p.m., the enemy kept up a very heavy fire on Lieutenant-Colonel Wood's column, whose right was extended into the bush east of Egginassie. . . . . . The officers commanding the columns performed their difficult task most excellently, and were efficiently aided by their staff. Lieutenant-Colonel Wood, V.C., was wounded while at the head of his troops.

"(Signed)   G. J. WOLSELEY."

On the 2nd of February, the whole force moved forward, and reached the river Ordah on the following day. The enemy attempted to hold the stream, but the advanced guard pressing steadily forward, they retired and took up a strong position on the thickly wooded rising on the north side of the river. A bridge was quickly thrown across the river; and on the 4th, the army moved forward, the advanced guard being commanded by Lieutenant-Colonel Wood, who had rejoined the previous day.

The moment the troops began to advance, the enemy opened fire on the head of the column, which pressed forward in the direction of Ordahsu. The fighting was very severe, and the native levies at one time held back, but animated by the gallant example set them by their officers, they struggled forward and gained the village, at the entrance to which Lieutenant Eyre fell mortally wounded

Captain Brackenbury, R.A., who was present on this **1874.** occasion, referring to the action in his narrative of the campaign, says :—

"This battle, too, had not been without loss, we had
"lost young Eyre, the Adjutant of Wood's regiment, as
"manly and true a young soldier as ever drew breath.
"The first day at Essaman had shown us all how strong
"he was to bear—how valiant he was to act. Always
"setting an example to his men of perfect apparent
"ignorance of the enemy's fire; he lost his life while
"thus facing the enemy without cover, at the very muzzles
"of their guns. Then and there we buried him, and the
"enemy's guns and our own joined in unison in firing the
"volleys over his grave."

Ordahsu once taken, the column pushed on, and fought its way through the village of Karsi, where the enemy made their last stand, and from which they were driven with heavy loss, to Coomassie, the capital of the Ashanti territory. Early on the 5th, the wounded were sent off, escorted by Wood's and Russell's regiments, and were followed on the next day by the remainder of the army. Before leaving, Sir Garnet Wolseley wrote his despatch to the Secretary of State for War, announcing the capture of Coomassie, from which the following is an extract :—

"Coomassie, February 5th, 1874.

"Sir,

" . . . . . The two native regiments raised
"on the coast were commanded throughout the war by
"Brevet Lieutenant-Colonel Wood, V.C., 90th Light In-
"fantry, and by Brevet-Major B. C. Russell, 13th Hussars.
"Both these officers have upon many occasions been
"placed in very difficult positions, requiring the exercise
"of high military qualities, and have invariably carried
"out their very arduous and trying duties most efficiently.
"(Signed)   G. J. WOLSELEY,
                      "Major-General."

1874. The many signal defeats he had sustained and the loss of his capital induced the King of Ashanti to come to terms, and the war being now at an end, Colonel Wood's regiment marched to Elmina, and was there disbanded, its late chief returning to England on the 4th of March.

For his services in the campaign Lieutenant-Colonel Wood was appointed a Companion of the Bath, and was promoted full Colonel by Brevet.

On the 1st July, 1874, the 90th Light Infantry, under the command of Lieutenant-Colonel Palmer, proceeded from Dover, by rail, to Aldershot, to take part in the second portion of the summer drills of that year. After a month of camp life, varied by the vicissitudes of a mimic war, the regiment returned to Dover, and was quartered in the Citadel barracks, whence, on the 15th of July, 1875, it proceeded on board H.M.S. *Simoom*, to Kingstown, Ireland, *en route* to Dublin, where, on arrival, it was quartered in the Richmond barracks. In 1877, the regiment moved to Limerick, whence, after a short stay it was ordered to proceed to Aldershot, where, on arrival, it was brigaded with the Guards, then stationed at the camp for the summer exercises.

1878. In January, 1878, the 90th stood first on the list of regiments for foreign service, and when it was found necessary to send troops to the Cape colonies to suppress the insurrection of the Caffres, the regiment received sudden orders to proceed to South Africa.

On the 10th, the first portion of the regiment left Southampton, in the Union Company's s.s. *Danube*, under the command of Major Rogers, V.C., accompanied by the following officers: Captains Hamilton, Wilson, and Lawrence; Lieutenants Hutchinson and Rawlins, and Dr. C. D. Heather. The head-quarters left Southampton on the 12th, in the s.s. *Nubian*, under the command of Lieutenant-Colonel Palmer, with whom went Major Cherry, Brevet-Major Hackett, Captain Stevens, Lieutenants Sandham, Maude, Smith, Saltmarshe, Campbell, Heathcote, and

Lomax; Sub-Lieutenants Gordon, Bright, and Hotham; **1878.**
Lieutenant and Adjutant Laye, Surgeon-Major Alcock,
and Quarter-Master Newman.

At this time Major and Brevet-Colonel Evelyn Wood,
V.C., C.B., held the appointment of Assistant-Quarter-
Master General at Aldershot. Soon after the departure
of his regiment he resigned his position on the Staff, and
on the 31st of January left England, in company with
Lieut.-General the Hon. F. A. Thesiger, C.B., for the seat
of war.

The companies under the command of Major Rogers,
V.C., landed at Durban, Natal, on the 9th of February.
The head-quarters arrived at East London on the same
day, having left Captain Lethbridge's company with the
band and colours, the whole under the command of Major
Cherry, at Cape Town, where the transports were detained
for a few days.

On landing at East London, Colonel Palmer, with four
companies, marched to King William's Town, where the
Governor, Sir Bartle Frere, and the Commander-in-Chief,
Lieutenant-General Sir Arthur Cunnyngham, were then
staying.

While at King William's Town the 90th was inspected
by General Cunnyngham.

On the 18th of February, Colonel Palmer was directed
to proceed to Fort Beaufort, and assume the command of
that district and of an expeditionary force, about to be
organized, to operate against Tini Macomo, a chief then
in open rebellion.

Colonel Palmer, accompanied by Captain Laye, his Staff
Officer, arrived at Fort Beaufort on the 21st, when he was
informed by W. B. Chalmers, Esq., the Special Commissioner, that his endeavours to come to a friendly under-
standing with the rebels had failed, and that they were
then in considerable force in the well-known fastnesses of
the Water and Schelm Kloofs.

Telegrams were sent to King William's Town reporting

1878. the state of affairs, resulting in the speedy despatch of a small column consisting of the head-quarters 90th Light Infantry, one company 1st batt. 24th Regiment, and four guns. At the same time, Colonel Palmer, in accordance with his instructions, called out the Burghers and Volunteers, and raised a few corps of Fingoes and Hottentots.

On the 2nd of March, Captain Lethbridge's company rejoined the head-quarters, accompanied by Major Cherry, who took over command of the regiment from Brevet-Major Hackett.

Lieutenant-General Thesiger and the officers accompanying him landed at Cape Town on the 25th of February, when the General assumed command of the forces at the Cape.

Active operations were commenced on the 3rd of March. A small force, commanded by Captain Stevens, 90th Light Infantry, consisting of 100 men of the 90th and two 7-pounder guns, was sent to occupy a position at the head of the Schelm Kloof. On the 4th, Colonel Palmer, with a column composed of 350 Europeans, 70 native police, and 200 Fingoes, left Fort Beaufort at 9 p.m., and making a night march reached Tini Macomo's village at Blinkwater at daylight on the 5th, and surrounded the huts.

Tini Macomo was absent, but many prisoners were taken, the cattle were seized, and the village was destroyed.

Heavy rains delayed the transport, causing a halt on the 6th; but on the 7th, an attack on the Schelm Kloof was made, Colonel Palmer's forces thoroughly working the lower Schelm Kloof.

On the 8th and 9th, the Upper Schelm Kloofs were searched and the rebels driven out, several being killed; 250 head of cattle were taken and sent into Fort Beaufort. Five posts were established to prevent the enemy from returning, the remainder of the troops returning to Fort Fordyce

Mr. Chalmers' efforts to induce the rebels, who still held out in the Water Kloof, to submit having again proved unavailing, an ultimatum was sent to them on the 14th, **1878.** and on the 16th, the troops once more took the field.

A company of the 90th Light Infantry occupied Batho's farm (a strong position at the foot of the Iron Mountains) with a force of 220 Burghers placed along the line of Meyer's Kloof on the south-west, and two guns on the eastern ridges, while the two most important passes were occupied by native police. The main body commanded by Colonel Palmer entered the pass from the south-west, with police in advance, flanked by Fingoes in the bush on either side, and followed by the mounted Burghers. The Fingo levy and native police held the pass until the artillery, two guns, and two companies of the 90th Light Infantry had passed through.

On arriving at the other side of the pass, it was found that the Burghers were engaged; they were reinforced by the Fingo levy, supported by 100 men of the 90th. As the Kaffirs retired, they came under the fire of the guns on the eastern ridges, and are supposed to have suffered severely. An advance was made, and the Kloofs and bush of the Iron Mountain were swept clear of the enemy. Their cattle and large stores of provisions and blankets, found in the caves of the various Kloofs, were brought away by the troops.

The success attending these operations had a most salutary effect on all the native inhabitants of the Stockenstrom district, who now gave up their arms and assumed a loyal and submissive tone.

Extract from a Despatch to the Secretary of State for War.

"I have visited the Beaufort district to see the "Waterkloof country, where Colonel Palmer has lately "carried out his operations, in order to judge for myself "how far it was now necessary to retain the Imperial "forces in that part of the colony. As I found the district "quiet, and the European farmers returning to their farms,

1878. "and no lack of Colonial forces there, to be called out if
"necessary, I had no hesitation in urging on Government
"the necessity of concentrating the five companies of the
"90th Light Infantry to the East, where they will be of
"very material assistance in the coming operations
"against Siyolo and Sandili, and will likewise be at
"hand, and ready to move to Natal and Transvaal if
"necessary.

"Active operations in the district having now ceased, I
"have the honour to forward a brief account of the opera-
"tions which Colonel Palmer, 90th Light Infantry, carried
"out in that difficult country. These had a successful
"issue, and reflect credit on him and the forces under his
"command.

"I have appointed this officer to the command of the
"Beaufort district, as his local knowledge of the country,
"and possibility of trouble again arising there, appeared
"to make such an arrangement desirable. The appoint-
"ment has given great satisfaction to the inhabitants of
"Beaufort district.

     "Signed F. A. THESIGER,
      "Lieutenant-General Commanding."

 "General Order.
      "King William's Town,
       "April 28th, 1878.

   "Active operations in the Fort Beaufort district
"being brought to a close by the rebels having been com-
"pletely driven out of the difficult country of which Fort
"Fordyce is the centre, the Lieutenant-General command-
"ing the forces in South Africa begs to offer his best
"thanks to Lieut.-Colonel Palmer, 90th Light Infantry,
"who directed those operations, and to all ranks of the
"Imperial and Colonial forces who took part in the same.

  * * * * * * * * * *

 "The Lieut.-General has already forwarded to the
"Secretary of State for War, an account of the military

"operations carried out in the Fort Beaufort district, as 1878. "furnished to him by Col. Palmer; and he feels assured "that the good service performed by Her Majesty's and "the Colonial troops, and the cordial and satisfactory "manner in which both worked together towards the "common end, will be duly appreciated by the Imperial "Government.

"By command, W. BELLAIRS, Col.
"Depty. Adjt.-Gen."

Sandili, one of the rebel chiefs, with a large number of followers having taken to the mountainous and thickly wooded country known as the Pirie Bush, General Thesiger, leaving Colonel Palmer in command at Fort Beaufort, went with all the available forces in his pursuit.

The bush held by the enemy was entered on the 18th of March by several small columns, the Caffres retiring with their cattle before them. On the 28th, another successful move was made, the enemy again retreating after a few shots had been exchanged.

On the 5th of April, about 700 Fingoes having arrived from the Transkei, the General organised a drive through the whole of the bush, from Mount Kempo on the north, to Haynes Mill on the south. This operation was unsuccessful, in so far that a vast quantity of ammunition was expended by the Transkei Contingent with very little result.

Siyolo, a disaffected chief, on this day threw off the mask, and crossing the Debe flats with about 500 men, took up a position near the Intaba Doda Mountain. They were attacked soon after their arrival, and driven out, losing several men from the well-directed fire of a party of the 90th, and Frontier Light Horse.

Skirmishes took place on the 7th and 9th, after which, the rebels remained unmolested for about three weeks, owing to the withdrawal of most of the volunteers. This cessation of hostilities naturally raised the spirits of the

1878. enemy, who at length descending from the mountains, burnt all the Fingo huts within two miles of the bush.

In the meantime, the five companies of the 90th being no longer required in the Fort Beaufort district, were ordered eastward, and more Fingoes and volunteers having been gathered together by the 29th, all was ready for the advance. The force was divided into two columns, one the eastern, commanded by General Thesiger, the western by Colonel Wood.

Siyolo, on his side, as was afterwards learnt from prisoners, undertook to hold the Makabalele ridge, and capture the guns if they were taken up the bush path leading up the ridge on to the Tutu plateau, while Tini Macomo was to hold the Tutu Bush. At daylight on the 30th of April, the General having gained the eastern crest of the Tamoika ravine, commenced shelling the rebel camp. Tini Macomo's men at once dispersed into the Tutu ravine, while Siyolo's men hastened westwards to support their picquets already ambushed on the Makabalele ridge. This feature of ground with precipitous sides, and covered with bush, but not of too dense a nature, was about 150 yards broad, and the forest on it extended for about half-a-mile, which the attacking force had to traverse before it could reach the open plateau. The column under Colonel Wood had already traversed about one-fourth of the distance when the Kaffirs formed across the bush path, and till now concealed by a turn of the path, charged the advanced guard, formed by Captain Stevens' company of the 90th Light Infantry. His men were immediately hotly engaged, and on the Captain being shot through the face, the rebels cheering charged, to be at once repulsed. Lieutenant Saltmarshe now took Captain Stevens' place, and within five minutes he was killed. The men, however, pressed on under Colour-Sergeant Smith, and by the time Major Cherry came up and took command of the leading company, which had in ten minutes **lost** two officers and eight or ten men killed and wounded, the enemy had given way. They, however, continued to hang about the path until Captain Smith's two guns opening fire upon them with grape, caused them to fall back and disperse. The open plateau was then gained without further loss, and Captain Stevens' company, now under Lieutenant Lomax, the adjutant, ran into the bush after some rebels and drove them away.

The column then passed on to the western bank of the Zamoika Ravine, where Colonel Wood was joined by Von Linsingen and Major Buller, commanding the Frontier Light Horse. Now having joined the western force, Buller's and Von Linsingen's men, with the 90th, formed line and moved down the Tutu ravine, in which they met two companies of the 90th, and a body of Fingoes advancing towards them. The rebels were thus surrounded, and many were slain. About 500 women eventually emerged from the thick bush, and it speaks well for the steadiness of the men that none were shot, for they frequently interposed between our troops and the rebels.

Many cattle were taken, and the rebels were completely dispersed without loss on our side, except that suffered by the 90th Regiment on the ridge, where, only, the enemy fought with determination.

From that day until the 8th of May, the rebels made but a passive resistance. On the 8th, however, an attack was made on the rebel camp, which was found deserted. In the subsequent movements, the Frontier Light Horse was fired upon while moving down a rocky path by a body of Kaffirs who had taken up a very strong position, from which they were driven, with some loss on both sides.

The death of Sandili at the end of May, and the surrender of several minor chiefs, induced the Kaffirs to give in, and brought the war in this part of the colony to a close. The Commander-in-Chief was thus enabled to turn his attention to the Transvaal and Zululand, where rumours of war were daily becoming louder and louder.

1878. *From Colonel Evelyn Wood, commanding troops on the Buffalo range, Kaffraria, to the Assistant Military Secretary.*

"Haynes Mill, June 18th, 1878.

" Sir,

" 1. In reply to your letter of the 15th instant, I
" have the honour to submit the names of the undermen-
" tioned officers :—

* * * * * * * * * * *

" Imperial troops.

* * * * * * * * * * *

"Lieutenant Rawlins, 90th L. I.
"Captain Stevens,   ,,
"Major Cherry,   ,,
"Bt.-Major Hackett,   ,,

* * * * * * * * * *

" 7. Lieutenant Rawlins, 90th Light Infantry, has com-
" manded the mounted men of the regiment throughout.
" He has been very often under fire, and leads his men
" boldly and skilfully, while he pays great attention to
" men and horses in camp and bivouac. I believe His
" Excellency saw the rebels turned back in the Jaiworka
" valley by the small party of mounted men under this
" officer on the 6th April.

" 8. When at Fort Beaufort I mentioned to the Lieu-
" tenant-General I was anxious to get Captain Stevens'
" company up to the front before we attacked the rebels.
" He is an excellent officer, and for this reason I acceded
" to his request to lead the advance up the Makabalele
" ridge on the 30th April. As I reported that day, he and
" the late Lieutenant Saltmarshe offered a fine example
" to all. I attribute the success of the front company in
" checking the rebel's advance to the gallant bearing of
" these officers.

" I trust I may be excused in adding that when Captain
" Stevens was wounded, within six paces of a large number
" of Kaffirs, Sergeant Jeffs and Private Graham, of the 90th

"Light Infantry, stepped coolly forward and removed their
"officer, under a heavy fire, and when Lieutenant Salt-
"marshe, who had taken his place, shortly afterwards
"was killed, Colour-Sergeant Smith, in my presence, en-
"couraged the men and caused them to advance.

"9. Major Cherry, 90th Light Infantry, who has com-
"manded the regiment since it came from Beaufort, has
"given me every assistance, he led the front company up
"through the last bit of bush on the 30th April, when its
"two officers were shot down.

"10. Brevet-Major Hackett held a detached command
"in the attack on the 30th April, in all of about 1200
"men, and later also in the Pirie Bush, and in every case
"his movements were conducted with decision and skill.

* * * * * * * * *

"I have etc.,
"EVELYN WOOD,
"Colonel."

To the Assistant Military Secretary, King William's Town.

"Fort Beaufort, June 19th, 1878.
"Sir,
"In reply to your letter of the 15th inst., I have
"the honour to solicit attention to my report of the 1st
"April last, addressed to the Deputy Adjutant-General,
"in which I brought to notice the names of various com-
"manding officers, heads of departments, and others,
"whose zealous co-operation had been of such material
"assistance to me. I would, however, again wish to avail
"myself of this opportunity to repeat my high opinion of
"Captain Laye, 90th Light Infantry, my staff officer,
"whose firmness, combined with tact, manifested his fitness
"for that class of appointment. I would beg to add the
"name of Quarter-Master Newman, 90th Light Infantry,
"who acted as Commissariat Officer during those four
"weeks' field operations, and I think the Commissary-

1878. "General will endorse my statement as to the satisfactory
"results arising from his zeal and accuracy."

* * * * * * * * * *

"I have, etc.,
"H. W. PALMER,
"Lt.-Col. 90th Light Infantry."

*Extract from a Despatch from Lieutenant-General the Hon.
F. A. Thesiger, C.B. to the Secretary of State for War.*

"26th June, 1878.

"1. The Kaffir war of 1877-78 being virtually brought
"to a close, it becomes my pleasing duty to bring to your
"notice the excellent service which has been performed
"by the troops under my command, both Imperial and
"Colonial, and to lay before you the names of those
"officers who have prominently distinguished themselves
"during the three months that I have been conducting
"active operations in the field.

"2. I trust that these services may receive such recog-
"nition as Her Majesty may be graciously pleased to
"bestow.

* * * * * * * * * *

"13. When I arrived at King William's Town on the
"4th March, 1878, operations in the Kroome range, under
"Colonel Palmer, 90th Light Infantry (which were soon
"after brought to a successful close), had just commenced,
"and a Colonial force, under Commandant General
"Griffith, C.M.G., was operating on the Thomas river
"against the Gaika rebels, under their chief Sandili, who,
"after the battle of Quintana, had returned to their own
"country, commonly known as the Gaika location.

* * * * * * * * * *

"62. Colonel Evelyn Wood, V.C., C.B., 90th Light
"Infantry, on special service in South Africa, has had
"command of a separate column of Imperial and Colonial
"troops from the time that I assumed the direction of
"military operations in the field.

"I cannot speak too highly of the good service rendered 1878.
"by this officer, he has exercised his command with marked
"ability and great tact.

"I am of opinion that his indefatigable exertions and
"personal influence have been mainly instrumental in
"bringing the war to a speedy close.

* * * * * * * * * * *

"64. Colonel Palmer, immediately on landing in South
"Africa, was entrusted with the responsible task of direc-
"ing the operations of a mixed Imperial and Colonial
"force against the rebels, under Tini Macomo, who had
"taken up their position in the Kroome range of
"mountains, of which the Schelm Kloof and Water
"Kloof form the most prominent features. The operations
"were entirely successful.

"On the departure of the five companies, 90th Light
"Infantry, from the Fort Beaufort district, Colonel Pal-
"mer, 90th Light Infantry, at the special request of the
"Civil Commissioner, was left in military charge.

* * * * * * * * * * *

"67. Major Cherry has commanded the head-quarters
"and five companies, 90th Light Infantry, from the date
"of their landing in South Africa, and is mentioned favour-
"ably by Colonel Palmer and Colonel Evelyn Wood, under
"whom he was serving.

"68. Colonel E. Wood has brought to notice the
"names of several officers, but I would particularly wish
"to draw attention to that of Captain Stevens who was
"dangerously wounded on the 30th April, 78."

* * * * * * * * * * *

At the end of June, Colonel Palmer received a communication from the Lieutenant-General Commanding-in-Chief,
stating that as the war was over in that part of the
Colony, and the head-quarters of the 90th Light Infantry
were about to undertake a march of several weeks' dura-

1878. tion to Natal, he could not ask him to accompany his regiment as he had already considerably exceeded his five years' tenure of command, and was, therefore, at liberty to proceed to England.

The following General Order was published on this occasion :—

" G.O.

" Military operations in the Fort Beaufort dis-
" trict having ended, Colonel Palmer, will, on the receipt
" of this order, hand over charge of the Colonial Forces
" under his command to the Civil Commissioner, and his
" duties in that district will cease.

" The Lieutenant-General Commanding begs to thank
" Colonel Palmer, and those who have co-operated with
" him, civil and military, for the satisfactory manner in
" which the military operations have been conducted and
" brought to a close.

" By Command,
" W. BELLAIRS,
" D.A.G."

On receipt of this order, Colonel Palmer bade farewell to the regiment, with which he had served since 1865, and soon after returned to England; Major and Brevet-Colonel Evelyn Wood, V.C., C.B., succeeded to the command of the 90th Light Infantry.

On the 26th June, 1878, a column composed of the headquarter companies of the 90th, a battery of Royal Artillery, and the Frontier Light Horse, the whole under the command of Colonel Evelyn Wood, marched from King William's Town for Natal.

The column was detained at Kokstadt for some weeks, owing to the unsettled state of Pondoland. Affairs were at length amicably settled, and the troops proceeded to Pieter Maritzburg, where they were encamped until the 19th of October.

Soon after their arrival at Durban, the three companies, **1878.** under command of Major Rogers, V.C., had marched, viâ Pieter Maritzburg, to Utrecht, on the borders of Zululand, where they were joined by the head-quarter companies from time to time, as they came in separately from Pieter Maritzburg. By the 2nd of November, the regiment was reunited, and Major Rogers assumed the command.

In November, Colonel Palmer was appointed a Companion of the Bath, and Major Cherry and Captain Stevens obtained brevet promotion for their services in the late war.

The defiant and threatening behaviour of Cetewayo, king **1879.** of the Zulus, having called forth remonstrances from the colonial authorities, to which he paid no heed, an ultimatum was finally despatched demanding certain guarantees for future good conduct, and stating that if these demands were not complied with, British troops would enter Zululand on the 1st of January, 1879.

Cetewayo's reply was so evasive, that preparations were at once made to invade his country.

The troops commanded by Lieut.-General F. A. Thesiger, Lord Chelmsford, K.C.B., were divided into four columns, and were stationed as follows :—

No. 1 column, under Colonel C. K. Pearson, was concentrated at Fort Williamson, near the mouth of the Tugela River. It numbered about 3,500 men, including the 2nd Batt. 3rd Buffs, and the 99th Regiment.

No. 2 column, under Colonel A. W. Durnford, R.E., at Middle Drift, numbered 3,000 men.

No. 3 column, under Colonel Glyn, C.B., numbering about 4,000 men, was stationed at Rorke's Drift.

No. 4 column, under Colonel Evelyn Wood, V.C., C.B., was at Utrecht, and was composed of the 1st Batt. 13th Light Infantry, the 90th Perthshire Light Infantry, 4 guns of the 11th Battery, 7th Brigade, R.A., the Frontier Light Horse, and some thousand native allies.

1879. Colonel Wood's column crossed the Blood River and entered Zululand on the 6th of January. Several skirmishes between the scouts of the column and the enemy took place, invariably ending in the defeat of the latter and the capture of their cattle. On the 10th, the troops moved in the direction of Rorke's Drift for the purpose of co-operating with No. 3 column in an attack upon a large force of the enemy, under Sirayo. The Zulus, however, in spite of the rapid movements of our troops, had received a timely warning and had retired. Several thousand head of cattle were captured, and after a consultation with Lord Chelmsford, Colonel Wood returned with his column to the Blood River.

On the 18th, No. 4 column left its camp near Bemba's Kop, moving in a north-westerly direction, and at 11.30 p.m. on the 21st, advanced against a large body of the enemy strongly posted on the Zlobani Mountain. The 90th, thirty Dutch volunteers, and 600 of Wood's Irregulars passed under the Insaka at daylight, and ascending the Zunguin heights passed over the top driving the enemy before them. The 13th and guns marched from Tinta's kraal, and encamped at the foot of the Zunguin. On this occasion Captain Wilson's company of the 90th having to escort some waggons back to camp, returned immediately that duty was performed, having marched thirty-six miles in twenty-four hours. A second attack was made on the enemy's position on the 24th, when the 90th advanced in line against 4,000 Zulus, who turned and fled. In both attacks the enemy suffered severely from our well-directed fire.

At this time the news of the disaster at Isandhlwana reached Colonel Wood, who determined to retire to the Umvolosi River for the purpose of covering Utrecht.

Compelled by circumstances to remain stationary, Col. Wood sought for a position, which, while guarding the main line into the Transvaal, would at the same time enable him to act on the offensive whenever an opportunity offered. A site for an entrenched camp was chosen on the 1879. Kambula Hill, commanding three lines of road, viz., that leading, viâ Derby, to Pretoria, that entering Natal at Rorke's Drift, and the main road to Utrecht.

The column arrived at this position on the 31st of January, and on the 1st of February, Lieut.-Colonel Buller, C.B., with two troops of Light Horse and some Dutchmen, under their gallant leader Piet Uys, left the camp to reconnoitre the Amaqulusi Kraal, hitherto supposed to be impregnable. Finding that the greater part of its defenders were absent, Colonel Buller dashed forward, and driving away the Zulus left in charge, set fire to and entirely destroyed this stronghold.

With the exception of frequent raids made by the mounted portion of the force, and expeditions into the district surrounding the camp, undertaken by Colonel Wood, with a view to inducing wavering chiefs to' come over to the English, nothing of any great importance occurred until the end of March, when reinforcements having arrived, Lord Chelmsford moved forward to relieve Colonel Pearson's column, which was blockaded at Fort Ekowe.

In order to create a diversion in favour of this movement, at Lord Chelmsford's request, Colonel Wood attacked, with his cavalry, the enemy, who, notwithstanding the defeat they had suffered there on the 24th January, still remained in great strength in the upper parts of the Zlobani mountain.

The following despatch from Colonel Wood fully describes the action :—

" Camp, Kambula, Zululand,
" March 30th, 1879.
" Sir,
" I have the honour to report that the Inhlobana
" mountain was successfully assaulted and its summit
" cleared at daylight on the 28th, by Lieutenant-Colonel

1879. " Buller, C.B., with the mounted riflemen and 2nd Bat-
" talion Wood's Irregulars, under the command of Second-
" Commandant Roberts, who worked under the general
" direction of Major Leet, commanding the corps.

" I append a copy of the orders I issued, and the reports
" of commanding officers, as I mentioned in my letter of
" 27th instant, addressed to His Excellency the Lieu-
" tenant-General commanding. I had heard all Cetewayo's
" army was about to move against this column, he having
" ordered that the local tribes only should remain about
" Ekowe to watch that line of advance. I considered that
" the great importance of creating a diversion of the
" Ekowe relief column justified me in making a recon-
" naisance in force, and moreover, the news which I
" received through Mr. Lloyd, showed me that on account
" of the delay made by Masipula for doctoring his men, it
" was improbable that Cetewayo's army could leave Undi
" till the 27th instant. As will be seen, however, from my
" instructions, I took precautions against the events which
" actually happened.

" I joined Colonel Russell's column at dusk on the 27th
" instant at his bivouac, about five miles west of the Inhlo-
" bana mountain. I had with me Captain the Hon. R.
" Campbell, Chief Staff Officer to No. 4 column, Mr. Lloyd,
" my political assistant, Lieutenant Lysons, 90th Light
" Infantry, Orderly Officer, and my mounted personal
" escort, consisting of eight men, 90th Light Infantry and
" seven natives, under Umtonga, one of Panda's sons.

" Soon after 3 a.m. I rode eastward with these details,
" and at daylight got on Colonel Buller's track, which we
" followed. Colonel Weatherley met me, coming westward,
" having lost his way the previous night, and I directed
" him to move on to the sound of the firing, which was
" now audible on the north-western face of the mountain,
" where we could see the rear of Colonel Buller's column
" near the summit. I followed Colonel Weatherley and
" commenced the ascent of the mountain, immediately

"behind the Border Horse, leading our horses. It is im-
"possible to describe in adequate terms the difficulty of
"the ascent which Colonel Buller and his men had suc-
"cessfully made—not without loss however, for horses,
"killed and wounded, helped to keep us on his track,
"where the rocks afforded no evidence of his advance. We
"soon came under fire from an unseen enemy on our right.
"Ascending more rapidly than most of the Border Horse,
"who had got off the track, with my staff and escort, I
"passed to the front, and, with half-a-dozen of the Border
"Horse, when within 100 feet of the summit, came under
"a well-directed fire from our front and both flanks,
"poured in from behind huge boulders of rocks. Mr.
"Lloyd fell mortally wounded at my side, and as Captain
"Campbell and one of the escort were carrying him on to
"a ledge, rather lower, my horse was killed, falling on me.
"I directed Colonel Weatherley to dislodge one or two
"Zulus, who were causing us most of the loss, but as his
"men did not advance rapidly, Captain Campbell and Lieu-
"tenant Lysons, and three men of the 90th, jumping over
"a low wall, ran forward, and charged into a cave, when
"Captain Campbell, leading in a most determined and
"gallant manner, was shot dead. Lieutenant Lysons and
"private Fowler followed closely on his footsteps, and one
"of them—for each fired—killed one Zulu and dislodged
"another, who crawled away by a subterranean passage,
"re-appearing higher up the mountain. At this time we
"were assisted by the fire of some of Colonel Buller's men
"on the summit. Colonel Weatherley asked for permission
"to move down the hill to regain Colonel Buller's track,
"which we had lost, and by which he later gained the
"summit without further casualties; by this time he had
"lost three men dead, and about six or seven wounded.

"Mr. Lloyd was now dead, and we brought his body and
"that of Captain Campbell about half-way down the hill,
"where we buried them, still being under fire, which,
"however, did us no damage.

1879. "I then rode slowly round under the Inhlobana mountain,
"to the westward to see how Colonel Russell's force had
"progressed, bringing with the escort a wounded man of
"the Border Horse, and a herd of sheep and goats, driven
"by four of Umtonga's men. We stopped occasionally to
"give the wounded man stimulants, unconscious of the
"fact that a very large Zulu force was moving on our left,
"across our front. We were about half-way under the
"centre of the mountain when Umtonga saw and ex-
"plained to me by signs, there was a large army close
"to us. From an adjacent hill I had a good view of the
"force; it was marching in five columns, with horns and
"dense chest, the Zulu normal attack formation.

"I sent Lieutenant Lysons to Colonel Russell, who,
"as it appeared, had seen the army previously, with the
"following written order: '10.30. a.m., 28th March, 1879,
"Colonel Russell, there is a large army coming this way
"from the south, get into position on the Zunguin neck,
"(signed) E. W.' Colonel Russell reports that he moved
"from the Inhlobana to the Zunguin's neck, but this is
"incorrect; on the contrary, he went away six miles to the
"west end of the range, misapprehending the position of
"the neck, which is at the eastern corner of the range,
"and for which Wood's Irregulars, the 1st battalion, and
"Oham's men, were making, driving the captured cattle.
"Colonel Russell ordered all the cattle to be abandoned,
"and moved off very rapidly under the western end of the
"range. He thus uncovered the retreat of Oham's people,
"about 80 of whom were killed by the Zulus running down
"from the Inhlobana, they being greatly encouraged by the
"sight of the large army now moving directly on the
"western end of that mountain. As Captain Potter,
"Lieutenant Williams, and Mr. Calverley were killed,
"and all Oham's men except one, who deserted that night.
"I cannot be yet sure of the numbers.

"The Ulundi army being, as I believe, exhausted by its
"rapid march, did not close on Colonel Buller, who des-

"cended, after Oham's people, the western point of the
" mountain; thus he was enabled, by great personal exer-
" tions and his heroic conduct, not only to bring away all his
" men, who had lost their horses, but also all his wounded
" who could make an effort to sit on their horses. Seeing
" from the Zunguin neck, where I had gone with my escort
" and some of Oham's men, that, although the Ulundi army
" did not come into action, yet some 200 or 300 Zulus were
" pursuing our natives, who still maintained possession of
" some hundreds of cattle, I sent an order to Colonel
" Russell, who was then ascending the western end of the
" range, to come eastward and cover the movement of our
" natives into camp. This he did, but before he could
" arrive, some of the natives were killed. We reached
" camp at 7 p.m., and Colonel Buller, hearing that some
" of Captain Barton's party were on foot some miles
" distant, at once started, in heavy rain, and brought in
" seven men, as we believe, the sole survivors of the
" Border Horse and Captain Barton's party, who, being
" cut off when on my track, retreated over the north end
" of the Itymtaka range.

"While deploring the loss we have sustained, it is my
" duty to bring to notice the conduct of the living and
" dead. In Mr. Lloyd, Political Assistant, I lose an officer
" whom I cannot replace. In writing to Sir Bartle Frere
" on the 12th instant, explaining that the success I had
" hitherto obtained, was, in a great measure, owing to my
" subordinates, I penned the following lines.—'I need not
" trouble you with the names of my military staff, but I
" am anxious to bring under your notice the name of
" Mr. Lloyd, who has been of the greatest assistance to
" me. To personal courage and energy, he adds a know-
" ledge of the Zulu language and character, and every
" attribute of a humane English gentleman.' Yesterday
" he showed great courage and devotion. His Excellency
" knew Captain the Hon. R. Campbell; he was an excel-
" lent Staff-Officer, both in the field and as regards office

1879. "work, and having showed the most brilliant courage, lost
"his life in performing a gallant feat, and though he fell,
"success was gained by the courageous conduct of Lieu-
"tenant Lysons and Private Fowler, 90th Light Infantry."

* * * * * * * * *

       I have, etc.,
        "E. WOOD,
          "Colonel."

 On the following day, March 29th, an attack was made on the camp at Kambula by the Ulundi army, which arrived at the Zlobani mountain during the action above-mentioned. Its strength was estimated at 20,000 men, who, after fighting with great determination for four hours, were repulsed with immense loss.

 The following extracts are from an account of the battle by the *Times* correspondent, with No. 4 column :—

          "March 29th.
 "The events of yesterday were sufficient to prepare
"us for an attack had any preparation been required. The
"troops fell into their assigned positions at réveille, about
"one hour before day broke. No bustle or excitement dis-
"turbed the ordinary daily routine, and at the usual hour
"over 2,000 oxen and horses were driven out some distance
"to graze. I was sitting in my tent writing the account
"of yesterday's doings, when a staff officer peeped in,
"and in the most business-like manner informed me
"that the Zulus were in sight. This occurred about
"noon. It appeared that Captain Raaf, who was on day
"patrol, had sent in one of Oham's men with the follow-
"ing story :—

 "Being left behind during yesterday's retreat, and
"seeing the *impi* approaching, he removed his distinguish-
"ing badge from his head and quietly joined the advancing
"throng, and so gleaned the following information :—The
"army left Ulundi on the 24th with orders to repeat the

" action of Isandlana and Rorke's Drift. Four regiments **1879**.
" were left behind near Ekowe, and four more with the
" King at Ulundi. The men stated they had marched about
" 20 miles a day, and had received no food, being promised
" a good dinner as soon as they got to Kambula! The
" chief command of the army was entrusted to Mnyamane,
" to whom I referred in a recent letter as having refused
" to join the attack against Luneberg on the 12th ult. This
" chief, however, did not come under fire throughout the day,
" but remained several miles in rear, the actual direction of
" the day's operations devolving on Tyingwayo. The force
" consisted of ten regiments, and was estimated at about
" 20,000 men.

" The bearer of the above news managed to disengage
" himself unperceived from the Zulu masses, and hurrying
" towards the camp was met by the patrols, and sent on
" with all possible despatch. Anxiously every telescope
" was turned in the direction of the black masses which
" now covered the hills to the north and north-west of our
" position. 'They will never be such fools as to run their
" heads against this wall,' I heard often repeated. 'One lot
" will go to our depôt at Balte Spruit and on to Utrecht,
" the other to Luneberg,' was an opinion very generally
" expressed, and indeed it was hard to believe that even
" the thousands, who every moment became more dis-
" tinct, would hazard an attack; but the majority of us
" were unaware that on the previous evening Colonel Wood
" had received news that not only would he be attacked,
" but that attacks would be made from the right and left at
" the 'white man's dinner time.' The information was
" correct, except that on this day the white man was com-
" pelled to dine a little earlier than usual. The men having
" dined, the mounted corps were ordered to saddle up, and
" when the head of the approaching column advanced to
" within about two miles the alarm bugle sounded. By
" this time all the oxen and horses were safely laagered.
" I was struck by the extreme quiet that prevailed. Thanks

R 2

1879. " to the careful arrangements and well-studied plans which
" with untiring zeal have been conceived and developed
" by Colonel Wood ; the entire machinery of his force was
" in perfect working order, and as the last tent was struck,
" and the last man fell into his place an expression of
" assurance and confidence seemed to gleam on the face
" of everyone. Faith in your helmsman is everything, and
" no one doubted the successful result of the coming
" struggle.

" It was evident that the first attack would be from the
" right, although the masses which were collecting on the
" distant hills to the south-east clearly showed that the
" main attack would be from that direction. At 1.30 p.m.,
" the mounted troops, under Lieut.-Colonel Buller, C.B.,
" and Lieut.-Colonel Russell, attacked the head of the right
" Zulu 'horn,' and were at once closely engaged. No
" doubt the intention of this column was to move round
" under the left of our position and complete the circle of
" attack. This was entirely frustrated by the 90th fire, and
" the fire from the Fort, for although the enemy bravely
" endeavoured to push forward, they eventually were
" obliged to fall back and seek shelter among the rocky
" ground, marked A. * * * * * * *

" The artillery, under Major Tremlett, were now only
" waiting to commence their part of the day's work, which
" once begun, never ceased until the close of the action.
" Four horse-guns, in position on the ridge sloping gently
" from the Fort to the north corner of the laager, now
" opened fire, and soon broke up the enemy's columns.
" The Fort, the fire from which throughout the engage-
" ment worked havoc among the troops of the centre and
" main attack, was commanded by Major Leet, 1st Bat-
" talion 13th Regiment. His force consisted of Laye's
" company, 90th Light Infantry, Fownes' and Evans' com-
" panies of the 1st Battalion 13th Light Infantry, and
" Nicholson's two mountain guns. At 2.15 p.m., heavy
" masses attacked the right front and right rear of the

KAMBULA CAMP MARCH 29 1879

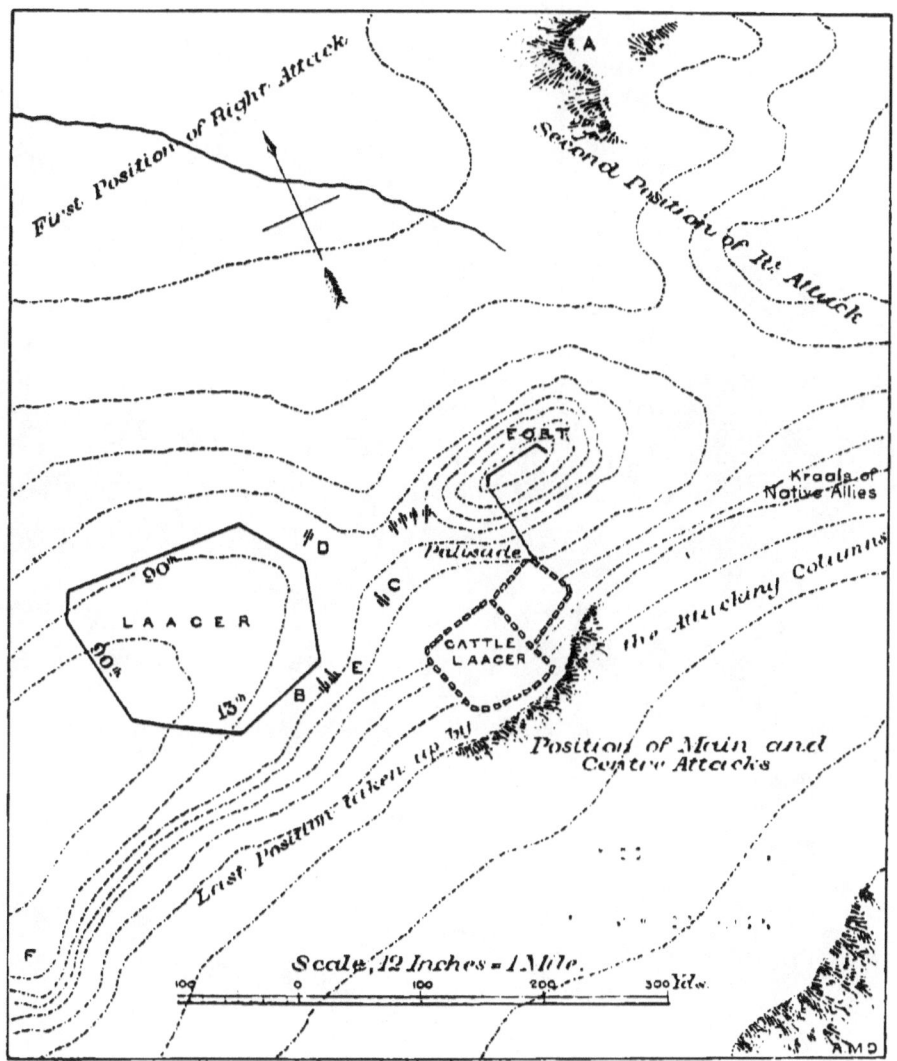

To face p. 244.

"camp, compelling the withdrawal of one company of
"the 13th, which had, until now, occupied a position
"on the right rear of the laager. At this time the artillery
"guns were divided, two under Lieutenant Bigge, moving
"to position marked D, two under Lieutenant Slade,
"to that marked C. The guns being exposed to the
"enemy's cross fire, Colonel Wood ordered the horses
"to be sent into laager, Lieutenant Slade's charger being
"shot during the change of position, Lieutenant Bigge's
"charger being wounded about the same time. Captain
"Cox's company of the 1st Battalion 13th still stoutly
"defended the cattle laager against the repeated
"rushes from the kraals or barracks of our native
"allies, but was at last obliged to withdraw, Captain Cox
"being shot through the leg, four of his men killed,
"and seven wounded. At this juncture, two companies
"of the 90th, under Major Hackett, were ordered out of
"the laager to advance over the ridge against the cattle
"laager. By this time a hot fire was opened from the
"knoll, marked F, enfilading the front of our position. I
"watched Major Hackett leading his men, with his pipe
"in his mouth, as cool and collected as man could be; he
"gallantly advanced over the ridge, where his men lay
"down and opened fire on the Zulus who were now under
"the waggons of the cattle laager. Almost at once the
"enfilade fire began to tell. A Colour-Sergeant was shot
"throught the head, and other casualties occurred in quick
"succession.

"Private Grosvenor, of the 13th, who had remained
"behind to save a wounded sergeant of his regiment, did
"so, but at the cost of his own life. He was assegaied
"before he could turn to defend himself. The gunners still
"were in the open, firing 'case' at the enemy, who were
"now within a hundred yards of the guns. Major
"Hackett was ordered to retire, and just before doing so,
"fell severely wounded in the head. Second-Lieutenant
"Bright, who was in temporary command of a company,

1879. "fell mortally wounded, the bullet passing through both
"legs. Some time before, Lieutenant Nicholson, Royal
"Artillery, when standing on the barbette battery in the
"fort, was shot through the body, and died on the follow-
"ing day. His place was filled by Captain Vaughan,
"Royal Artillery, Director of Transport to this column,
"and the guns continued to play upon the crowds of the
"enemy, who had established themselves among the
"kraals and on the rising ground above them. The fire
"now appeared to slacken, and Laye's company of the
"90th left the Fort, and advancing to the edge of the
"Krantz, poured a deadly fire into the enemy's ranks. On
"the right, Waddy's company, of the 13th, left the laager,
"and advanced down the slopes, the guns being run down
"by hand towards the edge of the rocks. The fire from
"point F. still continued, and several casualties occurred,
"Mr. Fereira, a civilian, who was watching the proceed-
"ings, being shot dead.

* * * * * * * * * * *

"The gallant Captain Raaf, cheering on his men, rushed
"from the laager and drove back the enemy, who still held
"to the rocks on the right of our position. At the same
"time a hearty cheer from the defenders of the Fort,
"told us that at last the Zulus were falling back. Redvers
"Buller, and his horsemen had been biding their time, and
"now galloped out of the laager, and the work of
"pursuit began. No need was there for the word of com-
"mand—'Disperse and Pursue.' Twenty-four hours ago
"those who were in full pursuit, were retreating before
"the assegais of the enemy. For nearly four hours to-day
"we had faced a fire of Martini Henry rifles, the loot of
"Isandlana and Luneberg. With such thoughts before
"them, the pursuers struck home the finishing blow of to-
"day's victory, and for seven miles the green 'veldt' was
"covered with hundreds of bodies of the slain. At 5.30
"p.m., the battle was over, and the day was ours.

"The medical staff, under Surgeon-Major O'Reilly, who

"had been fully employed throughout the action, were
"now hard at work among the wounded. Two officers
"were lying, alas! mortally wounded. Lieutenant Nichol-
"son only lived twenty hours, and in him the Royal
"Artillery have lost a brave and energetic officer and his
"comrades a valued friend. Second-Lieutenant Bright,
"90th Regiment, was a young officer of more than ordi-
"nary promise, and his loss is deeply deplored, not only
"by his regiment, but by all who knew him. He was a
"finished draftsman, and the last plan of this camp for-
"warded for publication was from his pen. Both these
"lamented officers were buried on the evening of the 30th,
"together with twenty-two non-commissioned officers and
"men. Major Hackett, I regret to say, remains in a most
"precarious state. As I write these lines the remains of
"Captain Sandham, of the 90th Regiment, are being car-
"ried to their last resting place, he having died yesterday
"from fever.

* * * * * * * * * *

"Throughout the engagement Colonel Wood and his
"staff were, of course, busily employed in making such
"dispositions of the troops as I have endeavoured to
"describe. Captain Woodgate, with his characteristic
"coolness, moved here and there carrying out the in-
"structions of his chief and advancing with the 90th
"Regiment under Major Hackett. Later in the day,
"he, together with Lieutenant Lysons, 90th Regiment,
"carried a wounded man from the Fort to the laager
"exposed to three cross fires. Captain Maude, 90th
"Regiment, who has temporarily succeeded Captain
"the Hon. R. Campbell as Staff Officer, ably assisted
"in directing the general operations. Lieutenant Smith,
"90th, and acting transport officer, assisted to bring
"out ammunition to the guns, and in helping a wounded
"man across the open was himself wounded in the right
"arm."

1879.

1879. *Report from Colonel Evelyn Wood, commanding No. 4 Column, to the Deputy-Adjutant General.*

"Camp, Kambula, March 30th, 1879.

"Sir,

"I have the honour to report that this camp was vigorously attacked yesterday by ten Zulu regiments from 1.30 p.m. to 5.30 p.m. The chief command was exercised by Myamana, who did not come under fire, and Tyingwayo. The army left Ulundi on the 24th instant, with orders to repeat the operations of the 22nd January, near Rorke's Drift. On the 24th instant, four regiments were left at Ulundi and four near Ekowe.

"Early in the forenoon, Captain Raaf who was out reconnoitring, sent in one of Uhamu's men; he told me that being behind with captured cattle he put his 'head badge' into his pouch, and being recognised by his friends who were ignorant that he had joined us, he marched with the Zulu army to the Umvolosi; at daylight he went out scouting, and giving his companions a message that they were recalled, he ran away to Raaf's men, and told us exactly how the attack would be made at 'dinner time.'

"About 11 a.m., we saw dense masses approaching in five columns from the Zunguin range and the Umvolosi. The two companies who were out wood-cutting were recalled, the cattle were brought in and laagered, with the exception of about 200, which had strayed away, owing to the desertion the previous evening of the natives whose duty it was to herd them. At 1.30 p.m. the action commenced, the mounted riflemen, under Colonels Buller and Russell, engaging an enormous crowd of men on the north side of our camp. Being unable to check them, our mounted men retired inside the laager, and were followed by the Zulus until they came to within 300 yards, when their advance was checked by the accurate fire of the 90th Light Infantry,

"and the Zulus spread out in front and rear of our camp.
"The attack on our left had slackened, when at at 2.15 p.m.
"heavy masses attacked our right front and right rear.
"The enemy well supplied with Martini-Henry rifles and
"ammunition, occupied a hill, not seen from the laager,
"and opened so accurate an enfilade fire, though at long
"range, that I was obliged to withdraw a company of the
"1-13th Light Infantry posted at the right rear of the
"laager. The front of the cattle laager was strongly held
"by a company of the 1-13th; they could not, however,
"see the right rear, and the Zulus coming on boldly, I
"ordered Major Hackett, 90th Light Infantry, with two
"companies, to advance over the slope. The companies
"moved down to the rear of the cattle laager, guided by
"Captain Woodgate, and well led by Major Hackett, who
"with Captain Woodgate, standing erect in the open under
"a heavy fire, showed a fine example to the men, as did
"Lieutenant Strong, who, sword in hand, ran on well in
"front of his company. The Zulus retired from their
"immediate front, but the companies being heavily flanked,
"I ordered them back. While bringing them in Major
"Hackett was dangerously and, I fear, mortally wounded;
"in any case I doubt his being able to serve again, and he
"will be a heavy loss to the regiment. The two mule guns
"were admirably worked by Lieutenant Nicholson, R.A.,
"in the redoubt, until he was mortally wounded, since
"dead, when Major Vaughan, R.A., Director of Transport,
"replaced him, and did good service. The horses of the
"other four guns, under Lieutenants Bigge and Slade,
"were sent inside the laager when the Zulus came within
"100 yards of them, but these officers with their men, and
"Major Tremlett, R.A., to all of whom great credit is due,
"remained in the open the whole of the engagement.

"In Major Hackett's counter attack, Lieutenant Bright,
"90th Light Infantry, an accomplished draughtsman, and
"a most promising young officer, was wounded, and he
"died during the night. At 5.30. p.m., seeing the attack

1879. "slackening, I ordered out a company of the 1-13th to the
"right rear of the cattle laager to attack some Zulus who
"had crept into the laager, but who had been unable to
"remove the cattle; and I took Captain Laye's company,
"of the 90th Light Infantry, forward to the edge of the
"Krantz on the right front of the cattle laager, whence
"they did great execution amongst a mass of retreating
"Zulus. Commandant Raaf, at the same time, ran for-
"ward with some of his men at the right rear of the
"camp, and did similar execution. I ordered out the
"mounted men, who, under Colonel Buller, pursued for
"seven miles the flying Zulus, retreating on our left front,
"chiefly composed of the Makulosini Kaffirs under Um-
"fonga, killing great numbers—the enemy being too
"exhausted to fire in their own defence.

"From prisoners we have taken, it appears that the
"column which attacked our left, and then, being repulsed,
"moved round to our front rear and right rear, was com-
"posed of the Nokenki, the Umbonamba, Ukandam-
"pemva regiments; the Makulosini, under Umfonga,
"attacked the front, the Undi the right front, and the
"Nkobamakosi the right. I append the list of our casual-
"ties, and we are still burying Zulus, of whom there are
"785 dead bodies lying close to the camp, and I cannot
"yet estimate their entire loss, which is, however, very
"heavy.

"Three hundred fire-arms have already been picked up
"close to the camp, several Martini Henry rifles being
"among them. I received every assistance from the
"officers commanding, Lieutenant-Colonel Gilbert, Lieu-
"tenant-Colonel Buller, Major Rogers, and from the
"following officers of my staff:—Captain Woodgate, who
"evinced great courage, for which I in vain recommended
"him for promotion after the Ashantee expedition; Cap-
"tain Maude, who, while replacing, temporarily, the late
"Captain the Hon. R. Campbell, rendered me very great
"assistance; Lieutenants Smith and Lysons—orderly

" officers, who, with Captain Woodgate, carried in a wounded
" soldier of the 13th, who was lying under fire, in doing
" which, Lieutenant Smith was himself wounded. The
" wounded were cared for most promptly by Surgeons
" O'Reilly, Brown, and staff, generally under fire."
" I have, etc.,
" (Signed) EVELYN WOOD, Colonel.
" Commanding No. 4. Column."

Eye-witnesses have described many acts of individual gallantry performed by officers and men during the fight of the 29th March, and all combine in their admiration of Major Hackett's advance towards the cattle laager.

Colour Sergeant McAllen, 90th Light Infantry, was wounded in the arm, and after the wound was dressed, ran out to his company, with which he continued to serve until shot dead.

Extract from District Orders.

" Camp, Kambula Hill,
" 30th March, 1879.

" No. 6.—The officer commanding the column
" desires to thank soldiers of all ranks for their behaviour
" before the enemy yesterday, which enabled us to gain
" a complete victory."

" 1st April, 1879.

" No. 5.—The officer commanding the column
" has much pleasure in recording his approbation of the
" soldierlike conduct of the under mentioned non-com-
" missioned officers and men on the 29th ultimo.
" The late Colour Sergeant McAllen, 90th Light Infantry,
" who being wounded, after having the wound dressed,
" ran out with his company, and performed his duty till
" he was shot dead.

* * * * * * * * * *

1879. "General Orders.
"High Commissioner's Office,
"Newcastle, Natal, 31st March, 1879.

"His Excellency the High Commissioner has "great pleasure in forwarding to His Excellency the "Administrator of Griqualand West, the Transvaal (and "to Ministers, Capetown), for general information, the "enclosed extracts from despatches received from Colonel "Wood, V.C., C.B., reporting the result of an attack on his "camp at Kambula by a force of Zulus, estimated at "20,000 men, comprising regiments which were the élite "of the Zulu army.

"The entire defeat of the determined attack made by "this large force, after an action of five hours' duration, "and the pursuit of the routed Zulus for several miles, "cannot fail to have a great effect on the whole of the "Zulu force, and on the future progress of the war. His "Excellency the High Commissioner, in congratulating "His Excellency Lieutenant-General Lord Chelmsford on "his decisive victory gained by the force under his com- "mand, begs that His Excellency will convey to Colonel "Wood, and to the officers and men specially named by "him, the High Commissioner's thanks, to which he feels "he may add, by anticipation, the cordial acknowledg- "ment of the Government, and people of all Her Majesty's "South African Colonies, for the effective services thus "rendered by the 4th Column of Lord Chelmsford's army.

"In deploring the loss of the many brave men and "officers who have fallen, the High Commissioner would "add his entire sympathy with Colonel Wood, in his ex- "pression of grief for the loss of Mr. Piet Uys, who, to the "valour and capacity of an accomplished soldier, added the "virtues and self denial of a high-minded and disinterested "patriot.

"By his distinguished services in life, not less than by "his death on the field of battle, Mr. Piet Uys offered a "noble example, which His Excellency feels assured will

"not be lost on his countrymen in South Africa, and will
"never be forgotten by Her Majesty's Government.
"By Command,
"(Signed) W. LITTLETON."
"Private Secretary to H. E. the High Commissioner,
"(By Command) W. BELLAIRS, D.A.G."

The casualties in the 90th Light Infantry, on the 29th of March, 1879, were, one officer, one colour sergeant, and ten privates killed.

Two officers, one sergeant, one corporal, and twenty privates wounded.

Captain George Sandham died of fever at Kambula on the 30th of March. When he heard the cheering of the victors on the day preceding his death he enquired the cause, and on being told that the Zulus were in full retreat, he attempted to join in the shouts of triumph. His loss was deeply regretted by the whole regiment.

A portion of the 90th, under Lieutenant Rawlins, formed part of the mounted force under Major Barrow, which operated so successfully at the battle of Ginghilova on the 2nd of April, and well maintained the reputation they had gained in the Gaika war. Major Barrow in his report on the pursuit of the retreating enemy says :—

"I succeeded in making a flank attack on the retreating
"Zulus with half a squadron of mounted infantry, under
"Lieutenant Rawlins (90th L. I.), who led his squadron
"with considerable dash and to my entire satisfaction.
"The half squadron drew swords and charged the Zulus,
"who were in large numbers, but utterly demoralized.
"The actual number of men killed with the sword were
"probably few, but the moral effect on the retreating Zulus
"as the swordsmen closed in on them was very great."

The Zulus had suffered so severely at Kambula and Ginghilov that the "impis" engaged in those battles were withdrawn to the neighbourhood of Ulundi, and with the exception of skirmishes between our and the enemy's scouts no fighting occurred for a time.

1879. The reinforcements had all arrived, and while adding to the strength of the English forces, at the same time proved a source of weakness. The means of transport at no time great, were now quite inadequate for the movement of an army numbering about 20,000 men; and anxious as Lord Chelmsford and Colonel Wood were to follow up their successes by an immediate advance they were forced to wait until a sufficient motive power had been accumulated.

On the 5th of May, Colonel Wood moved with his column from Kambula Hill and took up a position at Mayegwhana, about three miles north of Bemba's Kop, to cover a large depot of stores about to be formed at Conference Hill.

The British forces in the field were now arranged in two divisions under Generals Newdigate and Crealock, and No. 4 column, which became the Flying Column, under Colonel Wood.

The 1st Division was to advance on Ulundi from Fort Pearson by the coast road. The 2nd Division, under General Newdigate, was to move on the King's kraal from Conference Hill, preceded by the Flying Column.

On the 1st of June, the day on which Prince Louis Napoleon was killed, the 2nd Division moved from Koppie Allein to the Italezi river, the Flying Column crossed the Umyumyema river, and joined the division on the 2nd.

The troops moved forward daily, the Flying Column being in advance towards Babanango on the 5th. On the 7th, the 2nd Division reached the Mouwena river, and Colonel Wood with two and a half battalions (the 90th being one of them), four guns, two gatlings, half his mounted men and 400 empty waggons left for Landman's Drift for supplies, at which place he arrived on the 11th. The 2nd Division remained on the Mouwena, where Fort Newdigate was constructed, until the return of the Flying Column on the 16th. The convoy of which Colonel Wood had charge consisted of about 700 waggons and 9,000 oxen.

Extract from Regimental Orders. 1879.

"Camp Inhlambimkose,
"Zululand, 18th June, 1879.

"No. 1.—The Brigadier-General has much pleasure "in publishing for information of the troops under his "command the following extract from a despatch received "by H. E. the Lieutenant-General commanding, from the "Secretary of State for War, relative to the actions of "Kambula and Ginghilova.

"Having received the telegraphic intelligence of the "success gained by your Lordship and Colonel Wood, "I have the honour to express to you the general satis-"faction with which the news has been received in this "country, and I rejoice to note that the repulse of the "enemy was on both occasions complete and decisive.

"I have received Her Majesty's commands to convey to "you, and to the forces under your command, a gracious "message of congratulation."

The following communication to the Brigadier-General from H. E. the Lieut.-General commanding is published for information:—

"The Lieut.-General commanding desires to express "his thanks to you and those under you, who have worked "so zealously in carrying out and perfecting the arrange-"ments necessary for the safe conduct of the very large "convoy of supplies which reached this day from "Landman's Drift."

"Dated 17th June, 1879.

"The Brigadier-General commanding thanks all "ranks for their cheerful and soldierlike conduct while "engaged in the above duty."

On the 17th, the march was resumed, and on the 21st the 2nd Division reached the right bank of the Umlatosi. Brigadier-General Wood encamped on the opposite bank.

1879. Five kraals were burnt on the 24th near Usixepi, and a few Zulus were killed as they were making their escape.

Messengers from Cetewayo came into camp on the 27th, to treat for peace, bringing with them two elephant tusks as a pledge of sincerity, and desiring that the troops might retire. Lord Chelmsford returned the tusks, and stated that until all his conditions were fulfilled he would continue to advance; he accordingly crossed the White Umvolosi on the following day.

The Zulu monarch was given until the 3rd of July to comply with the demands made upon him. By noon that day, no messengers having come in, and the Zulus having fired upon our men when watering horses, Colonel Buller was ordered to cross the river, and make a reconnaissance in the direction of Ulundi; this he carried out with his usual dash, and having found a good position for the troops to occupy if necessary, and having forced the enemy to show his strength by inducing him to attack, he retired upon the camp.

On the 4th, leaving behind him a well-made and strongly garrisoned laager, Lord Chelmsford crossed the Umvolosi and advanced to the position chosen by Colonel Buller, with what results the following despatch will show :—

Telegram from Major-General the Hon. H. Clifford, to the Secretary of State for War (St. Vincent, July 23, 1879):—

"July 6.

" Following received from Chelmsford :—

" Cetewayo not having complied with my demands
" by noon yesterday, July 3, and having fired heavily on
" the troops at water, I returned the 114 cattle he had sent
" in, and ordered a reconnaissance to be made by the
" mounted force under Colonel Buller. This was effectually
" made, and caused the Zulu army to advance and show
" itself. This morning, a force under my command, con-
" sisting of the 2nd Division, under Major-General

" Newdigate, numbering 1,870 Europeans, 530 natives, and
" eight guns, and the flying column, under Brigadier-
" General Wood, numbering 2,195 Europeans and 573
" natives, four guns, and two gatlings, crossed the Um-
" volosi river at 6.15, and, marching in a hollow square,
" with the ammunition and intrenching tool carts and
" bearer company in its centre, reached an excellent
" position between Unodwengo and Ulundi, about half-
" past eight. This had been observed by Colonel Buller
" the day before. Our fortified camp on the right bank
" of the Umvolosi was left with a garrison of about 900
" Europeans, 250 Natives, and one gatling gun, under
" Colonel Bellairs. Soon after half-past seven, the Zulu
" army was seen leaving its bivouac and advancing on
" every side. The engagement was shortly after com-
" menced by the mounted men. By nine o'clock the
" attack was fully developed. At half-past nine the
" enemy wavered. The 17th Lancers, followed by the
" remainder of the mounted men, attacked them, and a
" general rout ensued. The prisoners state that Cetewayo
" was personally commanding, and had made all the
" arrangements himself, and that he witnessed the fight
" from Lickazi Kraal, and that twelve regiments took part
" in it. If so, 20,000 men attacked us. It is impossible
" to estimate with any correctness the loss of the enemy,
" owing to the extent of the country over which they
" attacked and retreated; but it could not have been less,
" I consider, than 1,000 killed. By noon, Ulundi was in
" flames, and during the day all the military kraals of the
" Zulu army, and in the valley of the Umvolosi, were de-
" stroyed. At 2 p.m., the return march to the camp of the
" column commenced. The behaviour of the troops under
" my command was extremely satisfactory. Their steadi-
" ness under a complete belt of fire was remarkable. The
" dash and enterprise of the mounted branches were all
" that could be wished, and the fire of the artillery very
" good. A portion of the Zulu forces approached our

1879.

S

1879. " fortified camp, and at one time threatened to attack it.
" The native contingent, forming a part of the garrison,
" were sent out after the action, and assisted in pursuit.
" As I have fully accomplished the object for which I
" advanced, I consider I shall now be best carrying out
" of Sir G. Wolseley's instructions by moving at once
" to Eulongamite, and thence towards Kwamagwasa, I
" shall send back a portion of this force with the empty
" waggons for supplies, which are now ready at Fort
" Marshall."

On the 4th July, eleven men of the 90th were wounded.

On the 5th of July, the Flying Column retired to Eutonjanene, thence, *via* Kwamagwasa to St. Paul's Mission Station, where it arrived on the 15th.

At the end of June, Sir Garnet Wolseley, who had been appointed to the supreme civil and military command of the Transvaal and adjoining districts, landed at Durban. After the delay necessary on assuming office, he proceeded to St. Paul's, where he met Lord Chelmsford, on the 16th July, and on the day following inspected the troops composing the Flying Column.

" At nine a.m., there was a general parade of the
" fighting men of the division, on a ridge just above the
" camp. The ground was about as unfavourable for the
" purpose as it well could be, but there was nothing better
" within reach. As is usual on such occasions, the troops
" were formed up in columns of batteries and battalions
" facing the saluting base—Buller's cavalry brigade on the
" right, Tremlett's battery of artillery, and Owen's two
" gatlings next them, the Royal Engineers, the 1st-13th
" Light Infantry, the 80th Regiment, the 90th Light In-
" fantry, and Wood's Irregulars on the left. They made
" an admirable show, being dressed as perfectly as on an
" Aldershot field-day, and as clean and neat as a long and
" arduous campaign would allow them to be."

Sir Garnet Wolseley inspected the troops, and ex-   1879.
pressed his high approval of the soldierly and efficient
appearance of the force.

" G.O.

"July 16th, 1879.

" The General commanding in South Africa con-
" gratulates Lord Chelmsford, and the officers and men
" serving under him, upon the brilliant success achieved
" by them, on the 4th instant, at the battle of Ulundi,
" whereby they defeated, with severe loss, the Zulu army,
" led by the King in person. The General commanding
" has learnt with great satisfaction from Lord Chelmsford
" of the admirable behaviour of all the troops serving
" under him, and hopes that their gallant conduct will
" have made the action of Ulundi decisive of the fate of
" the campaign."

With the victory at Ulundi the Zulu war came to an
end. The King, who escaped from the pursuing cavalry
after the battle, was captured a few weeks' later, and the
whole of the Zulu chiefs gave in their submission.

Colonel Wood, who had been appointed a Knight Commander of the Bath, for his services in the early part of
the campaign, returned home to receive the thanks of his
Sovereign, and the accolade at her hands.

Major Hackett, on his arrival in England, was received
by His Royal Highness the Prince of Wales, who thanked
him for his services, and expressed his sympathy for the
wound which had resulted in total blindness.

On the 14th June, when a sword of honor was presented
to Sir Evelyn Wood by the county of Essex, he made
mention of his regiment as follows :—

" I was fortunate during the recent campaign in being
" supported by such sterling personal leaders of troops as
" Colonel Gilbert '1-13th, and Major Rogers, V.C.

•   •   •   •   •   •   •   •

1879. " Nor were the 90th Light Infantry less fortunate in their
" leader. I have elsewhere testified to the courage and
" worth of some of the non-commissioned officers and
" privates; but no regiment could fail to be influenced by
" the steady guidance and well-tried courage of my loyal
" supporter, Major Rogers, V.C., who commanded the
" corps throughout the Zulu war, as I had been tempo-
" rarily promoted to the position of a General. The
" officers sustained well the character of their Major.
" Lieutenants Lysons and Smith went out in front of the
" position to a spot swept by fire to help a wounded
" soldier, and assisted by Captain Woodgate (4th Regt.)
" one of my staff, were carrying him in, when Lieutenant
" Smith fell severely wounded, which incident, however,
" failed to shake the composure of Woodgate and Lysons.
" George Sandham, the most popular captain of the corps,
" lay dying of enteric fever, unconscious of the strife
" raging round his tent, until aroused by the exulting
" shout, raised by the troops as the Zulus fell back dis-
" comfited. He spent his last remaining strength in
" clapping his hands and adding his failing voice to the
" cheers of the men."

Since its arrival in South Africa the casualties in the regiment amounted to 70 killed and wounded, including two officers killed and three wounded.

There being no longer any necessity for keeping so large a force in Natal, several regiments were sent home, and orders were issued directing the 90th to proceed to India in October. Accordingly, on the 20th October, the regiment left in H.M.S. *Serapis*, under the command of Major Rogers, V.C., and landed in India on 10th November.

ROLL OF OFFICERS

OF

THE 90TH LIGHT INFANTRY

From 1795.

ROLL OF OFFICERS, &c.

1795.

Lieut.-Col. Commt. Thos. Graham.

1st. Batt.

Lt.Col. George Moncrieffe.	Lieut. Francis Eddins.
Rowland Hill.	Alex. Drummond.
Major Kenneth Mackenzie.	James M'Donald.
Hugh Houston.	John C. T. Steward.
Capt. John Woodcock.	Wm. Cartwright.
Walter Farquhar.	Robert Showe.
Robert Cholmondeley	Ens. Wm. Austin.
James, Lord Ruthven.	— Webster.
John McNair.	And. Fra. Barnard.
John Knipe.	Wm. Cravan.
Cpt.Lt.George Vigoreux.	Samuel Colberg.
Lieut. George Parkin.	Chapl. James Grant.
Hon. Mark Napier.	Adj. Francis Eddins.
Edward Hodges.	Q.-M. David Hopkins.
James Edmund.	Surg. Wm. Russell.

2nd. Batt.

Lt.Col. Hon. Alex. Hope.	Lieut. M. W. Ferrebee.
Peter Heron.	Grainger S. Murray.
Major Thos. Cholmondeley.	Samuel Milner.
Lord Henry Murray.	— Oliphant.
Capt. Hendrick Molesworth	Ens. Alexander Hay.
Alexander Murray.	Charles M'Kay.
James Hutton.	— M'Andrew.
Tho. Bligh St. George	Chapl. Charles Webster.
John Graham.	Adj. Sam. Milner.
Lieut. Wm. Geddes.	Q.-M. Robert Mann.
Geo. Dixon Green.	Surg. William Ferguson.
Wm. Barclay.	

1796.

Lieut.-Col. Commt. Thos. Graham, c.

Lt.Col. George Moncrieffe.
 Rowland Hill.
Major Kenneth Mackenzie.
 Hugh Houston.
Capt. John Woodcock.
 Walter Farquhar.
 Alex. Murray.
 James Hutton.
 Rob. Cholmondeley.
 Lord Ruthven.
 John McNair.
 John Knipe.
 T. B. St. George.
 John Graham.
Cpt.Lt.Hon. M. Napier.
Lieut. George Parkin.
 Edward Hodges.
 Francis Eddins.
 Wm. Cartwright.
 Samuel Milner.
 C. Dixon Green.
 Robt. Snowe.
 Grainger S. Murray.
 Alex. Hay.
 Wm. Austin.
 Francis Herbert.

Lieut. Rich. Butler.
 Rich. Webster.
 Benj. Preedy.
 Sam. Colberg.
 — Tapp.
 Rich. Bowles.
 P. Burton Carter.
 P. Brereton.
 J. Willington.
 Edwd. Waldron.
Ens. Chas. M'Kay.
 — M'Andrew.
 James Patullo.
 Thos. Wright.
 John Blakeley.
 Wm. Holland.
 — Paterson.
 James Bracken.
 John D'Arcey.
 Harman Teesdale.
 — Power.
Chapl. James Grant.
Adj. Francis Eddins.
Q.-M. David Hopkins.
Surg. William Russell.

1797.

Lieut.-Col. Commt. Thos. Graham, c.

Lt.Col. George Moncrieffe.
 Rowland Hill.
Major Kenneth Mackenzie.
 Hugh Houston.
Capt. Alex. Murray.

Capt. Robert Cholmondeley
 James Lord Ruthven.
 John McNair.
 John Knipe.
 Thos. Bligh St. George

Capt. John Graham.
    William Barclay.
    James Murray.
Cpt.Lt.Hon. Mark Napier.
Lieut. Edward Hodges.
    Francis Eddins.
    Wm. Cartwright.
    Samuel Milner.
    Grainger S. Murray.
    Alex. Hay.
    Wm. Austin.
    Francis Herbert.
    Richard Butler.
    — Webster.
    Benj. Preedy.
    Sam. Colberg.
    P. Burton Carter.
    Edw. Waldron.

Lieut. — M'Andrew.
    James Patullo
    Thomas Wright.
    William Holland.
    Charles Paterson.
    John P. Dalrymple.
    David Graham.
    Harman Teesdale.
    Anthony Power.
Ens. Charles E. White.
    Adam Peebles.
    Wm. Cardon Seton.
    — Paterson.
    James Anderson.
Chapl. James Grant.
Adj. Francis Eddins.
Q.-M. David Hopkins.
Surg. Wm. Russell.

1798.

Lieut.-Col. Commt. Thos. Graham, c.

Lt.-Col. George Moncrieffe.
    Rowland Hill.
Major Kenneth Mackenzie.
    Hugh Houston.
Capt. Alex. Murray.
    Robert Cholmondeley
    James Lord Ruthven.
    John McNair.
    John Knipe.
    Thos. Bligh St. George
    John Graham.
    William Barclay.
    James Murray.
Cpt.Lt.Hon. Mark Napier.

Lieut. Francis Eddins.
    Wm. Cartwright.
    Sam. Milner.
    Alex. Hay.
    Wm. Austin.
    Richd. Butler.
    — Webster.
    Benj. Preedy.
    Sam. Colberg.
    P. Burton Carter.
    P. M'Andrew.
    James Patullo.
    Thomas Wright.
    Wm. Holland.

Lieut. Chas. Paterson.
 John P. Dalrymple.
 David Graham.
 Harman Teesdale.
 Anthony Power.
 Adam Peebles.
 Charles Gore.
 James Anderson.
 John Addison.

Ens. Charles E. White.
 — Paterson.
 David Hopkins.
 Andrew Wood.
 James Fitz Massey.
Adj. Francis Eddins.
Q.-M. David Hopkins.
Surg. Michael Egan.

1799.

Lieut.-Col. Commt. Thos. Graham, c.

Lt.-Col. G. Moncrieffe.
 Rowland Hill.
Major K. Mackenzie.
 Lyde Browne.
Capt. Alex. Murray.
 Rob. Cholmondeley.
 Lord Ruthven.
 John McNair.
 T. B. St. George.
 John Graham.
 William Barclay.
 James Murray.
 Hon. Mark Napier.
Cpt.Lt. Francis Eddins.
Lieut. Wm. Cartwright.
 Samuel Milner.
 William Austin.
 Richard Butler.
 — Webster.
 Benj. Preedy.
 Sam. Colberg.
 P. Burton Carter.
 — M'Andrew.

Lieut. James Patullo.
 Thomas Wright.
 William Holland.
 David Graham.
 Harman Teesdale.
 Anthony Power.
 James Anderson.
 John Addison.
 W. C. Browne.
 James Stuart.
 Edward Naish.
 George Clifton.
 John S. Hales.
 — Paterson.
Ens. Charles E. White.
 David Hopkins.
 Andrew Wood.
 J. F. Massey.
 B. Martin.
Adj. — Doolittle.
Q.-M. David Hopkins.
Surg. James Anderson.

1800.

Lieut.-Col. Commt. Thos. Graham, *c.*

Lt.Col. G. Moncrieffe.
    Rowland Hill.
Major K. Mackenzie, *l.c.*
    Lyde Browne, *l.c.*
Capt. A. Murray.
    Lord Ruthven.
    John McNair.
    T. B. St. George.
    John Graham.
    Hon. Mark Napier.
    W. Barclay.
    Fred. Thwaite.
Cpt.Lt.Francis Eddins.
Lieut. Wm. Cartwright.
    Samuel Milner.
    William Austin.
    Richard Butler.
    — Webster.
    Benj. Preedy.
    Sam. Colberg.
    — M'Andrew.
    James Patullo.
    Thos. Wright.

    William Holland.
    David Graham.
    Harman Teesdale.
    Anthony Power.
    James Anderson.
    John Addison.
    W. C. Browne.
    James Stuart.
    John S. Hales.
    — Paterson.
    John Gartside.
    William Dickson.
    Henry O'Grady.
    Andrew Wood.
    — Hanton.
    Thomas Acklom.
Ens. David Hopkins.
    J. F. Massey.
    B. Martin.
Adj. — Doolittle.
Q.-M. David Hopkins.
Surg. James Anderson.

1801.

Lieut.-Col. Commt. Thos. Graham, *c.*

Lt.Col. G. Moncrieffe, *c.*
    Rowland Hill, *c.*
Major K. Mackenzie.
    Geo. Vigoreux.
Capt. Lord Ruthven.
    John McNair.
    T. B. St. George.
    Hon. Mark Napier.

Capt. W. Barclay.
    Fred. Thwaites.
    Ch. Pickering.
Cpt.Lt.Francis Eddins.
Lieut. Wm. Cartwright.
    Sam. Milner.
    Wm. Austin.
    Richard Butler.

Lieut. — Webster.
    Benj. Preedy.
    Sam. Colberg.
    James Patullo.
    Thos. Wright.
    Wm. Holland.
    David Graham.
    Harman Teesdale.
    Anthony Power.
    John Addison.
    W. C. Browne.
    John S. Hales.
    — Paterson.
    — Gartside.

Lieut. Wm. Dickson.
    Andrew Wood.
    Henry O'Grady.
    Thomas M. Perryn.
    George Darley.
    George Scholey.
    Thomas Fairtlough.
Ens. B. Martin.
    David Hopkins.
    Wm. Hill.
Adj. — Doolittle.
Q.-M. David Hopkins.
Surg. James Anderson.
A. S. — Lamerte.

1802.

Lieut.-Col. Commt. Thomas Graham, c.

Lt.Col. Geo. Moncrieffe, c.
    Rowland Hill, c.
Major Geo. Vigoreux, l.c.
    John McNair.
Capt. Lord Ruthven.
    Thos. Bligh St. George.
    Hon. Mark Napier.
    Francis Eddins.
    Wm. Cartwright.
    David Stewart.
    Chas. Robert Fead.
    Chas. M'Gregor.
Cpt.Lt.Wm. Austin.
Lieut. Richard Butler.
    T. Webster.
    Benj. Preedy.
    Sam. Colberg.
    Thomas Wright.
    Wm. Holland.

Lieut. David Graham.
    Harmer Tisdall.
    Anthony Power.
    W. Christmas Browne
    John Scott Hales.
    John Paterson.
    — Gartside.
    Andrew Wood.
    Henry O'Grady.
    Thos. M. Perryn.
    George Darley.
    George Scholey.
    Thos. Fairtlough.
    Wm. Hill Milner.
    James Fitz Massey.
    Benj. Martin.
    Rich. Graves.
    John Graham Douglas
    Charles G. M'Mahon.

Adj. Dan. Doolittle. Surg. James Anderson.
Q.-M. David Hopkins.

1803.

Lieut.-Col. Commt. Thos. Graham, c.

Lt.Col. G. Moncrieffe, c. Lieut. Sir J. S. Hales, Bt.
Rowland Hill, c. John Paterson.
Major John McNair. — Gartside.
Lord Ruthven. Andrew Wood.
Capt. T. Bligh St. George. Geo. Scholey.
Hon. Mark Napier. Thos. Fairtlough.
Francis Eddins. William Hill.
C. R. Fead. John Hart.
Wm. Austin. B. Martin.
C. M'Gregor. F. North, Lord Greave
Cpt.Lt. Richard Butler. Wm. Wallace.
Lieut. Thos. Webster. Ens. Richard Graves.
Benj. Preedy. Chas. G. M'Mahon.
Sam. Colberg. Adj. Dan. Doolittle.
Thos. Wright. Pymr. H. Allison.
Wm. Holland. Q.-M. David Hopkins.
David Graham. Surg. J. Anderson.
Harmer Tisdall. A. S. Sam. Gissing.
Anthony Power. Rich. Webster.

1804.

Lieut.-Col. Commt. Thos. Graham, c.

Lt.Col. Geo. Moncrieffe, c. Capt. Wm. Austin.
Rowland Hill, c. Chas. M'Gregor.
Major John McNair. Richard Butler.
Lord Ruthven. Edward Currie.
Capt. Thos.BlighSt.George. Thos. Webster.
Hon. Mark Napier. Benj. Preedy.
Francis Eddins. Lieut. Thos. Wright.
Chas. Robert Fead. William Holland.

Lieut. John Paterson.
    John Gartside.
    Andrew Wood.
    George Jacob Wynter
    Manley Dixon.
    James Ferguson.
    Henry Hooper.
    John Hart.
    John Birch.
Ens. Tade Heatley.

Ens. Blacket M. Crofton.
    James Fraser.
    Richard Dogherty.
    Kenneth Snodgrass.
    William James.
Pymr. Harry Allison.
Q.-M. John Stevens.
Surg. James Anderson.
A. S. Richard Butler.
    Thos. M'Cready.

1805.

Lieut.-Col. Commt. Thos. Graham, *c.*

Lt.Col. George Moncrieffe, *c.*
    Rowland Hill, *c.*
    John McNair.
    John M. Mainwaring.
Major James Lord Ruthven.
    Thos. BlighSt. George.
    Hon. Mark Napier.
    Parry Jones.
Capt. Francis Eddins.
    Charles R. Fead.
    Wm. Austin.
    Chas. M'Gregor.
    Richard Butler.
    Edward Currie.
    Thos. Webster.
    Benj. Preedy.
    Thos. Wright.
    Wm. Holland.
    Andrew Pack.
    John Paterson.
    John Gartside.
    George Scott.

Capt. Andrew Wood.
Lieut. Wm. Hill Milner.
    Wm. Wallace.
    Manley Dixon.
    James Ferguson.
    Henry Hooper.
    John Hart.
    John Birch.
    Stephen C. Bowen.
    Blacket M. Crofton.
    James Fraser.
    W. F. Hutchinson.
    Archibald M'Intyre.
    Bolton Edw. Sargent.
    Aubery C. Bowers.
    Richard Dogherty.
    Wm. James.
Ens. James Macfarlane.
    David Cloag.
    Alex. Stewart.
    W. H. Pack.
    James Fraser.

Ens.	James Cotter.	Ens.	Francis Annesley.
	John Rains.	Pymr.	Harry Allison.
	James Dunbar.	Adj.	James Macfarlane.
	John Meynell.		Henry Hooper.
	John Tuckey.	Q.-M.	John Stephens.
	Henry Wilson.		James Crawford.
	Benj. Swift.	Surg.	Alex. Menzies.
	Henry M. Williams.	A. S.	Thos. M'Cready.
	George Wood.		Henry Hamilton.

1806.

Lieut.-Col. Commt. Thos. Graham, c.

Lt.Col.	G. Moncrieffe, m.g.	Lieut.	Wm. Hill Milner.
	Rowland Hill, m.g.		Manley Dixon.
	John McNair.		Jas. Ferguson.
	J. Mainwaring.		John Hart.
Major	Lord Ruthven.		J. Birch.
	Hon. M. Napier.		S. C. Bowen.
	P. J. Parry.		B. M. Crofton.
Capt.	F. Eddins.		Jas. Fraser.
	C. R. Fead.		W. F. Hutchinson.
	Wm Austin.		Bolton E. Sargent.
	C. M'Gregor.		R. Dogherty.
	Edw. Currie.		Wm. James.
	Benj. Preedy.		H. C. Wilson.
	Tho. Wright.		Alan M'Lean.
	Wm. Holland.		W. Reid.
	John Gartside.		F. Barallier.
	And. Wood.		Dav. Cloag.
	P. O. K. Boulger.		Alex. Stewart.
	Hec. M'Lean.		W. Bearda.
	D. A. Gilland.		F. Annesley.
	S. E. Bentley.		Jas. Fraser.
	Tho. Ware.		John Meynell.
	Arthur Bowen.		H. M. Williams.
	Albert D'Alton.		R. Peyton.

Ens. John Fisher.	Ens. P. Barailler.
H. English.	T. R. Stewart.
Rob. Thomson.	Adj. John Birch.
Rob. Coury.	Pymr. H. Allison.
J. L. Cox.	H. M. Williams.
Wm. Wood.	Q.-M. Jas. Crawford.
Fra. Mason.	— Dixon.
Tho. Jones.	Surg. Alex. Menzies.
C. O. C. Tuckey.	Rob. Stratton.
— Parry.	A. S. T. Macready.
Tho. Walsh.	H. Hamilton.

1807.

Lieut.-Col. Commt. Thos. Graham, c.

Lt.Col. Geo. Moncrieffe, m.g.	Capt. Albert D'Alton.
Rowland Hill, m.g.	Manley Dixon.
John McNair.	W. H. Wilby.
J. M. Mainwaring.	Wm. Boothby.
Major Lord Ruthven.	Chas. Gardiner.
Hon. M. Napier.	F. Livingstone.
Parry J. Parry.	Lieut. W. Hill Milner.
Rich. Butler.	Jas. Ferguson.
Capt. Fra. Eddins.	John Hart.
Wm. Austin.	John Birch.
C. M'Gregor.	S. C. Bowen.
Edw. Currie.	B. M. Crofton.
Benj. Preedy.	W. F. Hutchinson.
Thos. Wright.	R. Dogherty.
Wm. Holland.	Wm. James.
George Scott.	A. M'Lean.
And. Wood.	Wm. Read.
P. O. K. Boulger.	Wm. Barailler.
D. A. Gilland.	David Cloag.
S. E. Bentley.	Alex. Stewart.
Thos. Ware.	Wm. Bearda.
Arthur Bowen.	F. Annesley.

Lieut. Jas. Fraser.
John Meynell.
H. M. Williams.
R. Peyton.
John Costley.
Dan. O'Keefe.
Jas. Dongan.
Rob. Conry.
Fran. Mason.
Ens. Wm. Wood.
J. L. Cox.
C. O'C. Tuckey.
W. P. Jones.
W. Walsh.
P. Barailler.
T. R. Stewart.

Ens. Jas. Booth.
Rich. O'Meara.
Jas. Crawford.
D. Maclean.
Wm. Sweeny.
Alex. Cumming.
Thos. White.
Pymr. H. Allison.
Adj. John Birch.
Jas. Crawford.
Q.-M. Jas. Dixon.
Hec. Graham.
Surg. Alex. Menzies.
Rob. Stratton.
A. S. Thos. M'Cready.
H. Hamilton.

1808.

Lieut.-Col. Commt. Thos. Graham, *c.*

Lt.Col. Geo. Moncrieffe, *m.g.*
Rowland Hill, *m.g.*
John McNair.
J. M. Mainwaring.
Major Hon. M. Napier.
P. J. Parry.
Geo. Burrell.
Thos. Wright.
Capt. F. Eddins.
C. M'Gregor.
Edw. Currie.
Benj. Preedy.
Wm. Holland.
And. Wood.
D. A. Gilland.
Thos. Ware.
Arthur Bowen.

Capt. Albert D'Alton.
Manley Dixon.
W. H. Wilby.
W. Boothby.
C. Gardiner.
F. Livingstone.
Jas. Ferguson.
G. Williamson.
C. C. Dixon.
John Law.
J. M. Wallace.
Lieut. John Birch.
W. F. Hutchinson.
R. Dogherty.
Wm. James.
A. M'Lean.
W. Read.

Lieut. W. Barailler.
   A. Stewart.
   W. Bearda.
   Jas. Fraser.
   H. M. Williams.
   R. Peyton.
   D. O'Keefe.
   Jas. Dongan.
   W. J. Speed.
   R. Conry.
   F. Mason.
   Wm. Wood.
   J. L. Cox.
   Jas. Barrow.
   P. Barailler.
   J. Marsh.
   — Walsh.
   Jas. Crawford.
   D. Maclean.
   S. Fairtlough.
   G. D. Cranfield.
   H. Arden.
   And. Neill.
   Wm. Sweeny.
   J. Fleming.
   J. Bissett.
   W. H. Pack.
   W. H. Gibbons.
   Thos. White.

Lieut. C. Dowson.
   Jas. Johnston.
Ens. Henry Eager.
   John Grant.
   John Hinds.
   A. Campbell.
   G. Conry.
   Alex. Stewart.
   W. R. S. Webster.
   C. Le Hunte.
   — Allison.
   Wm. Laing.
   Pat. Lynch.
   Edw. Bevan.
   Wm. Beale.
   Wm. Walker.
   Dun. M'Dougall.
Pymr. H. Allison.
   E. P. Henslow.
Adj. John Birch.
   Jas. Crawford.
Q.-M. — Dixon.
   Hec. Graham.
Surg. Rob. Stratton.
   Wm. Wybrow.
A. S. Thos. M'Cready.
   H. Hamilton.
   John O'Dwyer.

1809.

Lieut.-Col. Commt. Thos. Graham, *c*.

Lt.Col. G. Moncrieffe, *m.g.*
   Rowland Hill, *m.g.*
   John McNair. (1)
   Rob. Smyth. (2)

Major Hon. M. Napier.
   Geo. Burrell. (2)
   Tho. Wright. (1)
   Tho. Steele, *l.c.* (2)

Capt. Fra. Eddins.
C. M'Gregor.
Edw. Currie.
Benj. Preedy.
Wm. Holland.
And. Wood.
D. A. Gilland.
Tho. Ware.
A. Bowen.
A. D'Alton.
M. Dixon.
W. H. Wilby.
C. Gardiner.
F. Livingstone.
Jas. Ferguson.
G. Williamson.
C. C. Dixon.
C. Silvertop.
Jas. Gauntlett.
John Dickins.
Lieut. J. Birch.
R. Dogherty.
W. James.
A. M'Lean.
W. Read.
F. Barailler.
A. Stewart.
Jas. Fraser.
H. Williams.
D. O'Keefe.
J. Dongan.
W. J. Speed.
Rob. Conry.
Fra. Mason.
Wm. Wood.
J. L. Cox.
P. Barailler.

Lieut. Jerem. Marsh.
J. Crawford.
D. Maclean.
S. Fairtlough.
G. D. Cranfield.
And. Neill.
J. Fleming.
J. Bissett.
W. H. Pack.
C. Dowson.
W. H. Gibbons.
J. Johnston.
Tho. Nicholl.
Henry Eager.
J. Grant.
A. Saunders.
W. G. Isdell.
C. C. Borton.
Ens. Wm. Hind.
Alex. Campbell.
Gilbert Conry.
Alex. Stewart.
C. Le Hunte.
— Allison.
Wm. Laing.
Edw. Bevan.
D. M'Dougall.
Wm. Beale.
Pat. Lynch.
E. Robinson.
Wm. Gibson.
D. Campbell.
T. Hovendon.
John Hawks.
E. S. Davis.
Pymr. H. Allison.
Chas. Jones.

Adj. J. Birch.
J. Crawford.
Q.-M. H. Graham.
J. Goddard.
Surg. R. Stratton.

Surg. T. Jones.
A. S. H. Hamilton.
P. Lawless.
J. Henley.

1810.

Col. Thos. Graham, *m.g.*

Lt.Col. G. Moncrieffe, *m.g.*
  John McNair. 1
  Rob. Smith. 2
Major Hon. M. Napier. 1
  Geo. Burrell. 1
  Tho. Wright.
  Tho. Steele, *l.c.*
Capt. C. McGregor.
  Edw. Currie.
  Benj. Preedy, *m.*
  Wm. Holland. (1)
  And. Wood. (1)
  D. A. Gilland. 1
  Tho. Ware. 1
  A. Bowen.
  Albert D'Alton.
  M. Dixon. 2
  W. H. Wilby.
  C. Gardiner.
  F. Livingstone.
  Ja. Ferguson.
  G. Williamson. 2
  C. C. Dixon (2)
  Ja. Gauntlett.
  John Dickins.
  J. Birch.
  Wm. Smith.
Lieut. R. Dogherty. 1
  Wm. James. 1

Lieut. Allan McLean. 1
  Wm. Read. (1)
  Alex. Stewart. 1
  Ja. Fraser. 1
  H. M. Williams. (1)
  D. O'Keefe.
  Ja. Dongan. 1
  W. J. Speed. 1
  Rob. Conry. 1
  J. L. Cox. 1
  Jeremiah Marsh. 1
  J. Crawford, *adj.* 2
  D. Maclean. 1
  Sam. Fairtlough. 1
  G. D. Cranfield. (1)
  And. Neill. 2
  J. Fleming. 2
  Cha. Dowson. (2)
  Tho. Nicholl. (2)
  W. H. Gibbons. (2)
  Ja. Johnston. 2
  Henry Eager. (2)
  John Grant.
  And. Saunders 2
  W. G. Isdell. (2)
  C. B. Norton.
  Wm. Hind.
  J. Parkinson.
  Gilbert Conry. 1

Lieut. C. Le Hunte. 1
 Rob. Allison.
 Wm. Laing.
 Cha. M'Anally.
Ens. Pat. Lynch.
 Wm. Gibson. (2
 D. Campbell. (2,
 John Hawks. (2)
 E. S. Davis. (2,
 John Walter. (2
 R. Bannerman. 2,
 Wm. Reid.
 Wm. Buchanan.
 Tho. Freer.

Ens. D. Campbell.
 David Miller.
 H. Graham.
 Cha. Boyd.
 Cha. McCartie.
Pymr. H. Allison. (1)
 Cha. Jones. (2,
Adj. J. Crawford, lt. (2,
Q.-M. P. Maitland. (2)
Surg. R. Stratton. (1)
 Isaac Silcock. (2,
A. S. P. Lawless. (1)
 J. Henley. (2)
 J. Ewing. (2)

1811.

Col. Thos. Graham, l.g.

Lt.Col. G. Moncrieffe, l.g.
 John McNair.
 Hon. Mark Napier. (1,
Major Geo. Burrell. (1)
 Tho. Wright.
 Tho. Steele. (2
 John Brown. (2,
Capt. C. M'Gregor.
 Edw. Currie.
 Benj. Preedy.
 Wm. Holland.
 And. Wood.
 D. A. Gilland.
 Tho. Ware.
 A. Bowen.
 Alt. D'Alton.
 M. Dixon.
 W. H. Wilby.
 C. Gardiner.

Capt. F. Livingstone.
 Jas. Ferguson.
 G. Williamson.
 C. C. Dixon.
 Jas. Gauntlett.
 John Dickins.
 J. Birch.
 S. Fairtlough.
Lieut. R. Dogherty.
 Wm. James.
 A. M'Lean.
 Wm. Read.
 Jas. Fraser.
 H. M. Williams.
 Dan. O'Keefe.
 W. J. Speed.
 Rob. Conry.
 J. L. Cox.
 Jerem. Marsh.

b

Lieut. J. Crawford.
D. Maclean.
G. D. Cranfield.
And. Neill.
J. Fleming.
Chas. Dowson.
Tho. Nicholl.
W. H. Gibbons.
Ja. Johnston.
Henry Eager.
John Grant.
A. Saunders.
W. G. Isdell.
C. B. Norton.
Wm. Hind.
J. Parkinson.
Gilbert Conry.
C. Le Hunte.
Wm. Laing.
Chas. M'Anally.
Pat. Lynch.
Wm. Gibson.
D. Campbell.
John Hawks.
Samuel Ball.
Ens. E. S. Davis.

Ens. John Walker.
R. Bannerman.
Wm. Reid.
— Buchanan.
Tho. Freer.
D. Campbell.
H. Graham.
Chas. Boyd.
Chas. M'Cartie.
Angus M'Donald.
Totten Alley.
Henry Terry.
Walter Gray.
Rob. O'Donnell.
Pymr. H. Allison. (1)
Chas. Jones. (2)
Adj. J. Crawford. (2)
W. James.
Q.-M. P. Maitland.
— Blood.
Surg. R. Stratton. (1)
Isaac Silcock. (2)
A.-S. P. Lawless.
J. Henley.
J. Ewing.
Jas. Cardiff.

1812.

Col. Thos. Graham, *l.g.*

Lt.Col. John McNair. (1)
Hon. M. Napier. (2)
Major Geo. Burrell. (1)
Tho. Wright. (1)
Tho. Steele, *c.* (2)
John Brown. (2)
Capt. C. M'Gregor.

Capt. Edw. Currie.
Benj. Preedy, *m.*
W. Holland.
And. Wood.
D. A. Gilland.
Tho. Ware.
A. Bowen.

Capt.	A. D'Alton.	Lieut.	Pat. Lynch.
	Manley Dixon.		Wm. Gibson.
	W. H. Wilby, *m*.		D. Campbell.
	C. Gardiner.		J. Hawks.
	F. Livingstone.		Samuel Bell.
	Jas. Ferguson.		E. S. Davis.
	G. Williamson.		John Walker.
	C. C. Dixon.		R. Bannerman.
	Jas. Gauntlett.		Wm. Read.
	John Dickins.		— Buchanan.
	J. Birch.	Ens.	Thos. Freer.
	S. Fairtlough.		D. Campbell.
Lieut.	R. Dogherty.		C. Boyd.
	Wm. James.		C. M'Cartie.
	A. M'Lean.		Angus M'Donald.
	Wm. Read.		Henry Terry.
	Jas. Fraser.		Walter Gray.
	H. Williams.		Rob. O'Donnell.
	Dan. O'Keefe.		James King.
	W. J. Speed.		John Wood.
	Rob. Conry.		Den. Dighton.
	J. L. Cox.		Edw. Warren.
	Jeremiah Marsh.	Pymr.	H. Allison. (1)
	J. Crawford.		Chas. Jones. (2)
	G. D. Cranfield.		John Orde.
	And. Neill.		Rich. Philips.
	J. Fleming.	Adj.	J. Crawford. (2)
	Chas. Dowson.		W. James. (1)
	Tho. Nicholl.	Q.-M.	P. Maitland.
	Henry Eager.		— Blood.
	John Grant.	Surg.	R. Stratton. 1,
	W. G. Isdell.		Isaac Silcock. (2)
	Wm. Hind.	A. S.	P. Lawless.
	Gilbert Conry.		J. Henley.
	C. Le Hunte.		J. Ewing.
	Wm. Laing.		Jas. Cardiff.
	C. M'Anally.		

1813.

Col. Sir Thos. Graham, K.B., *l.g.*

Lt.Col. John McNair.
Hon. Mark Napier.
Major George Burrell.
 Tho. Wright.
 John Brown.
 Chas. Gardiner.
Capt. Edw. Currie, *l.c.*
 Benj. Preedy, *m.*
 Wm. Holland.
 And. Wood.
 Dudley Gilland.
 Thos. Ware.
 Arthur Bowen.
 Albert D'Alton.
 Manley Dixon.
 W. H. Wilby, *m.*
 G. Williamson.
 C. Cranston Dixon.
 J. Gauntlett.
 John Dickins.
 John Birch.
 S. Fairtlough.
 Rich. Dogherty.
 And. Niel.
 Wm. James.
 Allan Maclean.
Lieut. W. Read.
 Jas. Fraser.
 H. M. Williams.
 Dan. O'Keefe.
 W. J. Speed.
 R. Conry.
 J. L. Cox.
 J. Marsh.
Lieut. J. Crawford.
 G. D. Cranfield.
 J. Fleming.
 C. Dawson.
 T. Nicholl.
 Henry Eager.
 John Grant.
 W. G. Isdell.
 W. Hind.
 Gilbert Conry.
 C. Le Hunte
 W. Laing.
 C. M'Anally.
 Pat. Lynch.
 W. Gibson.
 D. Campbell.
 J. Hawks.
 Sam. Bell.
 E. S. Davis.
 R. Bannerman.
 W. Reed.
 W. Buchanan.
 Thos. Freer.
 D. Campbell.
 Walter Gray.
 K. T. Ross.
 Chas. Boyd.
Ens. C. M'Cartie.
 Angus M'Donald.
 Henry Terry.
 James King.
 John Wood.
 Edw. Warren.
 John Orde.

Ens. John Green.
James Abbott.
N. Taylor.
J. Nunn.
H. J. French.
W. Macpherson.
W. H. Douglas.
Pymr. Harry Allison. (1)
Chas. Jones. (2)

Adj. J. Crawford.
Q.-M. Peter Maitland.
— Blood.
Surg. Rob. Stratton.
I. Silcock.
A. S. Pat. Lawless.
John Henley.
J. Ewing.
J. Cardiff.

1814.

Col. Sir Thos. Graham, K. B., *l.g.*

Lt.Col. John McNair, *c.*
Hon. Mark Napier.
Major George Burrell, *l.c.*
Tho. Wright, *l.c.*
James A. Hope, *l.c.*
A. Thistlethwaite.
Capt. Edw. Currie, *l.c.*
Benj. Preedy, *m.*
Wm. Holland.
And. Wood.
Dudley Gilland.
Thos. Ware.
A. Bowen.
A. D'Alton.
M. Dixon.
W. H. Wilby, *m.*
G. Williamson.
C. C. Dixon.
Jas. Gauntlett.
John Dickins.
John Birch.
S. Fairtlough.
R. Dogherty.
And. Neil.

Capt. W. James.
Allan Maclean.
Lieut. Wm. Read.
Jas. Fraser.
H. M. Williams.
Dan. O'Keefe.
W. J. Speed.
R. Conry.
J. L. Cox.
Jeremiah Marsh.
J. Crawford.
G. D. Cranfield.
J. Fleming.
C. Dowson.
T. Nickoll.
Henry Eager.
J. Grant.
W. G. Isdell.
W. Hind.
G. Conry.
C. Le Hunte.
W. Laing.
C. M'Anally.
P. Lynch.

Lieut. W. Gibson.   Ens. W. Macpherson.
    D. Campbell.   John Kerr.
    Sam. Bell.   Alex. Wilson.
    E. S. Davis.   J. Bayley.
    R. Bannerman.   Alex. Stuart.
    W. Reed.   Francis Newton.
    W. Buchanan.   M. G. Taylor.
    D. Campbell.   D. Thomson.
    Walter Gray.   Pymr. H. Allison. (1)
    K. T. Ross.   Charles Jones. (2)
    Chas. Boyd.   Adj. J. Crawford.
    C. M'Cartie.   Alex. Wilson.
    T. F. Uniacke.   Q.-M. P. Maitland.
Ens. A. M'Donald.   P. Blood.
    H. Terry.   Surg. Isaac Silcock.
    John Wood.   A. S. P. Lawless.
    Edw. Warren.   J. Henley.
    John Orde.   J. Ewing.
    James Abbott.   J. Cardiff.
    N. Taylor.   Hen. Hamilton.
    John Nunn.

1815.

Col. Thos. Lord Lynedoch, K.B., *l.g.*

Lt.Col. John McNair, *l.c.*   Capt. Albert D'Alton.
    Hon. Mark Napier.   M. Dixon.
Major G. Burrell, *l.c.*   W. H. Wilby, *m.*
    Tho. Wright, *l.c.*   G. Williamson, *m.*
    A. Thistlethwayte.   C. C. Dixon, *m.s.*
    E. Currie, *l.c.*   John Dickens.
Capt. Benj. Preedy, *l.c.*   J. Birch, *s.*
    Wm. Holland, *m.*   Sa. Fairtlough.
    And. Wood, *m.*   R. Dogherty.
    D. A. Gilland.   W. James.
    Tho. Ware, *m.*   Allan M'Lean.
    A. Bowen.   Wm. Read.

Capt. Ja. Fraser.
Lieut. H. M. Williams.
    Dan. O'Keefe.
    W. J. Speed.
    Rob. Conry.
    J. L. Cox.
    Jeremiah Marsh.
    J. Crawford, adj.
    G. D. Cranfield.
    J. Fleming.
    Cha. Dowson.
    Tho. Nickoll.
    Henry Eager.
    John Grant.
    Wm. Hind.
    Gilbert Conry.
    C. Le Hunte.
    Wm. Laing.
    Cha. M'Anally.
    Pat. Lynch.
    Wm. Gibson.
    D. Campbell.
    Samuel Bell.
    E. S. Davys.
    R. Bannerman.
    R. Buchanan.
    Walter Gray.
    K. T. Ross.
    Cha. Boyd.
    Cha. M'Cartie.
    J. F. Uniacke.
    A. Macdonald.

Lieut. Henry Terry.
    John Wood.
    Edw. Warren.
    John Orde.
Ens. Jas. Abbott.
    Nath. Taylor.
    John Nunn.
    Wm. Macpherson.
    John Kerr.
    A. Wilson, adj.
    John Bayley.
    Alex. Stuart.
    Fra. Newton.
    M. G. Taylor.
    Jacob Sankey.
    J. D. Bentham.
    Wm. Furlong.
    Edw. Last.
    N. G. White.
Pymr. H. Allison.
    Cha. Jones.
Adj. J. Crawford.
    A. Wilson.
Q.-M. P. Maitland.
    — Blood.
Surg. Isaac Silcock.
    H. Hamilton.
A. S. J. Henley.
    J. Ewing.
    Ja. Cardiff.
    A. Hamilton.

1816.

Col. Thos. Lord Lynedoch, G.C.B., *&c.*
Lt.Col. J. McNair, *c.* 1
    Hon. Mark Napier. 2
Major G. Burrell, *&c.*
    Tho. Wright, *&c.*

Major A. Thistlethwayte.
B. Preedy, *l.c.*
Capt. W. Holland, *m.*
And. Wood, *m.*
D. A. Gilland.
Tho. Ware, *m.*
A. Bowen.
A. D'Alton, *m.*
M. Dixon.
W. H. Wilby, *m.*
G. Williamson, *m.*
C. C. Dixon, *m.*
John Dickins.
J. Birch.
S. Fairtlough.
R. Doherty.
W. James.
Wm. Read.
Ja. Fraser.
Dan. O'Keefe.
W. J. Speed.
Lieut. H. M. Williams.
R. Conry.
J. L. Cox.
J. Marsh.
J. Crawford.
G. D. Cranfield.
J. Fleming.
C. Dowson.
Tho. Nickoll.
Henry Eager.
J. Grant.
W. Hind.
G. Conry.
C. Le Hunte.
W. Laing.
C. M'Anally.

Lieut. P. Lynch.
W. Gibson.
D. Campbell.
Sam. Bell.
E. S. Davys.
R. Bannerman.
R. Buchanan.
Walter Gray.
K. T. Ross.
Chas. Boyd.
Chas. M'Cartie.
T. F. Uniacke.
A. Macdonald.
H. Terry.
John Wood.
Edw. Warren.
John Orde.
Jas. Abbott.
Nath. Taylor.
John Nunn.
Ens. W. Macpherson.
J. Kerr.
A. Wilson.
J. Bayley.
Alex. Stuart.
Fra. Newton.
M. G. Taylor.
Jacob Sankey.
J. D. Bentham.
W. Furlong.
Edw. Last.
N. T. White.
Colin Rose.
John Wilson.
John Walker.
C. Baillie.
M. Pattison.

Ens. J. Fennell.
Pymr. H. Allison.
    C. Jones.
Adj. J. Crawford.
    A. Wilson.
Q.-M. P. Maitland.
    P. Blood.

Surg. Isaac Silcock.
    H. Hamilton.
A. S. J. Henley.
    J. Ewing.
    Jas. Cardiff.
    A. Hamilton.

1817.

Col. Thos. Lord Lynedoch, G.C.B., *l.g.*

Lt.Col. J. McNair, *c.*
Major George Burrell, *l.c.*
    Thomas Wright, *l.c.*
Capt. Will. Holland, *m.*
    Andrew Wood, *m.*
    Thos. Ware, *m.*
    Arthur Bowen.
    Albert D'Alton, *m.*
    Manley Dixon.
    W. H. Wilby, *m.*
    G. Williamson, *m.*
    C. Cranston Dixon, *m.*
    Honeyman Mackay.
Lieut. Robert Conry.
    John Lucas Cox.
    Jeremiah Marsh.
    James Crawford.
    George D. Cranfield.
    John Fleming.
    Chas. Dowson.
    Thos. Nickoll.
    Henry Eager.
    John Grant.
    Wm. Hind.
    Gilbert Conry.

Lieut. C. Le Hunte.
    Wm. Laing.
    Chas. M'Anally.
    Wm. Gibson.
    David Campbell.
    Samuel Bell.
    E. S. Davys.
    Robt. Bannerman.
    Robt. Buchanan.
    Walter Gray.
    Nath. Taylor.
Ens. John Kerr.
    Alex. Wilson.
    John Bayley.
    Alex. Stuart.
    Francis Newton.
    Monkhouse G. Taylor.
    Jacob Sankey.
    John Wilson.
Pymr. Harry Allison.
Adj. James Crawford.
Q.-M. Peter Maitland.
Surg. John Silcock.
A. S. Jos. Ewing.
    Mat. Farnan.

1818.

Col. Thos. Lord Lynedoch, G.C.B., *l.g.*

Lt.Col. J. McNair, *c.*
Major G. Burrell, *l.c.*
Tho. Wright, *l.c.*
Capt. W. Holland, *m.*
And. Wood, *m.*
Tho. Ware, *m.*
A. D'Alton, *m.*
M. Dixon.
W. H. Wilby, *m.*
G. Williamson, *m.*
C. C. Dixon, *m.*
Honeyman Mackay.
Carlisle Pollock.
Lieut. Rob. Conry.
J. L. Cox.
Jeremiah Marsh.
J. Crawford, *adj.*
G. D. Cranfield.
J. Fleming.
Cha. Dowson.
Tho. Nickoll.
Henry Eager.
John Grant.
C. Le Hunte.
Wm. Laing.

Lieut. Cha. M'Anally.
Wm. Gibson.
D. Campbell.
Samuel Bell.
E. S. Davys.
R. Bannerman.
R. Buchanan.
Walter Gray.
Nath. Taylor.
John Taylor.
Charles Shaw.
Ens. John Kerr.
A. Wilson.
John Bayley.
Alex. Stuart.
Fra. Newton.
M. G. Taylor.
Jacob Sankey.
John Wilson.
Pymr. H. Allison.
Adj. J. Crawford, *lt.*
Q.-M. P. Maitland.
Surg. Isaac Silcock.
A. S. J. Ewing.
M. Farnan.

1819.

Col. Thos. Lord Lynedoch, G.C.B., *l.g.*

Lt.Col. J. McNair, *c.*
Major G. Burrell, *l.c.*
Tho. Wright, *l.c.*
Capt. W. Holland, *m.*
And. Wood, *m.*
A. D'Alton, *m.*

Capt. M. Dixon.
W. H. Wilby, *m.*
G. Williamson, *m.*
C. C. Dixon, *m.*
Honey Mackay.
Carlisle Pollock.

Capt. C. Le Hunte.
Lieut. Rob. Conry.
J. L. Cox.
Jeremiah Marsh.
J. Crawford, *adj.*
G. D. Cranfield.
J. Fleming.
Cha. Dowson.
Tho. Nickoll.
John Grant.
Wm. Laing.
Cha. M'Anally.
Wm. Gibson.
D. Campbell.

Ens. A. Wilson.
    Alex. Stuart.
    Fra. Newton.
    M. G. Taylor.
    Jacob Sankey.
    John Wilson.
    J. Herris White.
    S. W. Popham.
Pymr. H. Allison.
Adj. J. Crawford.
Q.-M. P. Maitland.
Surg. Isaac Silcock.
A. S. M. Farnan.

1820.

Col. Thos. Lord Lynedoch, G.C.B., *l.g.*

Lt.Col. J. McNair, *m.g.*
  (w) Hen. Austen.
Major G. Burrell, *l.c.*
  Thomas Wright, *l.c.*
Capt. W. Holland, *m.*
  Andrew Wood, *m.*
  A. D'Alton, *m.*
  Manley Dixon, *m.*
  W. H. Wilby, *l.c.*
  G. Williamson, *m.*
  C. C. Dixon, *m.*
  Honeyman Mackay.
  Carlisle Pollock.
  C. Le Hunte.
Lieut. Robert Conry.
  J. L. Cox.
  Jeremiah Marsh.
  J. Crawford.
  G. D. Cranfield.
  J. Fleming.

Lieut. Chas. Dowson.
  Thos. Nickoll.
  John Grant.
  Wm. Laing.
  C. M'Anally.
  Wm. Gibson.
  Wm. Ewbank.
Ens. A. Wilson.
    Alex. Stuart.
    Francis Newton.
    M. G. Taylor.
    Jacob Sankey.
    John Wilson.
    S. W. Popham.
    H. J. Cotter.
Pymr. H. Allison.
Adj. J. Crawford.
Q.-M. P. Maitland.
Surg. J. Silcock.
A. S. M. Farnan.

1821.

Col. Thos. Lord Lynedoch, G.C.B., *l.g.*

Lt.Col. J. M'Nair, *m.g.*
   (w) Hen. Austen.
Major G. Burrell, *l.c.*
   Tho. Wright, *l.c.*
Capt. A. D'Alton, *m.*
   M. Dixon, *m.*
   G. Williamson, *m.*
   C. C. Dixon, *m.*
   Honeyman Mackay.
   Carlisle Pollock.
   C. Le Hunte.
   (w) S. Holmes.
   Robert Conry.
   Cha. Paget.
Lieut. J. L. Cox.
   G. D. Cranfield.
   Cha. Dowson.
   Tho. Nickoll.
   Wm. Laing.
   Wm. Ewbank.

Lieut. H. D. Maclean.
   A. Wilson.
   Hec. Munro, *adj.*
   Alex. Stuart.
   B. R. Ottley.
Ens. M. G. Taylor.
   Jacob Sankey.
   John Wilson.
   S. W. Popham.
   H. J. Cotter.
   Edw. Sneyd.
   J. W. Eyles.
   F. H. Buckeridge.
   Fred. White.
   G. C. M. L. W. S. John-
Pymr. H. Allison.   [ston.
Adj. H. Munro, *lt.*
Q.-M. P. Maitland.
Surg. W. Morrison.
A. S. Ja. McArthur.

1822.

Col. Thos. Lord Lynedoch, G.C.B., *g.*

Lt.Col. J. McNair, *m.g.*
   Sir F. Stovin, K.C.B.
Major G. Burrell, *l.c.*
   Tho. Wright, *l.c.*
Capt. A. D'Alton, *m.*
   M. Dixon, *m.*
   G. Williamson, *m.*
   C. C. Dixon, *m.*
   Honeyman Mackay.
   Carlisle Pollock.
   (w) S. Holmes.

Capt. Robt. Conry.
   H. B. Gamble.
Lieut. J. L. Cox.
   G. D. Cranfield.
   Chas. Dowson.
   Thos. Nickoll.
   Wm. Laing.
   Wm. Ewbank.
   H. D. Maclean.
   Hector Monro.
   Alex. Stuart.

xxix

Lieut. B. R. Ottley.
Ens. M. G. Taylor.
    Jacob Sankey.
    John Wilson.
    S. W. Popham.
    T. W. Eyles.
    F. H. Buckeridge.
    Fred. White.

Ens. G. C. M. L. W. S. Johnston.
    J. H. Baldwin.
Pymr. H. Allison.
Adj. H. Munro.
Q.-M. P. Maitland.
Surg. W. Morrison.
A. S. Jas. M'Arthur.

1823.

Col. Thos. Lord Lynedoch, G.C.B., *g*.

Lt.Col. J. McNair, *m.g.*
    Sir F. Stovin, K.C.B.
Major G. Burrell, *l.c.*
    Tho. Wright, *l.c.*
Capt. M. Dixon, *m.*
    G. Williamson, *m.*
    C. C. Dixon, *m.*
    Honeyman Mackay.
    Robert C. Pollock.
    W. S. Holmes.
    Robert Conry.
    Wm. Ewbank.
Lieut. J. L. Cox.
    G. D. Cranfield.
    Cha. Dowson, *d.*
    Tho. Nickoll.
    Wm. Laing.

Lieut. H. D. Maclean.
    Hec. Munro, *adj.*
    Alex. Stuart.
    Robert Read.
Ens. Jacob. Sankey.
    John Wilson.
    S. W. Popham.
    T. W. Eyles.
    F. H. Buckeridge.
    Fred. White.
    Wm. J. Owen.
    Wm. Beatty.
Pymr. H. Allison.
Adj. H. Munro, *lt.*
Q.-M. P. Maitland.
Surg. W. Morrison.
A. S. Ja. McArthur.

1824.

Col. R. Darling, *m.g.*

Lt.Col. J. McNair, *m.g.*
    Sir F. Stovin, K.C.B.
Major G. Burrell, *l.c.*
    Tho. Wright, *l.c.*
Capt. M. Dixon.

Capt. G. Williamson.
    C. C. Dixon.
    Honeyman Mackay.
    R. C. Pollock.
    W. S. Holmes.

Capt. Rob. Conry.
    Wm. Ewbank.
Lieut. J. L. Cox.
    G. D. Cranfield.
    Chas. Dowson.
    Tho. Nickoll.
    Wm. Laing.
    H. D. Maclean.
    Hec. Munro.
    Alex. Stuart.
    Robt. Read.
Ens. Jacob Sankey.

Ens. John Wilson.
    S. W. Popham.
    T. W. Eyles.
    F. H. Buckeridge.
    Fred. White.
    W. J. Owen.
    Wm. Beatty.
Pymr. H. Allison.
Adj. H. Munro.
Q.-M. P. Maitland.
Surg. W. Morrison.
A. S. J. M'Arthur.

1825.
Col. R. Darling, *m.g.*

Lt.Col. J. McNair, *m.g.*
    Sir F. Stovin, K.C.B.
Major G. Burrell, *l.c.*
    Man. Dixon.
Capt. C. C. Dixon, *m.*
    H. Mackay.
    Robt. Carlisle Pollock.
    (W. S. Holmes, *s.*
    Robert Conry.
    Wm. Ewbank.
    Cha. C. Blane.
    J. Lucas Cox.
Lieut. G. D. Cranfield.
    Tho. Nickoll.
    Wm. Laing.
    Hec. Munro, *adj.*
    Alex. Stuart.

Lieut. Robert Read.
    John Wilson.
    S. W. Popham.
    T. W. Eyles.
Ens. F. H. Buckeridge.
    Fred. White.
    Wm. J. Owen.
    Wm. Beatty.
    Hugh Massy.
    A. Mackenzie.
    Rich. Norman.
Pymr. H. Allison.
Adj. H. Munro, *lt.*
Q.-M. P. Maitland.
Surg. L. Whitney.
A. S. Ja. M'Arthur.

1826.
Col. R. Darling, *l.g.*

Lt.Col. J. McNair, *m.g.*
    Sir F. Stovin, K.C.B.

Major G. Burrell, *l.c.*
    Man. Dixon.

xxxi

Capt. C. C. Dixon, *m*.	Lieut. John Parker.
H. Mackay.	Fred. White.
Robt. Carlisle Pollock.	Ens. Wm. J. Owen.
Wm. Ewbank.	Wm. Beatty.
Cha. C. Blanc.	Hugh Massy.
H. Suckling.	A. Mackenzie.
G. D. Cranfield.	Rich. Norman.
Tho. Nickoll.	Fred. Eld.
Alex. Stuart.	Hen. H. Cuming.
Wm. Woollcombe.	Rob. Straton.
Lieut. Wm. Laing.	Dixon Foot.
Hec. Munro, *adj*.	H. R. Thurlow.
John Wilson.	Pymr. H. Allison.
S. W. Popham.	Adj. H. Munro, *ll*.
T. W. Eyles.	Q.-M. P. Maitland.
F. H. Buckeridge.	Surg. J. M'Arthur.
R. G. Daunt.	A. S. W. Blake.
Tho. Gleeson.	F. C. Huthwaite.
(w) J. Bowlby.	

1827.

Col. R. Darling, *l.g.*

Lt.Col. Sir F. Stovin, K.C.B.	Lieut. Hec. Munro.
Major G. Burrell, *l.c.*	John Wilson.
Manley Dixon.	R. G. Daunt.
Capt. C. C. Dixon, *m*.	Tho. Gleeson.
Honeyman Mackay.	George Pigot.
Wm. Ewbank.	W. J. Owen.
H. Suckling.	A. Mackenzie.
Tho. Nickoll.	Fred. Eld.
Alex. Stuart.	Henry H. Cuming.
W. Woollcombe.	Dixon Foot.
S. W. Popham.	Ens. Hugh Massy.
Marcus J. Slade.	Richard Norman.
(w) J. Bowlby.	Robt. Straton.
Lieut. W. Laing.	H. R. Thurlow.

Ens. Fred. Romilly.   Pymr. H. Allison.
John James.   Adj. H. Munro, *lt.*
Edm. P. Gilbert.   Q.-M. P. Maitland.
Marcus Geale.   Surg. J. McArthur.
John E. White.   A. S. W. Blake.
G. Douglas Bowyer.   F. C. Huthwaite.

1828.

Col. R. Darling, *l.g.*

Lt.Col. Sir F. Stovin, K.C.B.   Lieut. Fred. Eld.
Major G. Burrell, *l.c.*   Hen. H. Cuming.
Man. Dixon.   Dixon Foot.
Capt. H. Mackay.   Ens. Hugh Massy.
  Wm. Ewbank.   Rob. Straton.
  H. Suckling.   H. R. Thurlow.
  Alex. Stuart.   F. Romilly.
  (w) W. Woollcombe.   John James.
  M. J. Slade.   Edm. P. Gilbert.
  (w) J. Bowlby.   Marcus Geale.
  T. Woodw. Eyles.   John E. White.
  Fred. White.   G. Doug. Bowyer.
Lieut. Wm. Laing.   D. C. Mills.
  H. Munro, *adj.*   Pymr. H. Allison.
  John Wilson.   Adj. H. Munro, *lt.*
  R. G. Daunt.   Q.-M. P. Maitland.
  Tho. Gleeson.   Surg. J. M'Arthur.
  George Pigot.   A. S. W. Blake.
  Wm. J. Owen.   F. C. Huthwaite.
  A. Mackenzie.

1829.

Col. R. Darling, *l.g.*

Lt.Col. Sir F. Stovin, K.C.B.   Capt. H. Mackay.
Major G. Burrell, *l.c.*   Wm. Ewbank.
Man. Dixon.   H. Suckling.

Capt. W. Woollcombe. Lieut. Rob. Straton.
     M. J. Slade. Ens. H. R. Thurlow.
     J. Bowlby. F. Romilly.
     T. Woodw. Eyles. John James.
     Fred. White. Edm. P. Gilbert.
     Wm. Laing. Marcus Geale.
     Hon. F. G. Howard. John E. White.
Lieut. John Wilson. G. Doug. Bowyer.
     R. G. Daunt. D. C. Mills.
     Tho. Gleeson. Vere Caldwell.
     George Pigot. Rowland Alison.
     Wm. J. Owen. Pymr. H. Allison.
     A. Mackenzie, *adj.* Adj. A. Mackenzie, *lt.*
     Fred. Eld. Q.-M. P. Maitland.
     Hen. H. Cuming. Surg. J. McArthur.
     Dixon Foot. A. S. W. Blake.
     Hugh Massy. F. C. Huthwaite.

1830.

Col. R. Darling, *l.g.*

Lt.Col. Lord. G. W. Russell. Lieut. Wm. J. Owen.
Major G. Burrell, *l.c.* A. Mackenzie, *adj.*
     Man. Dixon. Fred. Eld.
Capt. H. Mackay. Hen. H. Cuming.
     Wm. Ewbank. Rob. Straton.
     H. Suckling. H. R. Thurlow.
     M. J. Slade. F. Romilly.
     J. Bowlby. W. H. Rogers.
     T. Woodw. Eyles. Ens. John James.
     Fred. White. Edm. P. Gilbert.
     Wm. Laing. Marcus Geale.
     Hon. F. G. Howard. John E. White.
     John Wilson. G. Doug. Bowyer.
Lieut. R. G. Daunt. D. C. Mills.
     Tho. Gleeson. Vere Caldwell.
     George Pigot. Rowland Alison.

Ens. S. B. Hobart.
P. P. Gallwey.
Pymr. H. Allison.
Adj. A. Mackenzie, *lt.*

Q.-M. P. Maitland.
Surg. J. M'Arthur.
A. S. W. Blake.
F. C. Huthwaite.

1831.

Col. R. Darling, *l.g.*

Lt.Col. Lord G. W. Russell.
Major Man. Dixon.
H. Mackay.
Capt. Wm. Ewbank.
H. Suckling.
M. J. Slade.
W. J. Bowlby.
T. Woodw. Eyles.
Fred. White.
Wm. Laing.
Hon. F. G. Howard.
John Wilson.
G. D. Griffith.
Lieut. R. G. Daunt.
Tho. Gleeson.
Wm. J. Owen.
A. Mackenzie, *adj.*
Fred. Eld.
Hen. H. Cuming.
Rob. Straton.

Lieut. H. R. Thurlow.
F. Romilly.
John James.
Ens. Edm. P. Gilbert.
Marcus Geale.
G. Doug. Bowyer.
Vere Caldwell.
Rowland Alison.
S. B. Hobart.
P. P. Gallwey.
Edm. T. Eyton.
J. H. Cotton.
Hon. Hen. Cav. Grey.
Pymr. H. Yielding Eager.
Adj. A. Mackenzie, *lt.*
Q.-M. P. Maitland.
Surg. J. M'Arthur.
A. S. W. Blake.
F. C. Huthwaite.

1832.

Col. R. Darling, *l.g.*

Lt.Col. C. G. J. Arbuthnot.
Major H. Mackay.
M. J. Slade.
Capt. Wm. Ewbank.
H. Suckling.

Capt. W. J. Bowlby.
T. Woodw. Eyles.
Fred. White.
Wm. Laing.
Hon. F. G. Howard.

Capt. John Wilson.
    G. D. Griffith.
    Fred. Eld.
Lieut. R. G. Daunt.
    Tho. Gleeson.
    W. J. Owen, *adj.*
    Hen. H. Cuming.
    Rob. Straton.
    H. R. Thurlow.
    F. Romilly.
    W. H. Rogers.
    John James.
    Edm. P. Gilbert.
    Cha. Spencer Bunyon.
Ens. Marcus Geale.

Ens. G. Doug. Bowyer.
    Vere Caldwell.
    P. P. Gallwey.
    Edm. T. Eyton.
    J. H. Cotton.
    Lord C. Lennox Kerr.
    B. G. F. Graham.
    T. Webb.
    Osborne Markham.
Pymr. Yielding Eager.
    Wm. J. Owen.
Q.-M. P. Maitland.
Surg. John Robertson.
    A. S. W. Blake.

1833.

Col. R. Darling, *l.g.*

Lt.Col. C. G. J. Arbuthnot.
Major H. Mackay.
    M. J. Slade.
Capt. Wm. Ewbank.
    H. Suckling.
    W. J. Bowlby.
    T. Woodw. Eyles.
    Fred. White.
    Hon. F. G. Howard.
    John Wilson.
    G. D. Griffith.
    Fred. Eld.
    Hen. H. Cuming.
Lieut. Tho. Gleeson.
    W. J. Owen, *adj.*
    Rob. Straton.
    H. R. Thurlow.
    F. Romilly.

Lieut. W. H. Rogers.
    John James.
    Edm. P. Gilbert.
    Marcus Geale.
    G. Douglas Bowyer.
    Vere Caldwell.
Ens. P. P. Gallwey.
    Edm. T. Eyton.
    J. H. Cotton.
    Lord C. Lennox Kerr.
    B. G. F. Graham.
    T. Webb.
    Osborne Markham.
    John F. Doxat.
    John H. Bringhurst.
    Lord Stephen Alg. Chichester.
Pymr. H. Yielding Eager.

Adj. Wm. J. Owen, *lt*.   Surg. John Robertson.
Q.-M. P. Maitland.   A. S. W. Blake.

1834.

Col. R. Darling, *l.g.*

Lt.Col. C. G. J. Arbuthnot.   Lieut. Marcus Geale.
Major H. Mackay.   G. Douglas Bowyer.
    M. J. Slade.   Vere Caldwell.
Capt. Wm. Ewbank.   Phil. P. Gallwey.
    H. Suckling.   Ens. Edm. T. Eyton.
    lu J. Bowlby.   J. H. Cotton.
    T. Woodw. Eyles.   Lord C. Lennox Kerr.
    Fred. White.   T. Webb.
    John Wilson.   John F. Doxat.
    G. D. Griffith.   John H. Bringhurst.
    Fred. Eld.   Lord S. A. Chichester.
    Hen. H. Cuming.   Lord J. Beresford.
    Tho. Gleeson.   C. Mont. Chester.
Lieut. W. J. Owen, *adj*.   Fred. Woodgate.
    Rob. Straton.   Pymr. H. Yielding Eager.
    H. R. Thurlow.   Adj. Wm. J. Owen.
    F. Romilly.   Q.-M. P. Maitland.
    W. H. Rogers.   Surg. John Robertson.
    John James.   A. S. W. Blake.
    Edm. P. Gilbert.

1835.

Col. R. Darling, *l.g.*

Lt.Col. C. G. J. Arbuthnot.   Capt. John Wilson.
Major H. Mackay.   G. D. Griffith.
    M. J. Slade.   Fred. Eld.
Capt. Wm. Ewbank.   Hen. H. Cuming.
    H. Suckling.   Rob. Straton.
    lu J. Bowlby.   Lieut. W. J. Owen, *adj*.
    T. Woodw. Eyles.   H. R. Thurlow.
    Fred. White.   W. H. Rogers.

Lieut. John James.
    Marcus Geale.
    G. Douglas Bowyer.
    Vere Caldwell.
    Phil. P. Gallwey.
    J. D. G. Tulloch.
    Edm. T. Eyton.
    J. H. Cotton.
Ens. T. Webb.
    John F. Doxat.
    John H. Bringhurst.
    Lord S. A. Chichester.

Ens. Lord J. Beresford.
    C. Mont. Chester.
    Fred. Woodgate.
    Digby F. Mackworth.
    J. E. Thackwell.
    Henry Fane.
Pymr. H. Yielding Eager.
Adj. Wm. J. Owen.
Q.-M. P. Maitland.
Surg. John Robertson.
    A. S. W. Blake.

1836.

Col. Sir R. Darling, K.C.H., *l.g.*

Lt.Col. C. G. J. Arbuthnot.
Major M. J. Slade.
    Geo. G. Nicolls.
Capt. H. Suckling.
    W J. Bowlby.
    T. Woodw. Eyles.
    John Wilson.
    G. D. Griffith.
    Fred. Eld.
    Hen. H. Cuming.
    H. R. Thurlow.
    John James.
    T. Graham Egerton.
Lieut. W. J. Owen.
    W. H. Rogers.
    Marcus Geale.
    G. Douglas Bowyer.
    Vere Caldwell.
    Phil. P. Gallwey.
    J. D. G. Tulloch.

Lieut. Edm. T. Eyton.
    J. H. Cotton, *adj.*
    Tho. Webb.
    John J. Doxat.
Ens. J. H. Bringhurst.
    Lord S. A. Chichester.
    Lord J. Beresford.
    C. Mont. Chester.
    Fred. Woodgate.
    Digby F. Mackworth.
    J. E. Thackwell.
    Henry Fane.
    C. Vaughan Pugh.
    Edw. Hickey.
Pymr. H. Yielding Eager.
Adj. J. H. Cotton, *lt.*
Q.-M. P. Maitland.
Surg. John Robertson.
    A. S. W. Blake.

1837.

Col. Sir R. Darling, G.C.H., *l.g.*

Lt.Col. C. G. J. Arbuthnot.
Major M. J. Slade.
   Geo. G. Nicolls.
Capt. H. Suckling.
      J. Bowlby.
   T. Woodw. Eyles.
   John Wilson.
   G. D. Griffith.
   Fred. Eld.
   Hen. H. Cuming.
   H. R. Thurlow.
   John James.
   T. Graham Egerton.
Lieut. W. J. Owen.
   W. H. Rogers.
   Marcus Geale.
   G. Douglas Bowyer.
   Vere Caldwell.
   Phil. P. Gallwey.
   J. D. G. Tulloch.

Lieut. Edm. T. Eyton.
   Tho. Webb.
   John J. Doxat.
Ens. J. H. Bringhurst.
   Lord S. A. Chichester.
   Lord J. Beresford.
   C. Mont. Chester.
   Fred. Woodgate.
   Digby F. Mackworth.
   J. E. Thackwell.
   C. Vaughan Pugh.
   Edw. Hickey.
   G. K. M. Dawson.
Pymr. H. Yielding Eager.
Adj. C. Mont. Chester.
Q.-M. P. Maitland.
Surg. John Robertson.
A. S. R. Dane.
R. K. Prendergast.

1838.

Col. Sir Hen. Sheehy Keating, K.C.B., *l.g.*

Lt.Col. C. G. J. Arbuthnot.
Major M. J. Slade.
   Geo. G. Nicolls.
Capt. H. Suckling.
      J. Bowlby.
   T. Woodw. Eyles.
   John Wilson.
   G. D. Griffith.
   Fred. Eld.
   Hen. H. Cuming.

Capt. H. R. Thurlow.
   John James.
   T. Graham Egerton.
Lieut. W. J. Owen.
   W. H. Rogers.
   Marcus Geale.
   G. Douglas Bowyer.
   Vere Caldwell.
   Phil. P. Gallwey.
   J. D. G. Tulloch.

Lieut. Edm. T. Eyton.
Tho. Webb.
John Doxat.
Ens. J. H. Bringhurst.
Lord S. A. Chichester.
Lord J. Beresford.
C. M. Chester, *adj*.
Fred. Woodgate.
Digby F. Mackworth.
J. E. Thackwell.

Ens. C. Vaughan Pugh.
G. K. M. Dawson.
Rob. Owen.
K. W. S. Mackenzie.
Pymr. H. Yielding Eager.
Adj. C. Mont. Chester, *ens.*
Q.-M. Wm. Newland.
Surg. John Robertson.
A. S. R. Dane.
R. K. Prendergast.

1839.

Col. Sir Hen. Sheehy Keating, K.C.B., *l.g.*

Lt.Col. John Peddie, K.H.
Major M. J. Slade.
J. Singleton, K.H.
Capt. H. Suckling, *m*.
T. Woodw. Eyles.
John Wilson.
G. D. Griffith.
Fred. Eld.
Hen. H. Cuming.
H. R. Thurlow.
Gervas S. Deverill.
Wm. H. Rogers.
G. Douglas Bowyer.
Lieut. Marcus Geale.
Vere Caldwell.
Phil. P. Gallwey.
J. D. G. Tulloch.
Edm. T. Eyton.
Tho. Webb.
John J. Doxat.
J. H. Bringhurst.

Lieut. Lord S. A. Chichester.
Lord. J. Beresford.
C. M. Chester, *adj*.
Ens. Fred. Woodgate.
Digby F. Mackworth.
J. E. Thackwell.
C. Vaughan Pugh.
Rob. Owen.
K. W. S. Mackenzie.
Tho. Ross.
W. P. Purnell.
Hen. Ashmore Evatt.
J. Bedford Woollcombe.
Pymr. H. Yielding Eager.
Adj. C. Mont. Chester.
Q.-M. Wm. Newland.
Surg. John Kinnis.
A. S. R. Dane
R. K. Prendergast.

1840.

Col. Sir Hen. Sheehy Keating, K.C.B., *l.g.*

Lt.Col. John Peddie, K.H.
Major M. J. Slade.
    J. Singleton, K.H.
Capt. H. Suckling.
    T. Woodw. Eyles.
    John Wilson.
    G. D. Griffith.
    Fred. Eld.
    Hen. H. Cuming.
    H. R. Thurlow.
    Gerv. S. Deverill.
    G. Douglas Bowyer.
    John B. Mann.
Lieut. Marcus Geale.
    Vere Caldwell.
    Phil. P. Gallwey.
    J. D. G. Tulloch.
    Tho. Webb.
    J. J. Doxat.
    J. H. Bringhurst.

Lieut. Lord S. A. Chichester.
    Lord J. Beresford.
    C. M. Chester.
    Fred. Woodgate.
Ens. Digby F. Mackworth.
    C. Vaughan Pugh.
    Rob. Owen.
    K. W. S. Mackenzie.
    Tho. Ross.
    W. P. Purnell.
    Hen. Ashmore Evatt.
    Hen. Lecky.
    F. Brockman Morley.
    J. W. B. Peddie.
Pymr. H. Yielding Eager.
Adj. C. Mont. Chester, *lt.*
Q.-M. W. Newland.
Surg. John Kinnis.
A. S. R. Dane.
    R. K. Prendergast.

1841.

Col. Sir Henry Sheehy Keating, K.C.B., *l.g.*

Lt.Col. J. Singleton, K.H.
Major T. W. Eyles.
    G. D. Griffith.
Capt. H. Suckling, *m.*
    John Wilson.
    Fred. Eld.
    Hen. H. Cuming.
    H. R. Thurlow.
    G. S. Deverill.
    G. Doug. Bowyer.
    John B. Mann.

Capt. Marcus Geale.
    P. P. Gallwey.
Lieut. J. D. G. Tulloch.
    Tho. Webb.
    J. H. Bringhurst.
    Lord S. A. Chichester.
    C. M. Chester.
    Fred. Woodgate.
    N. E. Blackall.
    C. Vaughan Pugh.
    J. MacNeale Walter.

Lieut. Rob. Owen.
K. Wm. S. Mackenzie.
Ens. Tho. Ross.
W. P. Purnell.
H. Ashmore Evatt.
Hen. Lecky.
F. Brockman Morley.
J. W. B. Peddie.
Rob. Grove.

Ens. D. Davies, *adj*.
W. Victor Johnson.
Hon. J. Tuchet.
Pymr. H. Yielding Eager.
Adj. D. Davies.
Q.-M. W. Newland.
Surg. John Kinnis.
A. S. R. K. Prendergast.
G. A. Cowper.

1842.

Col. Sir Alex. Leith, K.C.B., *l.g.*

Lt.Col. J. Singleton, K.H.
Major T. W. Eyles.
G. D. Griffith.
Capt. John Wilson.
Fred. Eld.
H. R. Thurlow.
G. S. Deverill.
G. Doug. Bowyer.
John B. Mann.
Marcus Geale.
P. P. Gallwey.
J. D. G. Tulloch.
Tho. Webb.
Lieut. J. H. Bringhurst.
C. M. Chester.
Fred. Woodgate.
C. Vaughan Pugh.
J. MacNeale Walter.
Rob. Owen.
K. W. S. Mackenzie.

Lieut. Tho. Ross.
W. P. Purnell.
H. Ashmore Evatt.
Ens. Hen. Lecky.
F. Brockman Morley.
Jas. W. B. Peddie.
Rob. Grove.
D. Davies, *adj*.
W. V. Johnson.
Cha. Fred. Thurston.
Tho. Smith.
Hor. John Suckling.
Wm. Davis.
Hen. P. Onslow.
Pymr. H. Yielding Eager.
Adj. D. Davies, *ens*.
Q. M. W. Newland.
Surg. Rob. Ellson.
A. S. R. K. Prendergast.
G. A. Cowper.

1843.

Col. Sir Alex. Leith, K.C.B., *l.g.*

Lt.Col. J. Singleton, K.H.
Major T. W. Eyles.

Major G. D. Griffith.
Capt. Fred. Eld.

Capt. H. R. Thurlow.
G. S. Deverill.
G. Doug. Bowyer.
John B. Mann.
Marcus Geale.
P. P. Gallwey.
J. D. G. Tulloch.
Tho. Webb.
J. H. Bringhurst.
Lieut. C. M. Chester.
Fred. Woodgate.
C. Vaughan Pugh.
J. MacNeale Walter.
Rob. Owen.
K. W. S. Mackenzie.
Tho. Ross.
W. P. Purnell.
H. Ashmore Evatt

Lieut. Hen. Lecky.
Ens. Jas. W. B. Peddie.
Rob. Grove.
D. Davies, *adj*.
W. V. Johnson.
Cha. Fred. Thurston.
Tho. Smith.
Horatio J. Suckling.
Wm. Davis.
Hen. P. Onslow.
Cha. S. Dowson.
T. de C. Hamilton.
Pymr. H. Yielding Eager.
Adj. D. Davies, *ens*.
Q. M. W. Newland.
Surg. Rob. Ellson.
A. S. R. K. Prendergast.
W. Maclise.

1844.

Col. Sir Alex. Leith, K.C.B., *l.g.*

Lt.Col. J. Singleton, K.H.
Major T. W. Eyles.
H. Vaughan, *l.c.*
Capt. Fred. Eld.
H. R. Thurlow.
G. S. Deverill.
G. Doug. Bowyer.
John B. Mann.
Marcus Geale.
P. P. Gallwey.
J. D. G. Tulloch.
Tho. Webb.
J. H. Bringhurst.
Lieut. C. M. Chester.
F. Woodgate.

Lieut. C. Vaughan Pugh.
J. MacNeale Walter.
Rob. Owen.
K. W. S. Mackenzie.
Tho. Ross.
W. P. Purnell.
H. Ashmore Evatt.
Hen. Lecky.
Ens. Jas. W. B. Peddie.
Rob. Grove.
D. Davies, *adj*.
W. V. Johnson.
C. F. Thurston.
T. Smith.
H. J. Suckling.

Ens. T. de Courcy Hamilton. Adj. D. Davies, *ens.*
  R. R. Wyvill. Q.-M. W. Newland.
  S. K. Ferrier Nazer. Surg. Rob. Ellson.
  J. A. Butler. A. S. R. K. Prendergast.
Pymr. H. Yielding Eager. Wm. Maclise.

1845.
Col. Sir Alex. Leith, K.C.B., *l.g.*

Lt.Col. J. Singleton, K.H. Lieut. Hen. Lecky.
Major T. W. Eyles.   J. W. B. Peddie.
  H. Vaughan. Ens. Robert Grove.
Capt. Fred Eld.   D. Davies.
  H. R. Thurlow.   W. V. Johnson.
  G. S. Deverill.   C. F. Thurston.
  G. D. Bowyer.   T. Smith.
  John B. Mann.   T. deCourcy Hamilton.
  Marcus Geale.   R. R. Wyvill.
  P. P. Gallwey.   S. K. F. Nazer.
  Tho. Webb.   J. A. Butler.
  T. H. Bringhurst.   Tho. J. Meredith.
  C. M. Chester.   W. L. Braybrooke.
Lieut. F. Woodgate. Pymr. H. Yielding Eager.
  C. Vaughan Pugh. Adj. D. Davies.
  J. MacNeale Walter. Q.-M. W. Newland.
  K. W. S. Mackenzie. Surg. Rob. Ellson.
  Tho. Ross. A. S. R. K. Prendergast.
  W. P. Purnell.   W. Maclise.
  H. Ashmore Evatt.

1846.
Col. Sir Alex. Leith, K.C.B., *l.g.*

Lt.Col. Marcus J. Slade. Capt. John B. Mann.
Major T. W. Elyes.   Marcus Geale.
  H. Vaughan.   Tho. Webb.
Capt. Fred. Eld.   J. H. Bringhurst.
  H. R. Thurlow.   C. M. Chester.
  G. S. Deverill.   F. Woodgate.

xliv

Capt. C. Vaughan Pugh.
Lieut. J. MacNeale Walter.
    Rob. Owen.
    Tho. Ross.
    W. P. Purnell.
    Hen. Lecky.
    J. W. B. Peddie.
    Rob. Grove.
    D. Davies, *adj.*
    W. V. Johnson.
    T. Smith.
    Purcell O'Gorman.
Ens. T.deCourcy Hamilton.
    R. R. Wyvill.

Ens. S. K. F. Nazer.
    J. A. Butler.
    Tho. Jas. Meredith.
    Jas. Perrin.
    Michael Foster Ward.
    H. McMahon Eager.
    J. Christ. Guise.
    J. Hardy Thursby.
Pymr. H. Yielding Eager.
Adj. D. Davies, *ll.*
Q.-M. Sam. Williams.
Surg. Rob. Ellson.
A. S. R. K. Prendergast.
    Wm. Maclise.

1847.
Col. Sir Alex. Leith, K.C.B., *l.g.*

Lt.Col. Marcus J. Slade.
Major T. W. Eyles.
    H. Vaughan.
Capt. Fred. Eld.
    H. R. Thurlow.
    G. S. Deverill.
    John B. Mann.
    Marcus Geale.
    Tho. Webb.
    J. H. Bringhurst.
    C. M. Chester.
    F. Woodgate.
    C. V. Pugh.
Lieut. MacNeale Walter.
    Rob. Owen.
    Tho. Ross.
    W. P. Purnell.
    Hen. Lecky.
    J. W. B. Peddie.
    Rob. Grove.

Lieut. D. Davies.
    W. V. Johnson.
    T. Smith.
    Purcell O'Gorman.
Ens. T.deCourcy Hamilton.
    R. R. Wyvill.
    S. K. F. Nazer.
    J. A. Butler.
    T. J. Meredith.
    Jas. Perrin.
    M. F. Ward.
    H. McMahon Eager.
    J. C. Guise.
    J. H. Thursby.
Pymr. H. Y. Eager.
Adj. D. Davies.
Q.-M. Sam. Williams.
Surg. Rob. Ellson.
A. S. W. Maclise.

1848.

Col. Sir Alex. Leith, K.C.B., *l.g.*

Lt.Col. Marcus J. Slade.
Major H. Vaughan, *l.c.*
    Fred. Eld.
Capt. H. R. Thurlow, *m.*
    G. S. Deverill, *m.*
    John B. Mann.
    Marcus Geale.
    Tho. Webb.
    J. H. Bringhurst.
    C. M. Chester.
    F. Woodgate.
    Tho. Ross.
    J. MacNeale Walter.
Lieut. W. P. Purnell.
    Hen. Lecky.
    J. W. B. Peddie.
    Rob. Grove.
    D. Davies.
    W. V. Johnson.

Lieut. T. Smith.
    Purcell O'Gorman.
    T. de C. Hamilton.
    R. R. Wyvill.
Ens. T. J. Meredith.
    Jas. Perrin.
    Michael F. Ward.
    H. McMahon Eager.
    J. Christ. Guise.
    J. H. Thursby.
    Herbert M. Vaughan.
    W. P. Tinling.
    Vere H. Close.
    R. D. Vaughton.
Pymr. J. W. B. Peddie.
Adj. Purcell O'Gorman.
Q.-M. Sam. Williams.
Surg. R. Ellson.
A. S. W. Maclise.

1849.

Col. Sir Alex. Leith, K.C.B., *l.g.*

Lt.Col. Marcus J. Slade.
Major H. Vaughan, *l.c.*
    Fred. Eld, *l.c.*
Capt. H. R. Thurlow, *m.*
    G. S. Deverill, *m.*
    John B. Mann.
    J. H. Bringhurst, *m.*
    Tho. Ross.
    Dun. Campbell.
    W. P. Purnell.
    W. Ben. Bastard.

Capt. Henry Lecky.
    Rob. Grove.
Lieut. D. Davies.
    W. V. Johnson.
    T. Smith.
    P. O'Gorman, *adj.*
    R. R. Wyvill.
    T. J. Meredith.
    Jas. Perrin.
    M. Foster Ward.
    J. Christ. Guise.

Lieut. Hon. Wm. Harbord.
J. H. Thursby.
Ens. H. McMahon Eager.
H. M. Vaughan.
W. P. Tinling.
Vere H. Close.
R. D. Vaughton.
Fred. Beatly.
Harry Denison.

Ens. Henry Butler.
Henry Hope Crealock.
Henry F. Every.
Pymr. Jas. W. Bainbrigge Peddie.
Adj. P. O'Gorman.
Q.-M. Sam. Williams.
Surg. R. Ellson.
A. S. W. Maclise.

1850.

Col. Sir Alex. Leith, K.C.B., *l.g.*

Lt.Col. Marcus J. Slade.
Major H. Vaughan, *l.c.*
Fred. Eld, *l.c.*
Capt. G. S. Deverill.
John B. Mann.
Tho. Ross.
Dun. Campbell.
W. P. Purnell.
W. Ben. Bastard.
Rob. Grove.
W. V. Johnson.
Thos. Smith.
Roger Barnston.
Lieut. P. O'Gorman, *adj.*
R. R. Wyvill.
T. J. Meredith.
Jas. Perrin.
M. Foster Ward.
J. Christ. Guise.
J. B. Thursby.

Lieut. H. M. Vaughan.
W. P. Tinling.
Vere H. Close.
Thos. Johns.
Ens. R. D. Vaughton.
Harry Denison.
Henry Butler.
Henry Hope Crealock.
Henry F. Every.
Jas. Herne Wade.
Chas. C. Maunsell.
R. H. Magenis.
Henry Preston.
Walter B. Persse.
Pymr. J. W. B. Peddie.
Adj. P. O'Gorman, *ll.*
Q.-M. Sam. Williams.
Surg. Rob. C. Anderson.
A. S. W. Maclise.

1851.

Col. Sir Alex. Leith, K.C.B., *l.g.*

Lt.Col. Marcus J. Slade. | Major H. Vaughan, *l.c.*

Major Fred. Eld, *l.c.*
Capt. G. S. Deverill, *m.*
    John B. Mann.
    Tho. Ross.
    Dun. Campbell.
    W. P. Purnell.
    W. Ben. Bastard.
    Rob. Grove.
    W. V. Johnson.
    Thos. Smith.
    Roger Barnston.
Lieut. P. O'Gorman, *adj.*
    R. R. Wyvill.
    T. J. Meredith.
    Jas. Perrin.
    M. Foster Ward.
    J. Christ. Guise.
    J. H. Thursby.
    H. M. Vaughan.

Lieut. W. P. Tinling.
    Vere H. Close.
    Cecil P. Pole.
Ens. R. D. Vaughton.
    Harry Denison.
    Henry Butler.
    H. H. Crealock.
    Henry F. Every.
    Jas. Herne Wade.
    Chas. C. Maunsell.
    R. H. Magenis.
    Henry Preston.
    Walter B. Persse.
Pymr. J. W. Bainbrigge
    Peddie.
Adj. P. O'Gorman, *lt.*
Q.-M. Sam. Williams.
Surg. Rob. C. Anderson.
A. S. W. Maclise.

1852.

Col. Sir Alex. Leith, K.C.B., *l.g.*

Lt.Col. Marcus J. Slade, *c.*
Major H. Vaughan, *l.c.*
    Fred. Eld, *l.c.*
Capt. G. S. Deverill, *m.*
    John B. Mann, *m.*
    Tho. Ross.
    Dun. Campbell.
    W. P. Purnell.
    W. Ben. Bastard.
    Rob. Grove.
    W. V. Johnson.
    Thos. Smith.
    Roger Barnston.
Lieut. P. O'Gorman, *adj.*

Lieut. R. R. Wyvill.
    T. J. Meredith.
    Jas. Perrin.
    M. Foster Ward.
    J. Christ. Guise.
    J. H. Thursby.
    H. M. Vaughan.
    W. P. Tinling.
    Vere H. Close.
    R. D. Vaughton.
Ens. Harry Denison.
    Henry Butler.
    H. H. Crealock.
    Henry F. Every.

Ens. Jas. Herne Wade. Pymr. Jas. W. Bainbrigge
Chas. C. Maunsell. Peddie.
R. H. Magenis. Adj. P. O'Gorman, *ll*.
Henry Preston. Q.-M. Sam. Williams.
Walter B. Persse. Surg. Rob. C. Anderson.
J. Clerk Rattray. A. S. W. Maclise.

1853.

Col. Sir Alex. Leith, K.C.B., *l.g.*

Lt.Col. Fred. Eld. Lieut. Vere H. Close.
Major Gervas S. Deverill. Rob. D. Vaughton.
Thos. Ross. Harry Denison.
Capt. John B. Mann, *m.* Henry Butler.
Duncan Campbell. Ens. Hope Crealock.
Wm. P. Purnell. Henry F. Every.
Wm. B. Bastard. Jas. Herne Wade.
Robt. Grove. Rich. H. Magenis.
Wm. V. Johnson. Henry Preston.
Thos. Smith. Walter B. Persse.
Roger Barnston. J. Clerk Rattray.
P. O'Gorman. Paul A. Phipps.
Richard R. Wyvill. Wm. John Rous.
Lieut. Thos. Jas. Meredith. A. Goodlad Daubeny.
Jas. Perrin. Pymr. J. W. B. Peddie.
Mich. Foster Ward. Adj. H. M. Vaughan.
John C. Guise. Q.-M. Sam. Williams.
John H. Thursby. Surg. Rob. C. Anderson.
Herb. M. Vaughan, *adj.* A. S. W. Maclise.
Wm. P. Tinling.

1854.

Col. Felix Calvert.

Lt.Col. Fred. Eld. Capt. Duncan Campbell.
Major G. S. Deverill. Wm. P. Purnell.
Thos. Ross. Wm. B. Bastard.

xlix

Capt. Rob. Grove.
    Wm. V. Johnson.
    Thos. Smith.
    Roger Barnston.
    P. O'Gorman.
    Tho. Jas. Meredith.
    R. H. P. Crauford.
Lieut. Jas. Perrin.
    Mich. F. Ward.
    John C. Guise.
    Herb. M. Vaughan, *adj.*
    Wm. P. Tinling.
    Vere H. Close.
    Robert Vaughton.
    Harry Denison.
    Henry Hope Crealock.

Lieut. Henry Flower Every.
Ens. J. Herne Wade.
    Rich. Magenis.
    Henry Preston.
    Walter B. Persse.
    J. Clerk Rattray.
    Paul A. L. Phipps.
    Wm. John Rous.
    A. Goodlad Daubeny.
    Hon. J. F. Pennington.
    Geo. Graham.
Pymr. Sam. Williams.
Adj. Herb. M. Vaughan.
Q.-M. W. Newland.
Surg. Rob. C. Anderson.
A. S. W. Maclise.

1855.

Col. **W.** Felix Calvert, C.B., *l.g.*

Lt. Col. Fred. Eld.
Major Gervas S. Deverill, *l.c.*
    Robert P. Campbell.
Capt. Duncan Campbell.
    Wm. P. Purnell.
    Robert Grove.
    Thos. Smith.
    Roger Barnston.
    P. O'Gorman.
    Rob. H. P. Crauford.
    James Perrin.
    John C. Guise.
    Herb. M. Vaughan.
    Wm. P. Tinling.
    Vere Henry Close.
Lieut. Rob. D. Vaughton.
    Harry Denison.

Lieut. H. Hope Crealock, *adj.*
    Garnet J. Wolseley.
    Jas. Herne Wade.
    Rich. Henry Magenis.
    Henry Preston.
    Walter B. Persse.
    J. Clerk Rattray.
    Paul A. L. Phipps.
    Wm. John Rous.
    A. Goodlad Daubeny.
    Hon. J. F. Pennington.
    Nicol Grahame.
    Rob. Hen. Evans.
    L. H. L. Irby.
Ens. P. J. Deverill.
    John Joshua Nunn.
    Chas. H. S. Raitt.

Ens. Sir C. Pigott, Bt.
Chas. B. Wynne.
Arthur D. Swift.
Pymr. Sam. Williams.
Adj. H. Hope Crealock.

Q.-M. David Jackson.
Surg. Rob. Anderson.
A. S. Rob. W. Jackson.
D. A. Reid.
Chas. Rob. Nelson.

1856.

Col. to Felix Calvert, C.B., l.g.

Lt.Col. R.P. Campbell, C.B.,c.
W. P. Purnell.
Major Robert Grove, l.c.
Thos. Smith.
Capt. Roger Barnston, m.
Jas. Perrin.
J. C. Guise.
W. P. Tinling.
Vere H. Close.
Rob. D. Vaughton.
Harry Denison.
H. Hope Crealock.
Garnet J. Wolseley.
J. Herne Wade.
R. H. Magenis.
W. B. Persse.
J. Clerk Rattray.
P. A. L. Phipps.
W. J. Rous.
A. G. Daubeny.
Lieut. Hon. J. F. Pennington.
Nicol Grahame.
R. H. Evans.
L. H. L. Irby.
P. J. Deverill.
Oswald W. Every.
J. J. Nunn.
C. H. S. Raitt.

Lieut. Sir C. Pigott, Bart.
H. J. Haydock.
H. H. Goodricke.
C. B. Wynne.
Ivan S. A. Herford.
A. A. Moultrie.
W. H. L. Carleton.
R. D. Synge.
Henry Bingham.
J. Barr.
W. Knight.
C. D. Barwell.
W. Rennie.
G. R. Miller.
H. C. Treacher.
Ens. Apsley Cherry.
E. C. Wynne.
Edward Carter.
M. Preston.
J. H. Rees.
J. W. Knox.
G. E. Perryn.
H. B. Savory.
W. H. Hassard.
L. W. Wilmer.
G. A. Agnew.
Annesley Eyre.
Pymr. Sam. Williams.

Q.-M. David Jackson.   A. S. D. A. Reid.
Surg. R. C. Anderson.   C. R. Nelson.
A. S. R. W. Jackson.

1857.

Col. to Felix Calvert, C.B., *l.g.*

Lt.Col. R.P.Campbell,C.B.,*c.*   Lieut. C. D. Barwell.
Major R. Grove, *l.c.*   W. Rennie.
    Thos. Smith, *l.c.*   G. R. Miller.
Capt. Roger Barnston, *m.*   H. C. Treacher.
    Jas. Perrin, *m.*   Apsley Cherry.
    J. C. Guise.   E. C. Wynne.
    W. P. Tinling.   Edward Carter.
    Vere H. Close.   M. Preston.
    Harry Denison.   Ens.   J. W. Knox.
    H. Hope Crealock, *m.*   G. E. Perryn.
    G. J. Wolseley.   H. B. Savory.
    J. Herne Wade.   L. W. Wilmer.
    R. H. Magenis.   G. A. Agnew.
    W. B. Persse.   Annesley Eyre.
    J. Clerk Rattray.   G. Gregg.
Lieut. Nicol Grahame.   A. R. Chute.
    L. H. L. Irby.   G. H. Powell.
    P. J. Deverill.   H. J. Edgell.
    O. W. Every.   Hugh Gordon.
    J. J. Nunn.   J. F. Haig.
    H. J. Haydock.   S. R. Handy.
    H. H. Goodricke.   Pymr. Sam. Williams.
    C. B. Wynne.   I.ofM. J. C. Guise.
    I. S. A. Herford.   Q.-M. David Jackson.
    A. A. Moultrie.   Adj. W. Rennie.
    W. H. L. Carleton.   Surg. Rob C. Anderson.
    R. D. Synge.   A. S. R. W Jackson.
    H. Bingham.   W. Bradshaw.
    W. Knight.

1858.

Col. Alex. F. Macintosh, K.H., *m.g.*

Lt.Col.R.P.Campbell,C.B.,*c.*
  Wm. P. Purnell.
Major Thomas Smith, *l.c.*
  Roger Barnston.
Capt. James Perrin, *m.*
  J. C. Guise, *I of M.*
  Wm. P. Tinling, *m.*
  Harry Denison.
  H. Hope Crealock, *m.*
  Garnet J. Wolseley.
  Jas. Herne Wade.
  Rich. Henry Magenis.
  J. Clerk Rattray.
  P. A. L. Phipps.
  L. N. D. Hammond.
  Leonard H. L. Irby.
Lieut. Nicol Grahame.
  Percy P. Deverill.
  Oswald W. Every.
  John Joshua Nunn.
  Hen. J. Haydock.
  H. H. Goodricke.
  Charles B. Wynne.
  Ivan S. A. Herford.
  Art. A. Moultrie.
  W. H. L. Carleton.
  Rob. D. Synge.
  Henry Bingham.
  William Knight.

Lieut. Chas. D. Barwell.
  Wm. Rennie, *adj.*
  Geo. Rob. Miller.
  Hen. C. Treacher.
  Apsley Cherry.
  Edw. C. Wynne.
  Edward Carter.
  M. Preston.
  Geo. E. Perryn.
Ens. Henry B. Savory.
  Louis W. Wilmer.
  Gerald A. Agnew.
  Annesley Eyre.
  George Gregg.
  Art. R. Chute.
  Geo. H. Powell.
  Henry J. Edgell.
  Hugh Gordon.
  James F. Haig.
  Sam. R. Handy.
  John Williamson.
Pymr. Samuel Williams.
I.ofM. J. C. Guise, *capt.*
Adj. Wm. Rennie, *lt.*
Q.-M. David Jackson.
Surg. Anth. D. Home.
A. S. Rob. W. Jackson.
  Wm. Bradshaw.
  Edw. J. Crane.

1859.

Col. Alex. F. Macintosh, K.H., *l.g.*

Lt.Col. W. P. Purnell, C.B.,*c.*
  Thos. Smith.

Major J. C. Guise, *l.c.*
  W. P. Tinling.

Capt. H. H. Crealock, *l.c.*
G. J. Wolseley, *m.*
J. Herne Wade, *m.*
R. H. Magenis, *m.*
J. Clerk Rattray.
L. N. D. Hammond.
L. H. L. Irby.
P. J. Deverill.
O. W. Every.
H. H. Goodricke.
Fred. E. Sorell.
W. T. M'Grigor.
Lieut. C. B. Wynne.
Ivan S. A. Herford.
Hen. Bingham.
Wm. Knight.
C. D. Barwell, *I of M.*
W. Rennie, *adj.*
G. R. Miller.
H. C. Treacher.
Apsley Cherry.
E. C. Wynne.
Edward Carter.

Lieut. G. E. Perryn.
H. B. Savory.
L. W. Wilmer.
G. A. Agnew.
Annesley Eyre.
G. Gregg.
Ens. H. J. Edgell.
J. F. Haig.
S. R. Handy.
J. Williamson.
D. P. Murray.
Fra. Russell.
O. W. De Thoren.
Fred. Hone Carleton.
Pymr. Sam. Williams.
I. of M. C. D. Barwell.
Adj. W. Rennie.
Q.-M. David Jackson.
Surg. Pat. Clarke.
A. S. Edw. J. Crane.
G. B. Poppelwell.
C. G. Lumsden.

1860.

Col. Alex. F. Macintosh, K.H., *l.g.*

Lt.Col. W. P. Purnell, C.B., *c.*
Thos. Smith, C.B.
Major John. C. Guise, *l.c.*
W. P. Tinling, *l.c.*
Capt. H. Hope Crealock, *l.c.*
Garnet J. Wolseley, *l.c.*
J. Herne Wade, *m.*
J. Clerk Rattray.
L. N. D. Hammond.
L. H. L. Irby.

Capt. P. J. Deverill.
O. W. Every.
H. H. Goodricke.
Fred. E. Sorell.
W. T. M'Grigor.
Robt. T. Knox.
Lieut. C. B. Wynne.
Ivan S. A. Herford.
H. Bingham.
W. Knight.

Lieut. C. D. Barwell.
    ŕ℃ Wm. Rennie.
    G. R. Miller.
    H. C. Treacher.
    Apsley Cherry.
    E. C. Wynne.
    Edw. Carter.
    L. W. Wilmer.
    G. A. Agnew.
    Annesley Eyre.
    George Gregg.
    C. H. Bindon.
    Joseph Outram.
Ens. H. J. Edgell.
    J. F. Haig.

Ens. S. R. Handy.
    J. Williamson.
    D. P. Murray.
    Fra. Russell.
    O. W. De Thoren.
    Fred. H. Carleton.
Pymr. Tho. Cassidy.
I. of M. C. D. Barwell.
Adj. Wm. Rennie.
Q.-M. David Jackson.
Surg. Pat. J. Clarke.
A. S. E. J. Crane.
    G. B. Poppelwell.
    C. G. Lumsden.

1861.

Col. Alex. F. Macintosh, K.H., *l.g.*

Lt.Col. Tho. Smith, C.B.
    ŕ℃ John C. Guise.
Major W. P. Tinling, *l.c.*
    H. H. Crealock, *l.c.*
Capt. G. J. Wolseley, *l.c.*
    J. Clerk Rattray.
    L. N. D. Hammond.
    L. H. L. Irby.
    P. J. Deverill.
    O. W. Every.
    H. H. Goodricke.
    F. E. Sorell.
    W. T. M'Grigor.
    R. T. Knox.
    Geo. H. Cox.
    H. R. H. Gale.
Lieut. Wm. Knight.
    C. D. Barwell.

Lieut. ŕ℃ Wm. Rennie.
    G. R. Miller.
    H. C. Treacher.
    Apsley Cherry.
    E. C. Wynne.
    Edw. Carter.
    L. W. Wilmer.
    G. A. Agnew.
    George Gregg.
    C. H. Bindon.
    Joseph Outram.
    H. J. Edgell.
    J. F. Haig.
    F. B. Bleazby.
    J. Williamson.
Ens. D. P. Murray.
    Fra. Russell.
    F. Hone Carleton.

Ens. R. I. Ward.　　　　　　Adj. Wm. Rennie.
R. A. Nolan.　　　　　　Q.-M. David Jackson.
J. Campbell.　　　　　　Surg. Wm. Lapsley.
Wm. Wilmer.　　　　　　A. S. Edw. J. Crane.
W. S. Hamilton.　　　　　　G. B. Poppelwell.
Pymr. Thos. Cassidy.　　　　　　C. G. Lumsden.
I.of M.C. D. Barwell.

1862.

Col. Alex. F. Macintosh, K.H., *l.g.*

Lt.Col. ✝︎C John C. Guise.　　Lieut. Hen. James Edgell.
Major Wm. P. Tinling, *l.c.*　　James F. Haig.
　　Garnet J. Wolseley, *l.c.*　　Fra. Bernard Bleazby.
Capt. J. Clerk Rattray.　　John Williamson.
　　L. N. D. Hammond.　　David P. Murray.
　　Leonard H. L. Irby.　　Francis Russell.
　　Percy J. Deverill.　　Randall I. Ward.
　　Oswald W. Every.　　Ens. Fred. Hone Carleton.
　　H. H. Goodricke.　　Rich. A. Nolan.
　　Fred. E. Sorell.　　John Campbell.
　　Wm. Tho. M'Grigor.　　Wm. Wilmer.
　　Fra. D. Wyatt.　　Wm. S. Hamilton.
　　✝︎C Rob. M. Rogers.　　John Hen. Hedges.
　　Apsley Cherry.　　Despréaux J. Boileau.
　　A. G. E. Morley.　　Art. Wm. Bowman.
Lieut. C. D. Barwell, *I of M.*　　Duncan Maclachlan.
　　✝︎C Wm. Rennie, *adj.*　　Pymr. Tho. Cassidy.
　　Geo. Rob. Miller.　　I.of M.C. D. Barwell, *lt.*
　　Hen. C. Treacher.　　Adj. ✝︎C W. Rennie.
　　Edw. C. Wynne.　　Q.-M. David Jackson.
　　Edward Carter.　　Surg. Wm. Lapsley.
　　Louis W. Wilmer.　　A. S. Edw. J. Crane.
　　Gerald A. Agnew.　　Geo. B. Poppelwell.
　　Chas. Hunt Bindon.　　T. T. Gardner.

1863.

Col. Wm. H. Eden, *m.g.*

Lt.Col. **VC** John C. Guise.
Major Wm. P. Tinling, *l.c.*
    J. Clerk Rattray.
Capt. L. N. D. Hammond.
    Leonard H. L. Irby.
    Percy J. Deverill.
    H. H. Goodricke.
    Fred. E. Sorell, *m.*
    Wm. Tho. M'Grigor.
    VC Robt. M. Rogers.
    Apsley Cherry.
    Thos. Carlisle.
    C. D. Barwell, *I of M.*
    Albert Seagrim.
    Hen. C. Treacher.
Lieut. **VC** W. Rennie, *adj.*
    Geo. Rob. Miller.
    Edw. C. Wynne.
    Edward Carter.
    Louis W. Wilmer.
    Gerald A. Agnew.
    Chas. Hunt Bindon.
    Hen. James Edgell.
    James F. Haig.

Lieut. Fra. Bernard Bleazby.
    John Williamson.
    David P. Murray.
    Randall I. Ward.
    Wm. Hen. Spooner.
    John Campbell.
Ens. Fred. Hone Carleton.
    Rich. A. Nolan.
    Wm. Wilmer.
    Wm. S. Hamilton.
    John Hen. Hedges.
    Despréaux J. Boileau.
    Art. Wm. Bowman.
    Duncan Maclachlan.
    Edwin Thackwell.
    Wm. Fred. Wilson.
Pymr. Tho. Cassidy.
I. of M. C. D. Barwell, *capt.*
Adj. **VC** W. Rennie, *lt.*
Q.-M. David Jackson.
Surg. Wm. Lapsley.
A. S. Edw. J. Crane.
    T. T. Gardner.
    P. Quinlan.

1864.

Col. Wm. H. Eden, *m.g.*

Lt.Col. **VC** John C. Guise.
Major J. Clerk Rattray.
    L. N. D. Hammond.
Capt. Leonard H. L. Irby.
    H. H. Goodricke.
    Fred. E. Sorell, *m.*
    VC Robt. M. Rogers.

Capt. Apsley Cherry.
    Thos. Carlisle.
    Chas. D. Barwell.
    Albert Seagrim.
    VC Wm. Rennie.
    Geo. E. Perryn.
    Geo. Robt. Miller.

Capt. Alex. Chas. Grant.
Lieut. Edw. C. Wynne.
 Edward Carter.
 Louis W. Wilmer.
 Gerald A. Agnew.
 Chas. Hunt Bindon.
 Hen. James Edgell.
 James F. Haig, *adj.*
 Fra. Bernard Bleazby.
 John Williamson.
 David P. Murray.
 Randall I. Ward, *I of M*
 Wm. Hen. Spooner.
 John Campbell.
 Fred. Hone Carleton.
 Rich. Albert Nolan.
Ens. Wm. Wilmer.

Ens. Wm. S. Hamilton.
 John Hen. Hedges.
 Despréaux J. Boileau.
 Art. Wm. Bowman.
 Duncan Maclachlan.
 Edwin Thackwell.
 Wm. Fred. Wilson.
 A. Nimmo Sandilands.
Pymr. Wm. Lawes.
I. of M. R. I. Ward, *lt.*
Adj. J. F. Haig, *lt.*
Q.-M. David Jackson.
Surg. Wm. Boyd.
A. S. Edw. J. Crane.
 T. T. Gardner
 P. Quinlan.

1865.

Col. Wm. H. Eden, *l.g.*

Lt. Col. Jas. Clerk Rattray.
Major L. N. D. Hammond.
 Hen. W. Palmer.
Capt. H. H. Goodricke.
 F C Robt. M. Rogers.
 Apsley Cherry.
 Thos. Carlisle.
 C. D. Barwell.
 Albert Seagrim.
 F C W. Rennie.
 Geo. E. Perryn.
 Geo. Robt. Miller.
 Hon. J. D. Drummond.
 Edward Carter.
 John Thomas French.
Lieut. Louis W. Wilmer.
 Gerald A. Agnew.

Lieut. Hen. James Edgell.
 James F. Haig, *adj.*
 Fra. Bernard Bleazby.
 David P. Murray.
 Randall I. Ward.
 Wm. Hen. Spooner.
 John Campbell.
 Fred. Hone Carleton.
 Rich. Albert Nolan.
 Wm. Wilmer.
 Wm. S. Hamilton.
 John Hen. Hedges.
 Duncan Maclachlan.
Ens. Art. Wm. Bowman.
 Edwin Thackwell.
 Wm. Fred Wilson.
 A. Nimmo Sandilands.

Ens. Jas. Hen. Jackson.   Pymr. Wm. Lawes.
Alex. M. Delavoye.   I. of M. R. I. Ward *ll*.
Chas. B. Norman.   Adj. J. F. Haig, *ll*.
J. M. W. Von Beverhoudt.   Q.-M. David Jackson.
   Surg. Wm. Boyd.
Rob. Lawrence.   A. S. Edw. J. Cran...
Gregory J. Buller.   T. T. Gardner.

1866.

Col. Wm. H. Eden, *l.g.*

Lt.Col. Jas. Clerk Rattray.
Major L. N. D. Hammond.
Hen. W. Palmer.
Capt. H. H. Goodricke.
    ✝C Robt. M. Rogers.
    Apsley Cherry.
    Thos. Carlisle.
    Chas. D. Barwell.
    ✝C Wm. Rennie.
    Geo. E. Perryn.
    Geo. Robt. Miller.
    Hon. J. D. Drummond.
    Edward Carter.
    John Thomas French.
    Robt. Hen. Hackett.
Lieut. Louis W. Wilmer.
    Gerald A. Agnew.
    Hen. James Edgell.
    James F. Haig.
    Fra. Bernard Bleazby.
    David P. Murray.
    Randall I. Ward, *adj.*
    Wm. Hen. Spooner.
    John Campbell.

Lieut. Fred. Hone Carleton.
    Rich. Albert Nolan.
    Wm. Wilmer.
    Wm. S. Hamilton.
    John Hen. Hedges.
    D. Maclachlan, *I of M.*
Ens. Art. Wm. Bowman.
    Edwin Thackwell.
    Wm. Fred Wilson.
    A. Nimmo Sandilands.
    Jas. Hen. Jackson.
    Alex. M. Delavoye.
    Chas. B. Norman.
    J. M. W. Von Beverhoudt.
    Rob. Lawrence.
    Gregory J. Buller.
Pymr. Wm. Lawes.
I. of M. D. Maclachlan, *ll*.
Adj. R. I. Ward, *ll*.
Q.-M. David Jackson.
Surg. Wm. Boyd.
A. S. C. J. Weir.
    A. Thomson.

1867.

Col. Wm. H. Eden, *l.g.*

Lt.Col. Jas. Clerk Rattray.
Major L. N. D. Hammond.
 Hen. W. Palmer.
Capt. Sir H.H.Goodricke,Bt
 ŦC Robt. M. Rogers.
 Apsley Cherry.
 Thos. Carlisle.
 Chas. D. Barwell.
 ŦC Wm. Rennie.
 Geo. E. Perryn.
 Geo. Robt. Miller.
 Hon. J. D. Drummond.
 Edward Carter.
 John Thos. French.
 Robt. Hen. Hackett.
Lieut. Louis W. Wilmer.
 Gerald A. Agnew.
 Hen. James Edgell.
 James F. Haig.
 Fra. Bernard Bleazby.
 David P. Murray.
 Randall I. Ward, *adj.*
 Wm. Hen. Spooner.
 John Campbell.

Lieut. Fred. Hone Carleton.
 Rich. Albert Nolan.
 Wm. Wilmer.
 Wm. S. Hamilton.
 John Hen. Hedges.
 D. Maclachlan, *I of M.*
Ens. Art. Wm. Bowman.
 Edwin Thackwell.
 Wm. Fred. Wilson.
 A. Nimmo Sandilands.
 Jas. Hen. Jackson.
 Alex. M. Delavoye.
 Chas. B. Norman.
 J. M. W. Von Beverhoudt.
 Rob. Lawrence.
 Gregory J. Buller.
Pymr. Wm. Lawes.
I.of M. D. Maclachlan, *ll.*
Adj. R. I. Ward, *ll.*
Q.-M. Robt. Gibbins.
Surg. Wm. Boyd.
A. S. C. J. Wier.
 A. Thomson.

1868.

Col. Wm. H. Eden, *l.g.*

Lt.Col. Jas. Clerk Rattray.
Major L. N. D. Hammond.
 Hen. W. Palmer.
Capt. Sir H.H.Goodricke,Bt
 ŦC Robt. M. Rogers.

Capt. Apsley Cherry.
 Thos. Carlisle.
 ŦC Wm. Rennie.
 Geo. E. Perryn.
 Hon. J. D. Drummond.

Capt. Edward Carter.   Lieut. Wm. Fred. Wilson.
      John Thos. French.   A. Nimmo Sandilands.
      Robt. Hen. Hackett.   Ens. Jas. Hen. Jackson.
      Hen. James Edgell.   Alex. M. Delavoye.
      John Caulfeild.   Chas. B. Norman.
Lieut. Louis W. Wilmer.   J. M. W. Von Bever-
      G. A. Agnew, *I of M*.   houdt.
      Fra. Bernard Bleazby.   Rob. Lawrence.
      David P. Murray.   Gregory J. Buller.
      Randall I. Ward, *adj*.   Edward Lethbridge.
      John Campbell.   F. Maitland Balfour.
      Fred. Hone Carleton.   Joseph Hen. Laye.
      Rich. Albert Nolan.   Pymr. Wm. Lawes.
      Wm. Wilmer.   I. of M. G. A. Agnew, *lt*.
      Wm. S. Hamilton.   Adj. R. I. Ward, *lt*.
      John Hen. Hedges.   Q.-M. Robt. Gibbins.
      Duncan Maclachlan.   Surg. Wm. Boyd.
      Arthur Wm. Bowman.   A. S. C. J. Weir.
      Edwin Thackwell.   A. Thomson.

1869.

Col. Wm. H. Eden, *l.g*.

Lt.Col. Jas. Clerk Rattray.   Lieut. Louis W. Wilmer.
Major L. N. D. Hammond.   G. A. Agnew, *I of M*.
      Hen. W. Palmer.   Fra. Bernard Bleazby.
Capt. Sir H. H. Goodricke, Bt.   Randall I. Ward, *adj*.
     ✝C Robt. M. Rogers.   John Campbell.
      Apsley Cherry.   Fred. Hone Carlton.
     ✝C Wm. Rennie.   Rich. Albert Nolan.
      Geo. E. Perryn.   Wm. Wilmer.
      Hon. J. D. Drummond.   Wm. S. Hamilton.
      Edward Carter.   John Hen. Hedges.
      John Thos. French.   Duncan Maclachlan.
      Robt. Hen. Hackett.   Arthur Wm. Bowman.
      John Caulfeild.   Edwin Thackwell.
      David P. Murray.   Wm. Fred. Wilson.

lxi

Lieut. A. Nimmo Sandilands.	Lieut. Joseph Hen. Laye.
Jas. Hen. Jackson.	Geo. Sandham.
Alex. M. Delavoye.	Herbert Flint.
Chas. B. Norman.	Pymr. Wm. Lawes.
J. M. W. Von Beverhoudt.	I. of M. G. A. Agnew.
	Adjt. R. I. Ward, *lt.*
Rob. Lawrence.	Q.-M. Robt. Gibbins.
Gregory J. Buller.	Surg. N. Norris.
Edward Lethbridge.	A. S. A. Thomson.
Fred. M. Balfour.	A. Minty.

1870.

Col. Wm. H. Eden, *l.g.*

Lt.Col. J. C. Rattray, *c.*	Lieut. Edwin Thackwell.
Major H. W. Palmer.	W. F. Wilson.
Sir H. H. Goodricke, Bt.	A. N. Sandilands.
Capt. ℣C R. M. Rogers.	J. H. Jackson.
Apsley Cherry.	Alex. M. Delavoye.
℣C W. Rennie.	Wm. Higgens.
G. E. Perryn.	Ens. J. M. W. Von Beverhoudt.
Edw. Carter.	
J. T. French.	Robt. Lawrence.
R. H. Hackett.	G. J. Buller.
John Caulfeild.	Edw. Lethbridge.
D. P. Murray.	F. M. Balfour.
John Lawrence.	J. H. Laye.
Lieut. L. W. Wilmer.	G. Sandham.
G. A. Agnew, *I of M.*	H. Flint.
F. B. Bleazby.	A. H. Eyre.
R. I. Ward, *adj.*	Pymr. W. J. Bampfield.
J. Campbell.	I. of M. G. A. Agnew.
R. A. Nolan.	Adj. R. I. Ward.
W. S. Hamilton.	Q.-M. Robt. Gibbins.
J. H. Hedges.	Surg. N. Norris.
D. Maclachlan.	A S. A. Thomson.
A. W. Bowman.	

1871.

Col. Wm. H. Eden, *l.g.*

Lt.Col. J. C. Rattray, *c.*
Major H. W. Palmer.
   Sir H. H. Goodricke, Bt.
Capt. ✝︎ R. M. Rogers.
   Apsley Cherry.
   ✝︎ Wm. Rennie.
   G. E. Perryn.
   Edw. Carter.
   J. T. French.
   R. H. Hackett.
   D. P. Murray.
   John Lawrence.
   R. I. Ward.
Lieut. John Campbell.
   W. S. Hamilton.
   J. H. Hedges, *I of M.*
   D. Maclachlan.
   A. W. Bowman, *adj.*
   Edwin Thackwell.
   W. F. Wilson.

Lieut. Alex. M. Delavoye.
   Wm. Higgens.
   Robt. Lawrence.
   W. J. Banbury.
Ens. J. M. W. Von Beverhoudt.
   G. J. Buller.
   Edw. Lethbridge.
   F. M. Balfour.
   J. H. Laye.
   G. Sandham.
   H. Flint.
   A. H. Eyre.
   A. W. Elliott.
Pymr. W. J. Bampfield.
I. of M. J. H. Hedges.
Adj. A. W. Bowman.
Q.-M. Robt. Gibbins.
Surg. N. Norris.
A. S. T. Seward.

1872.

Col. Wm. H. Eden, *l.g.*

Lt.Col. J. C. Rattray, C.B., *c.*
Major H. W. Palmer.
   ✝︎ H. E. Wood.
Capt. ✝︎ R. M. Rogers.
   Apsley Cherry.
   ✝︎ Wm. Rennie.
   G. E. Perryn.
   R. H. Hackett.
   D. P. Murray.
   John Lawrence.
   R. I. Ward.

Capt. John Campbell.
   W. S. Hamilton.
Lieut. D. Maclachlan.
   A. W. Bowman, *adj.*
   Edwin Thackwell.
   W. F. Wilson.
   R. Lawrence, *I of M.*
   W. J. Banbury.
   A. C. E. Welby.
   Fred. R. Hervey.
   Stephen J. Stevens.

lxiii

Lieut. Edw. Lethbridge.   Pymr. W. J. Bampfield.
       J. H. Laye.   I.of M.R. Lawrence.
Ens. F. M. Balfour.   Adj. A. W. Bowman.
      G. Sandham.   Q.-M. Robt. Gibbins.
      A. H. Eyre.   Surg. N. Norris.
      A. W. Elliott.   A. S. T. Seward.

1873.

Col. Wm. H. Eden, *l.g.*

Lt.Col. E. F. S. G. Dawson.   Lieut. Fred. Hervey.
Major H. W. Palmer.   Stephen J. Stevens
    VC H. E. Wood, *l.c.*   Edw. Lethbridge.
Capt. VC R. M. Rogers.   J. H. Laye, *adj.*
    Apsley Cherry.   F. M. Balfour.
    VC Wm. Rennie.   Geo. Sandham.
    G. E. Perryn.   A. H. Eyre.
    R. H. Hackett.   A. W. Elliott.
    D. P. Murray.   Sb.Lt. G. W. Hutchinson.
    John Lawrence.   A. M. Maude.
    R. I. Ward.   Wm. Hawley.
    John Campbell.   Pymr. W. J. Bampfield.
    W. S. Hamilton.   I.of M.R. Lawrence.
Lieut. D. Maclachlan.   Adj. J. H. Laye.
    W. F. Wilson.   Q.-M. Jos. Newman.
    Robt. Lawrence, *I of M*   Surg. N. Norris.
    W. J. Banbury.   A. S. T. Seward.
    A. C. E. Welby.

1874.

Col. Wm. H. Eden, *g.*

Lt.Col. H. W. Palmer.   Capt. R. I. Ward.
Major VC H. E. Wood, *l.c.*   John Campbell.
    VC R. M. Rogers.   W. S. Hamilton.
Capt. Apsley Cherry.   D. Maclachlan.
    G. E. Perryn.   W. F. Wilson.
    R. H. Hackett.   Lieut. R. Lawrence.
    John Lawrence.   W. J. Banbury.

Lieut. A. C. E. Welby.
    Fred. Hervey.
    Steph. J. Stevens.
    Edw. Lethbridge.
    J. H. Laye.
    F. M. Balfour.
    Geo. Sandham.
    A. H. Eyre.
    A. W. Elliott.

Sb.Lt. G. W. Hutchinson.
    A. M. Maude.
    Wm. Hawley.
    H. de C. Rawlins.
Pymr. W. J. Bampfield.
I. of M. Stephen J. Stevens.
Adj. J. H. Laye.
Q.-M. Joseph Newman.
Surg. N. Norris, *surg.-maj.*

1875.

Col. Wm. H. Eden, *g*.

Lt.Col. Hen. W. Palmer.
Major †℃ H.E. Wood, C.B., *c*.
    †℃ Robt. M. Rogers.
    Apsley Cherry.
Capt. Geo. E. Perryn.
    Robt. Hen. Hackett.
    Randall I. Ward.
    John Campbell.
    Wm. S. Hamilton.
    Duncan Maclachlan.
    Wm. Fred. Wilson.
    Rob. Lawrence.
    J. Bramley Ridout.
    Wm. Joseph Banbury.
Lieut. Alfred C. E. Welby.
    Fred. R. Hervey.
    S. J. Stevens, *I of M.*

Lieut. Edward Lethbridge.
    Joseph H. Laye, *adj*.
    Fred. M. Balfour.
    Geo. Sandham.
    Arthur Wood Elliott.
    Geo. W. Hutchinson.
    Francis Smith.
    Arthur H. Saltmarshe.
Sb.Lt. Aubrey M. Maude.
    Hen. de C. Rawlins.
    Hen. M. Campbell.
Pymr. Wm. Jno. Bampfield.
I. of M. S. J. Stephens, *lt.*
Adj. J. H. Laye, *lt.*
Q.-M. Joseph Newman.
Surg. N. Norris, *surg.-maj.*

1876.

Col. Wm. H. Eden, *g*.

Lt.Col. H. W. Palmer.
Major †℃ H.E. Wood, C.B., *c*.
    †℃ Robt. M. Rogers.
    Apsley Cherry.

Capt. Geo. E. Perryn.
    Robt. Hen. Hackett.
    R. I. Ward.
    John Campbell.

Capt. W. S. Hamilton.
 D. Maclachlan.
 W. F. Wilson.
 Robt. Lawrence.
 J. Bramley Ridout.
 W. J. Banbury.
Lieut. A. C. E. Welby.
 F. R. Harvey.
 S. J. Stevens, *I of M.*
 E. Lethbridge.
 J. H. Laye, *adj.*
 G. Sandham.
 A. W. Elliott.

Lieut. A. M. Maude.
 W. Hutchinson.
 H. de C. Rawlins.
 F. Smith.
 A. Saltmarshe.
Sb.Lt. H. M. Campbell.
 G. R. Heathcote.
 S. H. Lomax.
Pymr. W. J. Bampfield.
I.of M. S. J. Stevens.
Adj. J. H. Laye.
Q.-M. J. Newman.

1877.
Col. Wm. H. Eden, *g.*

Lt.Col. H. W. Palmer.
Major VC H.E.Wood,C.B.,*c.*
 VC R. M. Rogers.
 Apsley Cherry.
Capt. G. E. Perryn.
 R. H. Hackett.
 R. I. Ward.
 J. Campbell.
 W. S. Hamilton.
 D. Maclachlan.
 W. F. Wilson.
 R. Lawrence.
 J. B. Ridout.
 F. R. Harvey.
 J. Wilson.
Lieut. S. J. Stevens, *I of M.*
 E. Lethbridge.

Lieut. J. H. Laye, *adj.*
 G. Sandham.
 A. W. Elliott.
 A. H. Maude.
 W. Hutchinson.
 H. de C. Rawlins.
 G. R. Heathcote.
 S. H. Lomax.
 F. Smith.
 A. H. Saltmarshe.
 H. M. Campbell.
Sb.Lt. P. E. C. Sheehan.
Pymr. W. J. Bampfield.
I.of M. S. J. Stevens.
Adj. J. H. Laye.
Q.-M. J. Newman.

1878.
Col. Wm. H. Eden, *g.*

Lt.Col. H. W. Palmer. | Major VC H.E.Wood,C.B.*c.*

Major VC R. M. Rogers. Lieut. G. Sandham, *I of M.*
Apsley Cherry. A. W. Elliott.
Capt. G. E. Perryn, *m.* A. M. Maude.
R. H. Hackett, *m.* W. Hutchinson.
R. I. Ward. H. de C. Rawlins.
J. Campbell. G. R. Heathcote.
W. S. Hamilton. S. H. Lomax.
D. Maclachlan. F. Smith.
W. F. Wilson. A. H. Saltmarshe.
R. Lawrence. H. M. Campbell.
J. B. Ridout. P. E. C. Sheehan.
J. Wilson. 2nd Lt. A. Gordon.
S. J. Stevens. I. of M. G. Sandham.
E. Lethbridge. Adj. J. H. Laye.
Lieut. J. H. Laye, *adj.* Q.-M. J. Newman.

1879.

Col. Wm. H. Eden, *g.*

Lt.Col. VC H.E.Wood, C.B. *c.* Lieut. G. R. Heathcote.
Major VC R. M. Rogers. S. H. Lomax, *adj.*
Apsley Cherry, *l.c.* F. Smith.
Capt. R. H. Hackett, *m.* H. M. Campbell.
R. I. Ward. P. E. C. Sheehan.
J. Campbell. 2nd Lt. A. Gordon.
W. S. Hamilton. A. T. Bright.
W. F. Wilson. S. P. Strong.
R. Lawrence. H. E. Hotham.
J. B. Ridout. C. H. J. Hopkins.
S. J. Stevens, *m.* H. Lysons.
E. Lethbridge. A. O. White.
J. H. Laye. R. B. Fell.
G. Sandham. J. Ross.
A. M. Maude. Adj. S. H. Lomax.
Lieut. W. Hutchinson. Q.-M. J. Newman.
H. de C. Rawlins.

1880.

Col. Wm. H. Eden, *g.*

Lt.Col. F*C* R. M. Rogers.
Major Apsley Cherry, *l.c.*
Capt. Robt. Hy. Hackett, *l.c.*
    Randall I. Ward.
    John Campbell.
    Wm. S. Hamilton.
    Wm. Fredk. Wilson.
    J. Bramley Ridout.
    Edwd. Lethbridge.
    Joseph Henry Laye, *m*
    Aubrey M. Maude.
    G. W. Hutchinson.
    H. de C. Rawlins.
    John Mews Evetts.
Lieut. Gilbert R. Heathcote.
    S. Holt Lomax, *adj.*
    Francis Smith.
    Henry M. Campbell.

Lieut. P. E. C. Sheehan.
    Alex. Gordon.
    Sydney P. Strong.
    H. Edward Hotham.
    Andrew S. Parkinson.
    C. H. J. Hopkins.
2nd Lt. Henry Lysons, *d.*
    Arthur O. White.
    Robert Black Fell.
    John Ross.
    Hugh L. Custance.
    Wm. Henry Vicars.
    Wm. P. Anderson.
    John G. Blake.
Pymr.
I. of M.
Adj. S. H. Lomax, *lt.*
Q.-M. Joseph Newman.

www.ingramcontent.com/pod-product-compliance
Lightning Source LLC
Chambersburg PA
CBHW032050220426
43664CB00008B/937